The New Grammarians' Funeral

A critique of
Noam Chomsky's linguistics

IAN ROBINSON

Lecturer in English Language and Literature in the
University College of Swansea

We must plough over the whole of language.
—WITTGENSTEIN

CAMBRIDGE UNIVERSITY PRESS
CAMBRIDGE
LONDON · NEW YORK · MELBOURNE

Published by the Syndics of the Cambridge University Press
The Pitt Building, Trumpington Street, Cambridge CB2 IRP
Bentley House, 200 Euston Road, London NW1 2DB
32 East 57th Street, New York, NY 10022, U.S.A.
296 Beaconsfield Parade, Middle Park, Melbourne 3206, Australia

© Cambridge University Press 1975

Library of Congress catalogue card number: 75–6009

ISBN 0 521 20856 4 hard covers
ISBN 0 521 29316 2 paperback

First published 1975
First paperback edition 1978
Reprinted 1979

First printed in Great Britain by
Western Printing Services Ltd, Bristol
Reprinted in Great Britain at the
University Press, Cambridge

The New Grammarians' Funeral
A Critique of Noam Chomsky's linguistics

BOOKS BY IAN ROBINSON

Chaucer's Prosody (1971)
Chaucer and the English Tradition (1972)
The Survival of English, Essays in Criticism of Language (1973)
Cambridge University Press

(WITH DAVID SIMS)

The Decline and Fall of Mr Heath (The Brynmill Publishing Co.)
Edited by Ian Robinson, Robert Marchant, David Sims
The Human World, a quarterly review of English letters,
in sixteen issues, 1970–4. The Brynmill Publishing Co., Ltd,
130 Bryn Rd, Brynmill, Swansea SA2 OAT

To
F. R. LEAVIS
who twelve years since encouraged me to publish
an essay on the state of linguistics

Contents

If this be so, there is a connection between concern for truth and wondering at the world ... Also, since to wonder at the world is to wonder at a mystery, concern for truth has to do with being related to mystery.

R. F. HOLLAND

M. Jourdain: Qu'est-ce que tu fais?
Nicole: Je dis U.
M. Jourdain: Oui: mais quand tu dis U, qu'est-ce que tu fais?
Nicole: Je fais ce que vous me dites.
M. Jourdain: Oh! l'étrange chose que d'avoir affaire à des bêtes! Tu allonges les lèvres en dehors, et approches la mâchoire d'en haut de celle d'en bas: U, vois-tu? Je fais la moue: U.
Nicole: Oui, cela est biau.
Madame Jourdain: Voilà qui est admirable!

MOLIÈRE, *Le Bourgeois Gentilhomme*

Indeed, all that relates to language, that familiar but wonderful phenomenon, is naturally interesting if it is not spoiled by being treated pedantically.

MATTHEW ARNOLD, General Report for 1876

Preface

To offer a public discussion of Chomsky's linguistics may be thought a rash action on my part, for I have no qualifications for tackling the subject recognizable to professional linguists. I have read everything Chomsky has published in linguistics down to mid-1974, with the exception of a few inaccessible periodical pieces and some of the detail of *The Sound Pattern of English* (the latter omission because I have never been able to persuade my interest in language to take that direction), and I have been reading works in linguistics with a sort of desultory persistence for about fifteen years, but that is all. All I can offer is non-specialist thought. My reason for hoping, unabashed, that this is worth offering must show its strength as we go along. I do not think contemporary linguistics is enough of a discipline to make its standards those of thought about language, and the case of necessity cannot be made from within the discipline. I shall argue that the recent writer who said 'the study of language is **linguistics**' was overbold.

This monograph originated in my efforts to get help from linguistics with some of the problems which since the days of Plato have confronted all who try to think about language. I was forced on these questions, as one uncomfortably aware of being philosophically unqualified and unqualifiable, by the set of preoccupations that made me work concurrently on discussion of some of the English poets and the subjects of my *Survival of English*. The spur to say something about current linguistics was my increasingly exasperated sense of its inadequacy for my purposes—or, as far as I can see, for anything else that can really be called thought about language. Because *exasperated* is the word the book is as short and unencyclopaedic as I can make it.

Linguistics of all kinds is seed that falls in a rich academic field and brings forth an hundredfold. '*A high proportion*', however, '*of the material circulated and retrieved is without discernible value.*' This severe editorial pronouncement (italicized in the original) launches a huge volume from a series which, according to the same authority, 'was basically conceived and designed as a kind of *ad hoc* system of quality filters, to provide the linguistic community with one trustworthy device for restraining—if not curing—the cancerous spread of unneeded information'.[1] Some unfortunate malfunction of the filter appears in this case to have left the flow of untreated information unimpeded, in view of the size and weight of the volumes and the editorial promise for the future: 'Vol. xii, *Linguistics and Adjacent Arts and Sciences*, has expanded to colossal bulk. . .We now envisage a book, in at least three separate tomes, of some 2,500 pages [quarto]' (*ibid.* p. vi).

The dread of such an outcome, the shortness of human life, and my exasperation, have combined to prevent me from trying to discuss everything called 'linguistics', and I have made no show even of discussing in detail all Chomsky's works and doctrines. If I have concentrated on Chomsky it is because he is a serious man who has done his best to make linguistics a discipline and deserves attention from anyone who wants to know what light linguistics can shed on language, also because at present Chomsky appears to the general public to hold the field. But I have tried to discuss what I think interesting in Chomsky's work rather than to survey it. There are plenty of available Introductions to Chomsky with which I would not compete.

Fashions in linguistics come and go with a rapidity which in itself suggests something suspect about the essential claim of linguistics, that it is a science. Had I been writing fifteen years ago my examples would have been different, and I am pretty sure that in another fifteen years they will be out of date. Chomsky, further, is not *very* difficult to think about; he is a cause not worth spending *much* life on. Tackling Chomsky is not like tackling Plato, or Shakespeare.

What may make the effort nevertheless worthwhile is that it may possibly bring one up against real problems, if only by way of noticing their absence from linguistics, or their presence as unsound certainty. I believe that Chomsky's scientism is one of the *deep* fallacies. One thinks one has escaped, then finds oneself in its embrace. It is a hydra I shall not kill in the world or in myself; if I get one of its heads off I am sure two new ones will

[1] Thomas A. Sebeok (ed.), *Current Trends in Linguistics*, vol. ix, *Linguistics in Western Europe* (The Hague, 1972), vol. i, p. v.

sprout for the next comer. John of Salisbury maimed the monster once, I suspect, Occam again, and it has taken many more recent knocks. But she will always close and be herself. The continuing effort against the fallacy is nonetheless a necessary condition for clarity of thought about language. If I come back to comparable, related points from different directions that is because I *am* facing an authentic monster, not flogging a dead horse. To show again and again why the fallacy is fallacious is like that reminding oneself of the necessary conditions of criticism (that poetry be itself and not another thing, that only individual judgement based on individual response counts, that opinions are nevertheless not private whims. . .) which academic critics think repetitious and forget the minute they stop repeating.

So though I wish I were more familiar with the scholastic philosophers and with the great German retort to 'prose and reason' in the work of Hegel, Schopenhauer, Nietzsche, I do know enough to have the solid assurance that my position is not original. If I had been writing a more ambitious book I would have cried for more help to R. G. Collingwood, Croce and Vico; and I am sure that the great philosophers of language provide one of the measures for judging linguistics. As it is, I have aimed only at doing a useful job of work. Those familiar with linguistics will not mistake this for a small ambition.

My second hope, or the second aspect of the first, is, in showing what is lacking in linguistics, to *suggest*, however sketchily, a criterion for judging all linguistics, what will succeed Chomsky as well as what he succeeded.

The study of language is one mode of contemplating a mystery, and a proper awe is a measure of the sense and depth of what goes on in the study of language. I mean, not that linguists should talk about their wonder and awe or use it to gain recruits to the profession—for what is less awe-inspiring than a scholar *telling* us that his subject is wonderful?—but that awe at language should be present in linguistics and inform it. Whatever is the discipline in the subject ought to be what leads the student up to a sense of wonder.

Of course, there are mysteries and mysteries. When Mr Rush Rhees begins a discussion with something like 'What puzzles me about so-and-so is. . .' he is likely to have thought more about so-and-so than his auditors, the puzzlement being a measure of the depth of thought. To get the puzzle clear is then to see a

Preface

mystery. Chomsky's puzzles (and *a fortiori* his rivals'), unacknowledged as puzzlement and often taking the form of faith in the universal validity of scientific method, look to me more like ordinary, unilluminating confusion. The attempt to say so can be the effort to suggest the differences between the ill-founded confidence and the deep puzzles, the latter being eternal. I hope then that this little book might justify itself by provoking both literary critics and linguists to thought about language.

I am grateful to Mrs A. A. H. Inglis of the University of Sussex Library for help in obtaining scarce texts.

I am obliged to the colleagues and pupils who have listened patiently to some of this book in seminars for much of my sense of what is hard to others as well as myself, as well as for some useful questions and objections. I am particularly grateful to Mr David Sims for steady illumination, over a number of years, of some of the deeper problems.

Mr Michael Black made detailed comments that were both useful and encouraging. My debts to Charles F. Hockett's critique *The State of the Art* probably ought to have been greater, for I read it only after finding my own different way to what I wanted to argue against Chomsky. Hockett's elegant and humane book puts some things better than I can, but my reasons for thinking that he has not done all my work for me may be suggested by my conviction that he could not possibly find this monograph acceptable; the same is true of other scholars who have anticipated some of my things (see a handy catalogue by Robert A. Hall, Jr, 'Some Critiques of Chomskyan Theory', *Neuphilologische Mitteilungen* 78.1 (1977), 86–95). I hope the different context gives a different sense to my work.

It has no pretension to the great name of philosophy, but I have been much helped by the later work of Wittgenstein, particularly as mediated through the seminars of Mr Rush Rhees, without which I would hardly have ventured to tackle the subject. (Mr Rhees is of course quite free from responsibility for what I have made of his work.)

I must finally record my debt to William of Occam, Doctor Singularis et Invincibilis, for the use of his razor, an implement absolutely necessary for the paring of contemporary linguistics.

Swansea, 1964–77   I.R.

Preface to the 1978 Impression

The reprinting process allowed me to make only minor changes, which in fact were all I wanted. I have tidied up the discussion of 'knowing' at pp. 63 ff, corrected some mistakes and introduced some new examples.

The book generated a number of press controversies. There was a long-running and perhaps circulation-boosting one in the *TLS*, but it was incomplete because the Editor suppressed my last contribution, the only way left to him, I naturally concluded, of saving my opponent. The missing text is a good lead-in to this book, as well as the proper end to that series, and so I give the final paragraphs of it here:

Searle has confirmed and clarified my suspicion that the weakness [of transformational-generative grammar's treatment of adjectives] is generated by a mistaken notion of how grammar 'explains'. When grammarians fall into the belief that paraphrase into relative clauses is somehow an achievement of a new kind of clarity or that 'cause + become + not + alive' is somehow explanatory of 'kill', they are on the wrong track and if they persist in it must be told. When Chomsky wants, as Searle says, to make linguistics a branch of psychology, he is on a similar wrong track. The aim is to explain language in non-grammatical terms and 'psychology' is interpreted as the search for a bodily organ called the Language Acquisition Device; psychology, that is, becomes physiology and linguistics an exact science, viz. the formulation of mathematically precise rules for the behaviour of something belonging to the physical universe. In this way Chomsky, apparently blessed by Searle, relapses into the mistakes he began by trying to free linguistics from. But anyone who wants to follow the detail of the process or why I think it is a hopeless entry into a dead end will just have to read my *New Grammarians' Funeral*. . . .

In conclusion: is it not symptomatic that, having raised some questions about what linguistics is supposed to do, I find myself disputing with a linguistic philosopher about 'a pretty little girls' school' rather than about, e.g., language, or about actual uses of language?

and isn't it a mark of the plight of linguistics that 'linguists' find things like 'a pretty little girls' school' much more interesting than *Macbeth*?

I suppose it is an extravagance to hope that this book will provoke professional 'linguists' to think about language; but I hope its availability in paperback will allow it to reach some people able and willing to make that effort unimpeded by the restrictions of 'the science of language'.

September 1977   I.R.

Works by Chomsky

The following list is far from being a bibliography of Noam Chomsky. It is merely a list of works mentioned, together with abbreviations used. Of all works not listed here the author, title and date are given on first citation. Unless otherwise stated the place of publication, except of periodicals, is London.

The Logical Structure of Linguistic Theory, typescript, M.I.T. Library, 1955; positive microfilm 1968. (Abbreviated: *Logical Structure*)

Syntactic Structures, The Hague, 1957.

Review of B. F. Skinner's *Verbal Behavior*, *Language* 35 (1959), 26–58. (Abbreviated: First Skinner Review)

'Formal Properties of Grammars', in R. Luce *et al.*, *Handbook of Mathematical Psychology*, vol. II, New York, 1963, pp. 323–418.

'A Transformational Approach to Syntax', in J. A. Fodor and J. J. Katz (eds.), *The Structure of Language*, Englewood Cliffs, New Jersey, 1964, pp. 211–45.

Current Issues in Linguistic Theory, The Hague, 1964. (Abbreviated: *Current Issues*)

Aspects of the Theory of Syntax, Cambridge, Massachusetts, 1965. (Abbreviated: *Aspects*)

(with Morris Halle), 'Some Controversial Questions in Phonological Theory', *Journal of Linguistics* 1 (1965), 97–138.

Topics in the Theory of Generative Grammar, The Hague, 1966. (Abbreviated: *Topics*)

Cartesian Linguistics, New York, 1966.

'Recent Contributions to the Theory of Innate Ideas', *Synthese* 17 (1967), 2–23.

(with Morris Halle), *The Sound Pattern of English*, New York, 1968.

'Comments on Harman's Reply', in Sidney Hook (ed.), *Language and Philosophy*, New York, 1969, pp. 152–9.

'Some Empirical Assumptions in Modern Philosophy of

Language', in Sidney Morgenbesser *et al.* (eds.), *Philosophy, Science and Method*, Essays in Honor of Ernest Nagel, New York, 1969, pp. 260–85.

'Reply by Noam Chomsky' [to Max Black, 'Comment' on Chomsky's 'Problems of Explanation in Linguistics', later chapter two of *Language and Mind*], in Robert Borger and Frank Cioffi (eds.), *Explanation in the Behavioural Sciences*, Cambridge, 1970, pp. 462–70. (Abbreviated: Reply to Black)

'The Case Against B. F. Skinner', *The New York Review of Books* xvii (30 December 1971), 18–24. (Abbreviated: Second Skinner Review)

Language and Mind, second (enlarged) edition, New York, 1972.

Studies on Semantics in Generative Grammar, The Hague, 1972. (Abbreviated: *Studies*)

'Conditions on Transformations', in Stephen R. Anderson and Paul Kiparsky (eds.), *A Festschrift for Morris Halle*, 1974, pp. 232–86.

Reflections on Language (1976) appeared too late for my consideration here. Numbers of reviewers reacted to my demonstration, below, that Chomsky thinks of language as a physical object by denying it out of hand and ignoring the quotations in which his position is sufficiently clear. (Oddly enough the same reviewers were exasperated with me when I denied that language is a physical object.) *Reflections on Language* has the merit of boldness: Chomsky says what he thinks without academic caution and I do not see how after reading it anyone can be in any further doubt as to his belief that language is a part of our anatomy best studied by the neurologist. I am still waiting for neurologists to accept the invitation.

'The Science of Language'

Large and precise claims are made for Professor Noam Chomsky's contribution to linguistics. He is said by one linguist to have 'brought about a revolution in linguistics of exactly the kind Kuhn describes [in *The Structure of Scientific Revolutions*]'[1] and credited by another with having 'revolutionized the scientific study of language'.[2] A third draws support from a popular philosopher in saying that there has been a 'language revolution' which 'includes the linguistics revolution of 1957', that is, of Chomsky's *Syntactic Structures*.[3] Lyons's 'scientific' is used here, I shall show, in a quite exact, definable sense. It is not being asserted only that Chomsky has initiated an advance in an intellectual discipline. There may be some point, then, in showing firstly that Chomsky's real achievement has been reactionary not revolutionary, to steer linguistics back towards the Greek tradition of grammar it seemed to be trying to escape from, and secondly that Chomsky consistently fails when he tries to continue and extend the ambition of his predecessors to make linguistics a science.

That linguistics is a science is certainly the claim made for it by all its practitioners since Saussure, the founding father of the modern subject, indistinguishable for them from the claim that linguistics is serious thinking. 'Linguistics is the scientific study of human [*sic*] language. A study is said to be scientific when it is founded on the observation of facts and refrains from picking and choosing among the facts in the light of certain aesthetic or moral principles.'[4] This is the standard pre-Chomsky position

---

[1] James Peter Thorne, 'Models for Grammars', in Teodor Shanin (ed.), *The Rules of the Game, Cross-Disciplinary Essays on Models in Scholarly Thought* (1972), p. 179.

[2] John Lyons, *Chomsky* (Modern Masters Series, 1970), p. 9.

[3] Roger Fowler, *Understanding Language* (1974), p. ix. I have been told that Kuhn believes scientific revolutions to be only changes in intellectual fashion, so perhaps this remark is truer than its author intended or I realized.

[4] André Martinet, *Elements of General Linguistics*, transl. E. Palmer (1960), p. 15.

throughout the Western world. And although, as we shall see, Chomsky's impact has affected linguists' formulations of their ambitions, one still finds things like: 'The most important claim linguists make is that their study of language is scientific...Thus a scientific study should be **empirical, exact,** and, therefore, **objective.**'[5] Dinneen's notion of science differs a little from Martinet's, but the word *objective* is necessary to both.

The objective foundation on fact meant, for the American-trained linguistician of the 1940s, that in theory (though he would distrust 'theory') the study of a language would begin with a complete collection of the facts. He would not ask how, in the absence of scientific as well as moral principle, one knows a fact when one sees it. He would make a number of tape-recordings or written notes, at some point would declare them to be a 'corpus', and would then take this body home in order to observe it objectively, in the sure and certain hope that the categories appropriate to an explanation of the facts would emerge from such observation. This programme I shall call 'linguistic atomism'. It seems just the same as that variety of positivism of which Collingwood said, 'It was not very acute in the positivists to think that the "facts" of which a scientist speaks are observed by the mere action of our senses' (R. G. Collingwood, *An Essay on Metaphysics* (Oxford, 1940), p. 144).

At the beginning of *Language and Mind* Chomsky recalls the situation of American linguistics in the heyday of linguistic atomism, giving an example of a linguist who neglected even the observation of his corpus:

I recall being told by a distinguished anthropological linguist, in 1953, that he had no intention of working through a vast collection of materials that he had assembled because within a few years it would surely be possible to program a computer to construct a grammar from a large corpus of data by the use of techniques that were already fairly well formalized. At the time this did not seem an unreasonable attitude. (p. 2)

The absence of theory from this idea of science is certainly remarkable. The anthropologist in Chomsky's account did realize that something was needed beyond crude objective observation, some way of showing how the 'facts' hang together in a language

---

[5] Francis P. Dinneen, S.J., *An Introduction to General Linguistics* (New York, 1967), p. 4.

('grammar', as Chomsky calls it), but he did not see that this observation of structure must be as much a part of any discipline of linguistics as the collection of facts. Instead it was to be provided by 'the newly developed mathematical theory of communication, which, it was widely believed in the early 1950's, had provided a fundamental concept—the concept of "information"—that would unify the social and behavioral sciences and permit the development of a solid and satisfactory mathematical theory of human behavior on a probabilistic base' (*ibid.* p. 3). This 'probabilistic base' seems to appeal, as was not uncommon at the time, to a picture of language as a stimulus–response system. We are stimulated by what is said and emit a response (predictable in principle, hence probabilistic, hence within the domain of information theory) that in turn becomes the stimulus to the other party to the conversation. The violence of Chomsky's onslaught on B. F. Skinner comes from his surely true recognition that language is not an S–R system.

We shall see a little more of information theory later (Chapter 5); at present it is enough to say that to account for human behaviour in probabilistic terms is not plausible. There has never been any such technique of computation and Chomsky argues that there never can be. Although linguists frequently promised probabilistic analysis they never actually managed to supply any. The ambition, however, was strongly stated:

Suppose we go to some remote corner of the world and observe two persons conversing with one another. We ask ourselves whether these persons are speaking the same language... We make a tape recording of the sounds we hear, and upon careful study of this recording it turns out that the sounds uttered by the two persons have at least some similarities. Though many of the sounds may seem strange to our ears, we can learn to recognize, fairly well, the vowels and consonants which occurred in the speech of our subjects. Suppose we find that the various vowels and consonants we recognize sound approximately the same no matter which one of our subjects is talking, and that they occur on the average with about the same frequencies. This would be partial evidence for concluding that the two persons are speaking the same language...We analyze our tape recording further and find that the sounds often occur in similar sequences; if we listen carefully to the breaks between these sequences we might conclude that our subjects use many 'words' in common, and we would then have further evidence that they are speaking the same language. We could go on in this way, making

3

increasingly detailed analyses. (John B. Carroll, *The Study of Language* (Cambridge, Massachusetts, 1953), p. 7)

Carroll has abandoned objective observation in the first two quoted sentences. It is not by objective observation that we know that these two objects are persons, or that they are conversing. If I deny the description 'persons' Carroll might well—and not without reason—retort that I am crazy; but that will not show that his grounds for doing so have anything to do with objectivity. For 'objectivity' here must mean observation of facts the factuality of which is scientifically verifiable. But if we ask the great commonplace question, *How do you know?*, to what scientific procedure could Carroll go for proof that he has observed two persons conversing?

I am not raising the philosophical problem of perception, the question how we know *anything* exists as we see it; I am not suggesting that Carroll's observed persons may somehow be an illusion. Nor am I raising the philosophical questions about induction, about how we make inferences, about what counts as evidence, and so on. I ask the question within all the commonplace assumptions about the reality of the external world and the reliability of scientific reasoning about it which science needs, and I mean it in as ordinary a scientific sense as possible. What would the experiments be that proved these objects to be indeed persons conversing?

This is a very basic point and, as I know by experience, difficult for students of linguistics (including myself) to grasp. An analogy may help, though of course analogies are always dangerous to the same extent that they are useful. Here is one that I shall risk from time to time. Change the scene slightly and make our observer chance upon his two persons *singing*. How does he know that they are singing? and if, as may well be the case, he is genuinely doubtful, how will it be *proved* that they are singing? By measuring their noises against some standard of musical time, melody, harmony, and the other things we like to think of as elements of music? The problem might just be that our persons are singing outside the criteria we have brought with us of what singing is. If so one would have to get more familiar with the singing until one could take it *as* singing, thereby stretching one's conception of singing. But this process has nothing in common with Carroll's objective observation and probabilistic analysis,

4

and assumes we are familiar with singing before we observe the singers.

Scientific in the sense *careful, unprejudiced*, which nobody would deny to linguistics, has slid into *scientific* as the observer outside the thing observed, analysing and explaining it externally; and if one challenges the latter one is taken to be making a mad objection to the former. But the question 'whether these persons are speaking the same language' obviously means that 'language' is a conception we bring ready-made to this corner of the world. Whatever we discover by our objective observations it can't be what language is,[6] or what a person is.

Linguistic atomism will always accommodate its facts within a framework of assumptions which are merely those of common sense as influenced by millennia of grammatical thought, but it will not recognize the framework—will, in fact, jib at the existence of any such thing—but take it as somehow self-evident. This used to have harmful effects on the self-knowledge of linguistics, the clarity about the status of its own methods which is surely one mark of any intellectual discipline, at the time in question.

Grant, however, that by some not properly understood method Carroll satisfies himself that he is observing two people talking, and that he makes a lot of recordings of the sounds they make and begins his probabilistic analysis of this corpus of sound. If he is a genuinely objective observer he will have no way of knowing what sounds in the corpus are speech and what aren't.[7]

[6] One immediate line of defence for linguistics-as-objective-observation (through which we shall also drive the subject in the last chapter) is to say that the objections to 'objectivity' hold, *mutatis mutandis*, for the indisputable sciences. Physics also works outwards from common knowledge and in physics too our objective explanations depend on concepts we take with us to objects. Without everyday experience of phenomena like heat, speed, or chemical changes like burning or fermentation, and without everyday ways of thinking about them, there would not be the infinitely refined understanding of 'the same things' which constitutes the respective sciences. This, no doubt, is true, and the opening of a huge subject not of this book or within my capacity to tackle; but if so it must mean that physics itself is not quite the objective/explanatory thing the linguist is after, not that linguistics is.

[7] Hockett confesses that he suffered from such notions of objectivity in his description of the Amerindian language Potawatomi (before the second war the sanity of American linguists was regularly preserved by their important fieldwork): 'The facts could be stored in notebooks and file boxes as they were gathered; they did not also have to be stored in my head. It is not surprising that my account of the language ... was so inadequate' (Charles F. Hockett, *The State of the Art* (The Hague, 1968), pp. 30–1). Hockett claims, optimistically I think, that by 1950 'we had quite

It is so natural for us to think that when we have recorded the sound we have really got hold of the language. 'What we apprehend, in the first place, is sounds; in other words, phenomena which properly belong to the domain of physics.'[8] Yes, *sound* sounds comfortingly objective, and in practice the insistence on objectivity used to mean for linguistics the primacy of phonology. H. A. Gleason, the author of the standard textbook *An Introduction to Descriptive Linguistics* (later revised to make room for Chomskyan grammar), somewhere has an essay called 'In the Beginning was the Sound'; and the first edition of his book, like all its rivals including Hockett's, spends what now looks like a very disproportionate time, at the beginning, on sound. Unfortunately, as Wartburg observes, the study of sound is a well-established branch (called acoustics) of a respectable discipline (called physics): how sound becomes language is another matter altogether, not to be dealt with by the observation of sound as sound. Another recent book eschews the 'science of language' formula and begins instead with an attempt at foolproof definition of the linguist's object of study (called not *language* but *speech*; cf. below pp. 174 ff.):

When we enter a foreign country, the first thing that strikes us is the fact that the inhabitants make strange noises with their mouths ...This phenomenon is the object of our study: the production of vocal sounds by human beings in order to influence the behaviour of their fellows...(Leonard R. Palmer, *Descriptive and Comparative Linguistics* (1972), p. 14)

If this were true, and, stepping off our hovercraft at Boulogne, we really did observe porters, customs officials, police etc. making strange noises with their mouths (whistling, shall we say, or howling), our problem both as travellers and linguists would be different. What we do notice, on the contrary, is that on the Continent people speak foreign languages. But that is not an observation about sound in itself, and it is made from a secure base not in objective observation but in our own language.[9]

recovered' from these 'queer views' (p. 30). His 'stored in my head' still unfortunately suggests a collection of unrelated objects.

[8] Walter V. Wartburg, *Problems and Methods in Linguistics* (Oxford, 1969), p. 1.

[9] Not all speech, incidentally, is meant to influence behaviour. Some people pray, some talk to themselves, some even recite poems. On the other hand some 'vocal sounds' that are not speech are intended to influence the behaviour of other human beings: a woman's scream when she is pinched, a war cry, some sobbing.

If Carroll's corpus were made in Kensington Gardens on a hot day after three dry weeks at the end of June he would have no probabilistic way of showing that sneezes were not speech: they might imaginably be more frequent than some of the sounds of speech. What, too, of the noises made by a man as he feeds the ducks or calls and whistles to his dog, and the other noises, sighs and odd words, made by pairs of lovers? The reasons for saying that all these do or do not belong to speech cannot belong to the statistics of their probable occurrence. I see no way of separating the question from what the sounds *mean* in language.

Carroll tries to work up to meaning from sound. The objective listener to the tapes will, he says, notice 'that the sounds uttered by the two persons have at least some similarities'.

One of the most amazing powers of all users of a language is to understand one another despite very different voices. A fifty-year-old bass's voice is not acoustically much like a five-year-old girl treble's, but if they speak the same language the former can correct the latter by telling her to imitate him. 'Say it like this!' he may say, and she will then make some quite different noise which he may nevertheless recognize as having obeyed his command. But the relevant similarity is there just because it is heard as language. Outside language, observing objectively, one might notice *any* kinds of similarity/dissimilarity between the two voices—that one is husky, treble, young, the other loud, gasping, interrupted by giggles—without having any way of knowing which of the similarities constitute the sounds of language (below, Chapter 4). Unless one knows what one is looking for there is nothing to find, and such knowing is not a result of objective observation.

That Carroll does in fact know what he is looking for is proved by his use of quite advanced grammatical terms like 'vowels' and 'consonants', categories (like 'language') which he takes out with him.

Once established, phonemes would, it was hoped, somehow add themselves together into morphemes, the smallest meaningful units of language (which is very like trying to add inches up into gallons) and so on all the way up to words, sentences and beyond. But 'words', in or out of inverted commas, are no more objective than phonemes. How could the category 'word' arise from the fitting together of sounds? And even if there were some way of knowing the words in this corpus there could be no statistical method of discovering what they meant. All kinds of statistical games can be played with corpora; mathematicians can certainly calculate the probability of occurrence of words; in fact this can be done purely numerically by a mathematician who doesn't know he is dealing with words at all.[10]

Carroll seems to be taking elaborate pains, in the interests of 'objectivity', to avoid the only way of finding out whether the two imagined creatures are really persons conversing in the same language, namely to understand what they are saying, and to prove it by joining in the conversation. The extent to which that can be done is the precise extent of our certainty that they are indeed persons conversing. In a word Carroll is suffering from atomism, the belief that if one stares long enough at the *bits*, at the sounds as sounds, they will somehow cohere into language.

Linguistics is much like religion in that the dogmas of previous ages, replaced by a new orthodoxy, do not die but hang on in out-of-the-way corners, sometimes to make a successful comeback: this kind of 'objective observation' is still found, for instance, in Allen D. Grimshaw, 'Data and Data Use in an Analysis of Communicative Events', an essay published as recently as 1974 (in Richard Bauman and Joel Sherzer (eds.), *Explorations in the Ethnography of Speaking*, Cambridge). 'Once pattern and variation begin to emerge', he says, 'taxonomies seem naturally to follow' (p. 422). Actually the pattern *is* the taxonomies: my point is just that it is still thought to 'emerge' from pure observation of data; for though Grimshaw, less naive that Carroll, does know that the data must be *'relevant'* (p. 420) he has 'left unasked many questions about conceptual frames used in the collection and analysis of those data' (p. 424). If he had asked them he must have realized that the way of talking is inappropriate to the observation of language.

It is not my contention that in the years before Chomsky linguistics was wholly nonsensical. Saussure did not suffer from atomism and contributed to the subject the true picture of language as an organism, or a system to which there are many possible points of entry. Bloomfield, too, if I dare say so at the present moment of linguistic fashion, is a writer who with what-

---

[10] The point is made by Peter Winch, *The Idea of a Social Science* (1958), p. 115; he also says, ' "Understanding", in situations like this, is grasping the *point* or *meaning* of what is being done or said. This is a notion far removed from the world of statistics and causal laws.'

ever lapses and crudities is well worth attention. And the history of American linguistics between Bloomfield and Chomsky is of a complexity I have no wish to coarsen. (Cf. the first chapter of Charles F. Hockett, *The State of the Art*.) The name 'structuralism' itself ought to undermine atomism, for it seems to recognize that the bits of language can be studied only in their inter-relationships. My strictures are aimed at the impression American linguistics in its ordinary textbook formulations would make on people beginning the subject in the years between the Second World War and the decisive impact of Chomsky. This common linguistics was saved from being complete conceptual and methodological nonsense only by the unconscious infiltration of common sense. However much the ordinary linguistics courses in those years talked of objective observation, of statistical analysis of a corpus etc., they kept going without formal collapse into dementia only by the surreptitious introduction of what every schoolboy knows.

Lyons makes this claim for 'the scientific study of language':

In one sense of course we all know what we mean by 'language'; and our use of the word in everyday conversation depends upon the fact that we all interpret it. . .in the same or in a very similar way. There is, however, a difference between this kind of unreflecting and practical knowledge of what language is and the deeper or more systematic understanding that we should want to call 'scientific'. (*Chomsky*, pp. 10–11)

The difference as regards Carroll's probabilistic analysis is that the 'scientific' conception of language is false and the everyday one true.

Chomsky's first contribution to linguistics has been to see clearly that the old notion of linguistic atomism will not do. There is no finished thing to be observed; living languages are not bodies. On the other hand if linguistics is the scientific study of language it will hardly do to begin with Saussure's suave 'conventional simplification of the evidence' from *le langage* (everything said) so as to make the object of study manageable. 'The normal use of language characteristically involves new sentences, sentences that bear no point-by-point resemblance or analogy to those in the child's experience' (*Language and Mind*, p. 171).[11] The linguist's task is therefore how to study something infinite, without leaving anything out.

[11] The assertion that we speak new sentences is not, of course, empirically

Even if there were a corpus (as in the case of dead languages) objective observation would not in itself yield any rules or framework for the body of observed objects: it could not even show them to *be* one thing, i.e. belonging to the same language.

This last is one of the traditional aims of grammar. There are, to make the claim of grammar minimally, certain likenesses within every language. One use of a sound or a word may be very like another; it is not difficult in some cases to see two groups of words as both sentences, and to justify the description by pointing out that they both have a subject and a main verb. One may even say without immediate chaos resulting (though difficulties will later transpire) that language follows rules, however one understands the word, including the rules of traditional grammar.

Now there are other things to be observed of language as well as its 'rules'. It is possible to be more interested in particular manifestations and contemplate poetry; I even believe that a linguist is lacking if he confines his interest to the likenesses between uses of language and is never surprised by the uniqueness of a particular utterance. But the ambition to state the regularities of language is reasonable in a linguist, and Chomsky's first programme is, accordingly, to formalize a set of the rules of language that will govern not only what is to be found in any 'corpus', but whatever could be added to it and still be recognized as the same language. Chomsky calls the set of rules he formulates 'competence': 'The central task of descriptive linguistics is to construct grammars of specific languages, each of which seeks to characterize in a precise way the competence that has been acquired by a speaker of this language' (*Studies on Semantics*, p. 11).

In due course we shall recognize some problems in this way of putting things—the difficulty of connecting 'competence' with 'performance' and of getting evidence for 'competence' from what people really say, the troubles associated with 'acquired', and so on. But both in objecting to the notion of a 'corpus' and in seeing that if linguistics is to be in any sense a science it must

demonstrable: the linguist cannot begin by collecting all the sentences a speaker has heard. There are difficulties, too, about 'analogy', which we shall touch on. Chomsky is really, I think, offering a note on our mythology of language, the conditions given to us by our language for understanding it (though he wouldn't say so) and has the truth possible to such a mode of discussion.

have more of a method than can be suggested by 'objective observation', Chomsky seems to me wholly right, and his influence salutary.

It does not follow that he is right to retain the scientific ambitions and pretensions of his predecessors. He insists that he is more of a scientist than they. One result has been a development in the usual definitions of linguistics. John Lyons begins in his little book *Chomsky* with the very traditional 'It is the aim of theoretical linguistics to give a scientific answer to the question "What is language?"' (p. 11), but he later qualifies 'a *scientific* description' as 'one that is carried out systematically on the basis of objectively verifiable observations and within the framework of some general theory...' (p. 16). Objectivity and the verifiable are still with us; the new Chomskyan thing is the insistence on a body of theory to provide a home for the observations. We shall see that Chomsky means 'theory' quite precisely, and that his insistence on it subserves the ambition to give, in a load-bearing phrase we shall see much of, a 'language-independent explanation' of language. If Carroll accounted for facts by placing them in traditional categories which he did not recognize as such, Chomsky will try to explain language in terms altogether independent of language.

It remains to be shown that 'What is language?' is a question that can have a scientific answer, that grammar or any development of it can be made to do duty as scientific theory or that, even if there can be something called 'the science of language', the understanding of language will automatically benefit from it. 'Obviously', Chomsky writes, 'any rational person will favor rigorous analysis and careful experiment' (*Language and Mind*, p. xi); and he adds no limiting clause such as 'in the areas where they are illuminating'. The methods of science are, he feels, always best where they are possible. 'We cannot specify, a priori, what postulates and hypotheses are legitimate' (Second Skinner Review, p. 19). But we can, it seems, restrict disciplined discussion to what can be so described.

All thought, thinks Chomsky, is science or speculation. The former is always preferable but when science is not available our licence to speculate is complete.

Given the primitive character of the study of man and society and its general lack of intellectual substance, we can only speculate about the essential and basic factors that enter into human behavior, and it would be quite irresponsible to claim otherwise. Speculation about these matters is quite legitimate, even essential. It should be guided, where this is possible, by such limited and fragmentary knowledge as exists. But speculation should be clearly labeled as such and clearly distinguished from the achievements of scientific inquiry. (*Language and Mind*, p. x)

I deny, however irresponsibly, that the study of man and society is primitive and lacking in intellectual substance in the work of the great historians, novelists and philosophers, though there it is not scientific at all. But if the world of mind were, as Chomsky suggests, restricted to science on the one hand and undisciplined speculation on the other it would be hard to understand the importance he attaches to the latter. If all true thought is scientific why must not Chomsky follow Hume? 'If we take in our hand any volume, of divinity or school metaphysics, for instance, let us ask, *Does it contain any abstract reasoning concerning quantity or number?* No. *Does it contain any experimental reasoning concerning matters of fact and existence?* No. Commit it then to the flames: for it can contain nothing but sophistry and illusion.'

These ideas that disciplined thought is restricted to science on the one hand and free-range speculation on the other, widespread as they are,[12] are just what a truly disciplined study would begin by questioning.

Hockett gives only two alternatives to linguistics, opting firmly for the former: 'Is linguistics then, after all, an empirical science like chemistry? Or is it a formal discipline, like logic and mathematics?' (*The State of the Art*, pp. 56–7). Must it really be one or t'other? Linguists should at least consider two possibilities, firstly that scientific method is usable in their subject, if ever, only on peripheral questions or only if we are content to gain no illumination from its use; secondly that linguistics is a *sham* science.

[12] 'The present title was deliberately chosen to avoid any impression that the contents are restricted to a particular school of thought', says the editorial in the prospectus for *Question*, before going on in the next paragraph, 'The only commitment of *Question* itself is to rational inquiry. For although this implies an assumption that science offers the most systematically rational interpretation of common experience. . . .' I don't believe that science interprets common experience at all: it is physics, or biology, or thermodynamics or whatever; but the point here is just that *Question* is, in the act of proclaiming its open-mindedness, restricting itself rigidly to one style of thought. Cf. remarks on W. G. Runciman's sociology, *The Human World* no. 3 (1971), 85–8 and no. 7 (1972), 90–1.

The criterion of success for any linguistics can only be the depth of understanding of language the subject makes possible. Chomsky's insistence that linguists' theories must be 'nonvacuous' and 'nontrivial' certainly enriches the literature of the subject; but scientific method, even where it is genuine, is no more a guarantee of understanding than 'speculation' is. According to Wittgenstein there are in the science to which Chomsky finally assimilates linguistics, 'experimental methods and *conceptual confusion*'.[13] Chomsky himself is well aware of the odd sense given to 'science' by much of what is done under that name in the 'social sciences': 'To a considerable degree, I feel, the "behavioral sciences" are merely mimicking the surface features of the natural sciences; much of their scientific character has been achieved by a restriction of subject matter and a concentration on rather peripheral issues' (*Language and Mind*, p. xi).

The 'depth of understanding' permitted by a subject can only be judged by proficients in the subject. Bruce L. Derwing makes the point well: 'I also concede with Kuhn that "...there is no standard higher than the assent of the relevant community." For me, the relevant community must be that contemporary body of fellow linguists, and I am perfectly content to leave the judgment in their hands' (*Transformational Grammar as a Theory of Language Acquisition* (Cambridge, 1973), p. 23). Yes, this is the only test in any discipline worth the name. There must still be a non-specialist condition of making sense. It remains possible that conceptual confusions within a subject go deep enough to make the approval or disapproval of its professors no more valuable than the judgements in their subjects of alchemists, phrenologists or astrologers. Phrenology's possible interest (like astrology's) was as a framework within which acute psychological observation could imaginably be made; but it did not justify itself as explanation of observation; it had to be rejected as science if general standards of sense were to be maintained and science not to be engulfed in quackery.[14]

[13] Ludwig Wittgenstein, *Philosophical Investigations*, translated by G. E. M. Anscombe, second edition, English text (Oxford, 1963), p. 232e.

[14] In point of fact few linguists have the first-hand experience of real scientific work which is the best guarantee of sense to the phrase 'scientific method'. Before linguistics began to occupy its own space on the campus linguists were predominantly classical dons who took up philology after a thorough grounding in Latin and Greek. I can't easily call to mind any eminent linguist who began life as a physicist. The only scientific qualification of most of the present generation of professional linguists is a degree

The last clause is important, though. There are no impregnable fortresses, no final guarantees in affairs of the mind except a kind of central sense which we have constantly to renew in judging what does indeed make sense. Even if we say, rather optimistically, with Arthur Koestler, that 'the atomistic concepts of the last century...have been abandoned in all other branches of contemporary science [than psychology]'[15] they can still be found flourishing in many of the pseudo-sciences from which our century enjoys no special immunity,[16] in sociology, for instance, and the work of the 'mind–brain identity' school. But this can only be said from a position of common sense outside the pseudo-sciences. 'Scientific method' will not save us, if we lose our common criteria of sense and understanding, from repeating the most arrant nonsense for evermore and using it to flatter ourselves about how much more strictly, scientifically and deeply we understand the world than our ancestors could. 'Truth has bounds, error none.'

in linguistics, hardly likely to impress real scientists. Chomsky himself is a mathematician, which, as we shall see, affects his notion of the 'rules' of language.

[15] Arthur Koestler, *The Ghost in the Machine* (reprint 1970), p. 30. I cite this non-member of the Linguists' Union, and shall do so again, sometimes in disagreement, just because he richly *does* make sense about the misapplications of scientific method, much more so than many professional linguists.

[16] 'Cosmologists' assert their claims to be considered scientists by telling the tall story that the universe did (or did not) start with a big bang, and firmly interpret the colours of stars as meaning that the universe is expanding, for which there is no corroborative evidence—confusing here the specialist terminology of science which cannot make sense in common speech ('the curvature of space', 'real time') with what might be *ordinarily* true. And although life is at present only found on earth other 'scientists' assert that life *cannot* exist uniquely on earth: 'If our model is correct it is certain that life exists on other planets. [if!]...The animals would have two eyes but the ears would appear anywhere on the body'—Open University broadcast, 16 August 1973. On the other hand, even if life became extinct on earth it must automatically reappear: 'We [sic] have another chance. If life disappeared overnight it would automatically appear again' (*ibid.*). The experimental test of this would necessarily involve the extinction of the experimenter.

Chomsky's Grammar to the Rescue

Chomsky has reinstated grammar, in the old school sense of the word, because only by grammar, he thought, could the theory missing from post-war American linguistics be supplied. I put it this way to point to the strength and weakness of his work, respectively the recognition that linguistics must contemplate the regularities of language, and the belief that this activity can be a kind of natural science.

The most obviously available regularities of language are the rules of traditional grammar. Linguistics used to look off-puttingly technical to outsiders; Chomsky, though he has introduced specialist terminology of his own, uses without fuss such well-known terms as *word, noun, verb* and *phrase* and asks very traditional questions about the grammaticality of *sentences.*

His attachment to traditional grammar is quite unlike Carroll's determination to view all linguistic phenomena with an open mind; and Chomsky is able to avoid Carroll's consequent dilemma of having no grounds for knowing what is and what is not language, for Chomsky can identify as language the sentences that follow the rules of grammar. We shall go on to consider the difficulties in which this lands Chomsky in his turn. Immediately it will be convenient to follow the development of his case about grammar in its first full public statement, *Syntactic Structures.*

There Chomsky distinguishes three kinds of grammar (in my view the possible number of grammars for any language is infinite and the actual number the same as the number of grammarians); transformational grammar, with which Chomsky's name will always be associated, is the third and most 'powerful' of these three. The first is an application of 'finite state Markov processes':

Suppose that we have a machine that can be in any one of a finite number of different internal states, and suppose that this machine switches from one state to another by producing a certain symbol (let us say, an English word). One of these states is an *initial state*; another is a *final state*. Suppose that the machine begins in the initial state, runs through a sequence of states (producing a word with each transition), and ends in the final state. Then we call the sequence of words that has been produced a 'sentence'. Each such machine thus defines a certain language; namely, the set of sentences that can be produced in this way. Any language that can be produced by a machine of this sort we call a *finite state language*; and we call the machine itself a *finite state grammar*. (pp. 18–19)

Chomsky's first example is a grammar that generates only two sentences:

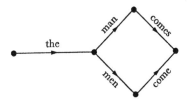

No explanation or illumination is here being offered; the grounds of correctness or incorrectness are merely the design of the machine, which can nevertheless be called a 'grammar' because it chooses from several possibilities and says only two are correct. You could disobey the 'rules' and read the words back to front, or cross the lines and generate 'the men comes' or 'the man come': these are possible strings of the words but would be declared ungrammatical because they fail to follow the quite arbitrary rules of the grammar. So this 'language' can begin a sentence in only one way and can continue it in only one of two ways. The 'machine' is a kind of catalogue of these possibilities, and I am not altogether clear why it is not ruled out as a possible grammar of a natural language by Chomsky's previous objection to 'any attempt to present directly the set of grammatical phoneme sequences', that 'it would lead to a grammar so complex that it would be practically useless' (p. 18). A finite-state grammar which tried to catalogue all the grammatical continuations of sentences beginning with only a few common English nouns would be everlasting as well as unilluminating. As Chomsky frequently says, 'The most striking aspect of linguistic competence is what we may call the "creativity of language", that is, the speaker's ability to produce new sentences' (*Topics*,

p. 11).[1] Chomsky's basic notion therefore is that a grammar must be a finite set of rules 'generating' an infinite number of sentences that follow the rules; and that, one would have thought, puts paid to finite-state grammar as portrayed in *Syntactic Structures*.

Before abandoning it, however, Chomsky rather confusingly offers a development of finite-state grammar which *can* generate an infinite number of sentences, and it is worth some consideration as exemplifying Chomsky's mathematically exact notion of a grammatical rule. He adds 'closed loops' to the basic model quoted (*Syntactic Structures*, p. 19). A closed loop is a rule permitting though not requiring a word (or part of a sentence?) to be repeated an indefinite number of times. Thus by introducing 'old' into the first example on a closed loop between 'the' and 'man' or 'men' we can generate 'the old man comes' and 'the old men come', 'the old old man comes', 'the old old men come', 'the old old old man comes'. . .and so on *ad infinitum*. (Chomsky will make it important to his case to say *ad infinitum* not *ad nauseam*.)

These closed loops, making possible an infinite number of sentences generated by the grammar, making the sentences of the language, that is, a mathematically well-defined but infinite set, and also giving the speaker a new element of choice, alter so radically the finite-state grammar originally described that I think the version with loops should have a different name. I shall call it 'B' finite-state grammar and the original 'A' finite-state grammar.

Chomsky wants to show that 'it is *impossible*, not just difficult, to construct a device of the type described above ['A' or 'B' finite-state grammar]. . .which will produce all and only the grammatical sentences of English' (*Syntactic Structures*, p. 21). His first argument is mathematical and not, as far as I understand it, as conclusive as he thinks. He imagines 'several languages whose alphabets contain just the letters a, b, and whose sentences are defined' in three sets of rules (*ibid.*). The first is 'ab, $aabb$, $aaabbb$, . . . , and in general, all sentences consisting of n occurrences of a followed by n occurrences of b and only these'. Below,

---

[1] This is why Derwing's analogy between speaking and performing music from a score won't do (Derwing, *Transformational Grammar*, p. 262); speaking is more like improvising, and the task of grammar is to state its kind of rules for linguistic improvisation. A finite-state grammar of English would have to score all possible English sentences, as alternatives of possible beginnings.

Chomsky says, 'We can easily show that each of these three languages is not a finite state language.' But he does not do so and I do not see how he could. The one I have quoted could be represented as a 'B' finite-state language by the diagram:

Similar diagrams would cover the other cases Chomsky discusses. Moreover a more complicated diagram could allow his second and third 'languages' to appear as optional loops of the first:

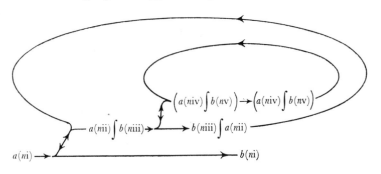

where $\int$ = 'or vice versa' and ni-v are any natural numbers

(There would have to be refinements to permit these complications in different orders within the sentence.)

These diagrams do go beyond finite-state 'B' grammars in making the number of repetitions in the earlier parts of a sentence control those in the later, and also beyond 'B' in allowing a clause rather than a word to appear on a loop. I don't think this is such a great innovation as allowing loops into 'A'; but let us recognize it by calling my last diagram an example of a finite-state 'C' grammar. Ignoring certain difficulties about seeing this as a grammar at all, one can say that it has the essential finite-state characteristic (see below) of treating a sentence as a linear series of successively restricted choices; and Chomsky certainly includes 'C' within finite-state grammar when he writes,

We might arbitrarily decree that such processes of sentence formation in English as those we are discussing cannot be carried out more
than n times, for some fixed n. This would of course make English a
finite state language as, for example, would a limitation of English
sentences to length of less than a million words. (p. 23)

That is to say, unless n can be infinite there can be a finite-state
grammar of English. But is not a sentence by definition finite?
Even if we crudely interpret 'infinite' as very like 'more than a
million words' I am not convinced by Chomsky's application of
his argument to English:

It is clear, then, that in English we can find a sequence $a + S_1 + b$,
where there is a dependency between a and b, and we can select as
S_1 another sequence containing $c + S_2 + d$, where there is a dependency between c and d, then select as S_2 another sequence of this
form, etc. . .Thus we can find various kinds of non-finite state models
within English. (pp. 22–3)

Far too much work is being done by Chomsky's 'etc.': this is
where it must mean *ad infinitum*. English sentences are not in
fact ever of more than a million words; it is also a fact that no
English sentence contains more than a few 'nestings' or 'embeddings'. If this were not so we would be accustomed to sentences
like the following.

I asked him to say whether the man who was wearing what he had
inherited from, a woman who had earned, after several years working in that famous island inhabited successively in historic times,
for we cannot venture beyond the limits imposed by, as certain
theologians would, if they were not of the persuasion of the, as he
then was, though he is now Dean of one of the, as I am informed,
better-known Cambridge colleges, King's, Bishop of Woolwich,
have us believe, an omniscient deity, by Greeks, Romans, Moors,
Normans, Italians and the Mafia—Sicily—a living in the Plutocrat
Nightclub, his mother, an old blue coat, had had chicken-pox.

Chomsky would not claim that anyone would ever speak or
write such a sentence outside discussions of grammar, or that
anyone would understand it if spoken. It is, however, a well-
formed English sentence, analysable (on paper), if there is no
limit to the number of embedded clauses or the width of their
separation of parts. For Chomsky the sentence would be not
ungrammatical but unacceptable. In a later discussion he writes

'repeated nesting contributes to unacceptability' (*Aspects*, p. 13), and explains the fact as 'simply a consequence of the finiteness of memory' (p. 14). So my sentence would be impossible not because it breaks any grammatical rule but because of its demands on memory. This of course raises the problem of Chomsky's sharp distinction of 'competence' from 'performance' to which we shall return in Chapter 4. The immediate question is whether a grammar ought not to rule out such impossible sentences if they are, as Hockett says (p. 60), an 'empirical absurdity'. If the cause of unacceptability is our mental limitations the effect on language is just the same as if there were a grammatical rule forbidding too many embeddings and nestings. 'Assuming the set of grammatical sentences of English to be given, we now ask what sort of device can produce this set...' (*Syntactic Structures*, p. 18). But how can we assume as given a set that includes impossible sentences? Even if Chomsky's explanation is correct, one might reasonably argue that our mental limitations are expressed in the rules of grammar; if we are to see grammar as an account of *all* the regularities of language I think we must say something of the kind. But if grammar is not to describe all the regularities of language, on what grounds can it decide what to omit?

Chomsky's notion of a grammatical rule is unduly restricted here to the mathematically precise. He is right to say that to rule out as ungrammatical any sentence with more than a fixed number of these constructions would be arbitrary. The arbitrariness would be in fixing the number. But that does not mean that no rule can be formulated.

Some rules are, of course, mathematically 'well-defined' and depend on so being for their status as rules. Chess, as Hockett points out, is a finite-state system; the rules constitute the well-definition of the system. Every game of chess begins in one initial state, and passes through a series of discrete alternative states before reaching one of a very small number of final states; the number of possible moves at chess, though large, is finite. (Hockett suggests it would take a computer the size of the earth 10^{37} years to print out the best move for each player at every possible state of the game.) A well-defined rule may generate an infinite series, too, like the formula for π, which can be expressed numerically in a series every member of which is exactly predictable, but which has no end. It won't do, in such mathematical cases, to say things like 'the formula for the circumference of a circle is, in a very large number of cases, $2\pi R$', or 'two plus two is, often enough, four'.

Chomsky sometimes (below, Chapter 4) writes as if rules constituted language, like the formula for π generating its series of integers, or perhaps like the rules of chess defining actual games as chess.[2] He *always* writes as if all rules are mathematically precise. And the obvious danger is that grammar then becomes logically *analytic*, rather than a way of referring to language. If the language happens not to fit the well-defined systems of rules it is declared ungrammatical: rules take precedence over language and grammar returns to prescriptivism. It may be that Chomsky's rules are mathematically precise to the extent that they are not the regularities of language. But not all rules are precise.

One might say, 'An English sentence cannot have too many of these constructions.' If you then ask precisely how many 'too many' is, you are asking the wrong question, just as if (to borrow a Wittgenstein image) I say 'Stand roughly there' and you stand roughly there and say 'Am I exactly where you told me to be?' you are asking the wrong question. So when Chomsky truly says that 'there is no human language in which it is possible, in fact or in principle, to specify a certain sentence as the longest sentence meaningful in this language' (*Language and Mind*, p. 118) one can still retort that it is possible also to say truly that some sentences are too long to be grammatical, and that the question of the exact borderline is playing its favourite role of red herring. (For if we cannot say at what precise moment day becomes night does that mean we don't know day from night?) I concur here with Hockett in his discussion of 'flexible constraints' that 'are, in my opinion, *part of the language*' (*The State of the Art*, pp. 60–1) and agree with his memorable dictum that 'all constraints in a language [are] more or less rubbery' (p. 61).

So although I shall conduct discussions which imply that English is not a finite-state language, I cannot see that Chomsky has made the case.

The reason that nobody is ever likely to attempt a finite-state 'C' grammar of English is just that it wouldn't help anybody to

---

[2] Cf. Hockett, to whom my formulations here are much indebted, *The State of the Art* especially pp. 47, 57; cf. also John R. Searle, *Speech Acts* (Cambridge, 1969), pp. 33, 55. The *deep* grammatical dilemma suggested by the chess analogy, that one cannot know the moves except in the rules of the game, but that the understanding can only be shown in games, in the moves, is one of Wittgenstein's topics in the *Philosophical Investigations*.

understand or do anything. I spent some time in the flinty field to make for the first time the point that grammar is not, so to speak, an absolute study. 'The form of the justification will vary with the purposes of the grammar', as Chomsky says (*Logical Structure*, 3.1). The answers grammar gives must vary with the questions asked, but the questions behind finite-state grammar are not about the regularities of language.

One great limitation of finite-state grammar is that it can contain no sufficient concept of a sentence. My finite-state 'C' does permit the first part of a sentence to control a later part; but nothing I could call a finite-state grammar would permit the latter part of a sentence to control the former part. This is, however, within the capacity of English sentences. We can sometimes say a word and later decide what word it is.

Banks and braes o' bonnie Doon. . .
Banks are an imposition of the capitalist system.
Banks' profits are swollen by inflation.
Banks of fifty degrees are forbidden in Concorde.
Banks told me that tale.
Bank's a word with many uses.

There seems little point here in saying that 'banks. . .' limits the choice of following words, when what word *banks* itself is depends on its relation to the rest of the sentence. (What, by the way, of the sentence 'Banks. . .no that isn't what I mean.' Is that governed by its first word?)

The dependence of words on a whole sentence is like our taking words themselves as wholes. The parts of a word derive from the whole word. If language were explicable as a line of successively restricted choices it is not clear why the element of choice should not enter at the end of the first syllable of a word, but nobody is embarrassed by saying the word *country*.

It is even sometimes possible to change a word in a sentence that has already been completed. It is natural when the Countess reads Bertram's letter in Act III scene ii of *All's Well that Ends Well* to hear, 'I have sent you a daughter-in-law: she hath recovered the king, and undone me. I have wedded her, not bedded her; and sworn to make the knot eternal.' This would express his chagrined acceptance of his fate. But when the letter continues 'You shall hear I am run away' we realize that what he has sworn to make eternal is the 'not'.

Chomsky's Grammar to the Rescue

If we want the understanding of sentences possible to traditional grammar we must go beyond finite-state grammar.[3] Chomsky does so in the second grammar discussed in *Syntactic Structures*, phrase-structure (or Σ, F) grammar, in his later work called the grammar of the 'base phrase marker' and similar variant phrases. Phrase-structure grammar is, quite simply I think, the 'analysis' that used to be taught in schools when they used to teach grammar. It immediately goes beyond any finite-state grammar in beginning with the notion of the sentence; and it consists of the analysis of sentences into the syntactic functions of their words and phrases, together with the categorization of words as parts of speech. (These two should not be confused: a noun, for instance, may be the subject or the object of a verb: *noun* is classification as part of speech, *subject* or *object* according to syntactic function.)

At my old-fashioned school we used to analyse sentences into their syntactic parts by using boxes or labels; Chomsky favours brackets, or lists of 'rewrite rules', or 'tree diagrams', but the principles are in all these cases identical. (Chomsky virtually says so in *Aspects*, pp. 63–4.) The first example in *Syntactic Structures* is 'the man hit the ball'. At school we would have said something like: the subject is 'the man', the predicate 'hit the ball' in which 'hit' is the verb and 'the ball' the object. We would also categorize the words, 'the' as the definite article, 'man' as a common noun in the singular, etc. Chomsky instead defines a primitive phrase-structure grammar then uses it to construct a 'derivation' of the sentence:

(13) (i) *Sentence*→*NP*+*VP*
    (ii) *NP*→*T*+*N*

[3] Finite-state grammar is not, however, mere feeble-mindedness: it has its applications in mathematics and might even illuminate some bits of natural languages. The game in which you complete an advertising slogan in not more than six words could be seen as governed by a finite-state grammar, because the judges would be unlikely to admit neologisms. So could some card games like Lexicon. So, possibly, might the frenzy that results from a publisher's requiring an author to replace a paragraph (by return of post) in the same number of words. Perhaps finite-state grammar might even sometimes extend to the old-fashioned kind of rhetoric, much practised by politicians and eminent divines until recently, where one speaks extremely slowly, with pauses between clauses and sentences long enough to allow one, if need be, to change one's mind about what to say next. In writing it must be more common to begin a sentence before allowing inspiration, within the limits dictated by what one has written, to dictate the completion of the sentence. But these are much more problematic.

(iii) $VP \rightarrow Verb + NP$
(iv) $T \rightarrow the$
 (v) $N \rightarrow man, ball$, etc.
(vi) $Verb \rightarrow hit, took$, etc.

Suppose that we interpret each rule $X \rightarrow Y$ of (13) as the instruction 'rewrite X as Y'. We shall call (14) a *derivation* of the sentence 'the man hit the ball,' where the numbers at the right of each line of the derivation refer to the rule of the 'grammar' (13) used in constructing that line from the preceding line.

(14) *Sentence*

$NP + VP$	(i)
$T + N + VP$	(ii)
$T + N + Verb + NP$	(iii)
$the + N + Verb + NP$	(iv)
$the + man + Verb + NP$	(v)
$the + man + hit + NP$	(vi)
$the + man + hit + T + N$	(ii)
$the + man + hit + the + N$	(iv)
$the + man + hit + the + ball$	(v)

Thus the second line of (14) is formed from the first line by rewriting *Sentence* as $NP + VP$ in accordance with rule (i) of (13); the third line is formed from the second by rewriting NP as $T + N$ in accordance with rule (ii) of (13); etc.

Chomsky then does the same thing with a tree diagram:

(15)

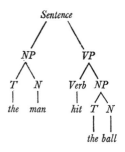

Syntactic Structures, pp. 26–7

What is going on here is, in the light of traditional grammar, plain enough; but the qualification is necessary. Chomsky never defines any of his key terms—'sentence', 'phrase', 'verb', 'noun' or even 'word'—outside the whole system; that is to say he never gives any objective or experimental evidence that they refer to

things which exist. I don't at all intend this as an objection, but
as a way of getting clear the logical status of Chomsky's discussions, as a variety of the common Western grammatical tradition.
What he means by 'sentence', 'word' etc. is then based firmly on
what we mean by them in common speech or common grammar,
and when he goes further what he means by his terms is simply
what they do in his system of grammar. I repeat that this is not
an objection.

It is noticeable that when Chomsky offers definitions they are
system-bound. For instance:

Suppose further that we propose the following general definitions:
(11) (i) Subject-of: [NP, S]
    (ii) Predicate-of: [VP, S]
    (iii) Direct-Object-of: [NP, VP]
    (iv) Main-Verb-of: [V, VP]
In this case, we can now say that...*sincerity* is the Subject-of the
sentence *sincerity may frighten the boy* and *frighten the boy* is its
Predicate; and *the boy* is the Direct-Object-of the Verb Phrase
frighten the boy and *frighten* is its Main-Verb. (*Aspects*, p. 71)

Yes. This is all right so long as no claim is made that such analyses
are language-independent explanation or that anything is being
said about linguistic universals (below, Chapter 4).

If we keep this clearly in mind, the discussion of Σ, F grammar
in *Syntactic Structures* is, minor cavils apart, unexceptionable,
though I shall suggest below that we need to keep the rather
specialized use of 'rule' in 'rewrite rule' quite clearly distinct
from rules in functional grammars that actually tell one what to
do. The analysis does make, in its own way, a kind of sense—the
kind of sense, merely, that it is. And if so, it does show the initial
step, the identification of these words as a Sentence, to have been
(within all the assumptions of traditional grammar) justified.

'Domination' is similarly unobjectionable as long as one
remembers that its sense is identically system-dependent. 'What
is meant by "domination"', says Lyons, 'should be clear, without formal definition, from the tree diagrams' (*Chomsky*, p. 61).
Chomsky himself says that 'the interpretation of such a diagram
is transparent' (*Aspects*, p. 64). When Lyons suggests that there
could be formal definition, presumably independent of anything
like the tree diagrams or labelled bracketings, he is understating
his case. 'Domination' is *only* definable by the working of the
system: domination is the sense made by our seeing that S covers

the whole sentence, that a V dominates the whole VP, and so on. Once again this is not an objection so long as we remain clear about the status of the word.

The same must be said of 'string'. I am not much worried by the rather loose use of the word to mean the result of any 'rewrite' rule's application, but we must be clear about the way in which Σ, F grammar develops *via* 'strings' into Chomsky's third and most famous kind, transformational grammar, in order to keep a grasp on the kind of understanding of language transformational grammar can offer.

Transformational grammar is not an alternative to phrase-structure grammar (as finite-state grammar tries to be): in Chomsky's account in *Syntactic Structures* phrase-structure grammar becomes an essential component of transformational grammar, and the complete system is called transformational-generative (TG) grammar. From time to time throughout his career Chomsky has given sketches of what a complete grammatical description of a sentence would be. They differ somewhat, as does the place of the phrase-structure component within the system, but essentially in all of them the phrase-structure grammar will derive base strings by inserting 'lexical items' into 'phrase markers' such as the tree quoted, and the transformational component will then generate all the sentences of the language from this set of strings. The sentences generated will include, as well as the simple declarative active 'kernel' sentences closest to the underlying base string, negatives, passives, interrogatives, 'nominal phrases', conjunction and relativization.[4] Finally, the 'surface structure' generated by the transformations contains the phonological component of the grammar which gives phonetic instructions for converting surface structure into sound. Starting the other way round, with sound, as seems to me much more natural with Chomskyan grammar which is essentially a form of syntactic analysis, a complete Chomsky grammar will derive surface structure (the words of the sentence) from sound, will analyse surface structure transformationally into the 'deep structure' of the kernel sentences 'underlying' it, and this deep structure through all the steps of the phrase structure

[4] 'The kernel consists of simple, declarative, active sentences (in fact, probably a finite number of these), and . . . all other sentences can be described more simply as transforms' (*Syntactic Structures*, p. 80).

derivation to S on the one hand, and to 'lexical items' (which may themselves be analysed into their underlying universal semantic components) on the other.[5] Here is one of Chomsky's statements:

The syntactic component consists of a base that generates deep structures and a transformational part that maps them into surface structures. The deep structure of a sentence is submitted to the semantic component for semantic interpretation, and its surface structure enters the phonological component and undergoes phonetic interpretation. The final effect of a grammar, then, is to relate a semantic interpretation to a phonetic representation—that is, to state how a sentence is interpreted. This relation is mediated by the syntactic component of the grammar, which constitutes its sole 'creative' part. (*Aspects*, pp. 135–6)

Thus, given (by Σ, F grammar) the sentence 'the man hit the ball', a transformational grammar will 'generate' from it 'did the man hit the ball?', 'the man did not hit the ball', 'the ball was hit by the man', as well as the phrases '...who hit the ball...', 'if the man hit the ball...', 'the man's hitting of the ball...' and from it and other strings the forms 'the (adjective) man hit the (adjective) ball', 'the (adjective and adjective) man...' and so on. I suppose transformational grammar must also generate '...and the man hit the ball' and 'the man hit the ball and...' though I cannot recall any treatment of this sort of conjunction, and it seems a little grandiose to call the placing of *and* before or after a sentence a 'recursive transformation'.

Some years after *Syntactic Structures* it began to be important to the Chomskyans to distinguish these two kinds of trans-formation, 'recursive' and 'non-recursive'. The 'non-recursive' transformations (passive, interrogative, negative...) convert the string underlying a simple declaratory active sentence into another simple sentence of their respective syntactic kind. They are very limited in number (the number cannot be finally fixed because what belongs to the transformational and what to the phrase-structure parts of the grammar is debatable)—a dozen at the outside. If then English has a 'highly restricted (perhaps finite) set of *basic strings*, each with an associated structural description called a *base Phrase-marker*' (*Aspects*, p. 17), the number of simple sentences that can be generated will be the

[5] On the belief that meaning is whatever semantic universals underlie words, see below, Chapters 5 and 6.

(perhaps finite) number of strings multiplied by the number of usable non-recursive transformations.

'Recursive' transformations are the ones that can be repeated to build an infinite number of complex sentences from a finite number of strings; transforms are thus, in Chomsky's view as quoted, the 'sole "creative" part' of language. Relatives are one obvious example. '...who hit the ball...' demands an antecedent and a main verb to follow and can only belong to a complex sentence.

The transformations are related to each other by way of the strings underlying kernel sentences. A string is just the words of the kernel sentence understood in the syntactic relations (or 'labelled bracketing') that constitute the kernel sentence, as:

$$\text{NP}_1 \text{——— V ——— NP}_2$$

$$\underbrace{\text{the man}} \qquad \text{hit} \qquad \underbrace{\text{the ball}}$$

Transformations operate upon the syntactic relations so understood; 'To specify a transformation explicitly we must describe the analysis of the strings to which it applies and the structural change that it effects on these strings' (*Syntactic Structures*, p. 61; cf. p. 111). The terms 'string' and 'transformation' are defined within the whole grammar just like Chomsky's other terms and are therefore pure grammatical abstractions existing nowhere but in grammar.

The exact borders between the phrase-structure and transformational parts of Chomsky's grammar vary from time to time, which doesn't matter much. (He also points out in *Aspects* that the phrase-structure component itself, now modified into the 'base string', has certain transformational features, but I will not discuss this.) Traditional grammar can, of course, discuss complex sentences in its own ways; and even Chomsky's Σ, F model is taken a lot further at the end of *Syntactic Structures* than in the passage I quoted. There he for instance gives a rule about singular and plural NPs and another about *Aux*, together with a fairly complicated list of the alternatives of *Aux*. In this phrase-structure grammar of *Aux* Chomsky includes '(*have* + *en*)' and '(*be* + *ing*)', i.e. past and present tenses, but not (*be* + *en*), the passive. This is not because the passive *cannot* be included in a phrase-structure grammar; Chomsky offers a way of doing so earlier in *Syntactic Structures*. But he argues that the passive is best dealt with in the transformational part of the grammar.

Chomsky's Grammar to the Rescue

This is the claim Chomsky makes for the *Syntactic Structures* version of TG grammar:

We can greatly simplify the description of English and gain new and important insight into its formal structure if we limit the direct description in terms of phrase structure to a kernel of basic sentences (simple, declarative, active, with no complex verb or noun phrases), deriving all other sentences from these...by transformation, possibly repeated. (pp. 106–7)

Let us consider the claim as it relates to the passive, which is Chomsky's third and clinching example in *Syntactic Structures* of transformational grammar's superiority.

As a third example of the inadequacy of the conceptions of phrase structure, consider the case of the active–passive relation. Passive sentences are formed by selecting the element $be + en$ in rule (28iii) [an extended phrase-structure grammar]. But there are heavy restrictions on this element that make it unique among the elements of the auxiliary phrase. For one thing, $be + en$ can be selected only if the following V is transitive (e.g., $was + eaten$ is permitted, but not $was + occurred$); but with a few exceptions the other elements of the auxiliary phrase can occur freely with verbs. Furthermore, $be + en$ cannot be selected if the verb V is followed by a noun phrase, as in (30) (e.g., we cannot in general have $NP + is + V + en + NP$, even when V is transitive—we cannot have 'lunch is eaten John'). Furthermore, if V is transitive and is followed by the prepositional phrase $by + NP$, then we *must* select $be + en$ (we can have 'lunch is eaten by John' but not 'John is eating by lunch,' etc.). Finally, note that in elaborating (13) [the skeletal phrase-structure grammar, above, p. 23] into a full-fledged grammar we will have to place many restrictions on the choice of V in terms of subject and object in order to permit such sentences as: 'John admires sincerity,' 'sincerity frightens John,' 'John plays golf,' 'John drinks wine,' while excluding the 'inverse' non-sentences 'sincerity admires John,' 'John frightens sincerity,' 'golf plays John,' 'wine drinks John.' (pp. 42–3)

Instead Chomsky proposes a transformational rule:

(34) If S_1 is a grammatical sentence of the form
$$NP_1 \text{——} Aux \text{——} V \text{——} NP_2$$
then the corresponding string of the form
$$NP_2 \text{——} Aux + be + en \text{——} V \text{——} by + NP_1$$
is also a grammatical sentence.

(p. 43)

Chomsky's first claim is that this is a general rule which gets round the difficulties he has been discussing:

> We can now drop the element *be* + *en*, and all of the special restrictions associated with it, from (28iii). The fact that *be* + *en* requires a transitive verb, that it cannot occur before $V + NP$, that it must occur before $V + by + NP$ (where V is transitive), that it inverts the order of the surrounding noun phrases, is in each case an automatic consequence of rule (34). This rule leads to a considerable simplification of the grammar. But (34) is well beyond the limits of $[\Sigma, F]$ grammars. Like (29ii), it requires reference to the constituent structure of the string to which it applies and it carries out an inversion on this string in a structurally determined manner. (*ibid.*)

The strength of the claim seems to me to be at the end, and I shall come back to saying why. But I doubt whether the grammar of English is simplified by this way of talking. Granting that the transformational rule is true, we shall not have removed the difficulties about transitivity etc. out of our discussion, but only into another (and now unspecified) part of our grammar. For though it is true that if the active is a well-formed sentence of the appropriate structure the passive will also be well-formed, the transformational rule will not tell us whether the active is well-formed; but this must somewhere be said if the grammar is to generate all and only the well-formed sentences of the language.[6] If by some mistake we accept a sentence with an intransitive main verb and a direct object as well-formed there will be nothing to prevent our calling the passive well-formed too, for the transformation will apply quite regularly: 'John sat the apple' and 'the apple was sat by John'. To explain why both are ill-formed we simply have to start talking about transitivity again. Or, to take cases where we would have to consider 'collocability' rather than transitivity: the passive transformation cannot in itself rule out Chomsky's own examples 'golf plays John', 'wine drinks John' etc., but will form from them the equally ungrammatical 'John is played by golf', 'John is drunk by wine' etc.

At one point, though, Chomsky has done more with the passive than he claims. Chomsky thinks it quite important to establish that the strings on which the transformations operate are closer

---

[6] In *Aspects* the 'somewhere' becomes the lexicon, for Chomsky argues on pp. 94ff. that the lexicon should contain the items which will, in an older terminology, decide whether a verb is transitive or not.

to simple declarative active sentences than, e.g., to passives. In logic or psychology this may be so, but I know of no grammatical reason other than a preference for simplicity why we should not, for instance, take negative interrogative passives as kernels and derive declaratory actives as well as all other forms from them. Chomsky tries to support his position by arguing that it is easier to derive the passive from the active than vice versa: in fact it seems to me exactly as easy to transform passive into active as active into passive, and I believe this strengthens the system as pure grammar. We can merely state Chomsky's rule the other way round to derive active from passive:

$$NP_1 \text{——} Aux + be + en \text{——} V \text{——} by + NP_2$$
$$\rightarrow NP_2 \text{——} Aux \text{——} V \text{——} NP_1$$

Chomsky objects that such a rule will not allow for a case like 'John was drunk by midnight' but will generate from it an active *'midnight drank John' (*Syntactic Structures*, p. 80). All one does there is say that 'John was drunk by midnight' is not a passive. It is not the function of the transformation to identify passives, only to derive them from actives. Chomsky could handle this case with his distinction between deep and surface structure (below, Chapter 4): in one way or another the grammarian will say that the sentence may look superficially like a passive but that really the last phrase is adverbial of time, not instrumental. If this example does cause problems, however, they will be found equally in active to passive. Chomsky (unlike T. S. Eliot) may well be of the opinion that 'midnight shakes the memory' is not well-formed, but if it is we can generate from it a passive 'the memory is shaken by midnight', where 'by midnight' looks more like an adverb of time than an agent in the passive. (See below, pp. 125 ff.)

What Chomsky *has* done with his discussion of the passive, and, in general, with transformational grammar, is to make a refined definition of one part of the domain of traditional syntax. He has shown how to relate to a simple declarative sentence all the other forms which this area of syntax can recognize as so related. His transformational rules do show the ways in which different sentences may be different syntactic forms of one another; they also exclude carefully all other matters from this area of discussion. The area of discussion is thus defined as what can be so transformed: transformational grammar is what can meaningfully be discussed as such. The validation of such discussion is still within the system.

The longest and most careful discussion in *Studies on Semantics in Generative Grammar* is the chapter 'Remarks on Nominalization'. The question at issue is whether what Chomsky calls 'gerundive nominals' can be brought within the transformational system, i.e. whether they are relatable to the kernel in the same system of rules as the negative, interrogative and passive. For instance can 'John's refusing the offer' be related to 'John refused the offer' by the same kind of rule that will generate from the latter 'the offer was refused by John', 'did John refuse the offer?', 'John did not refuse the offer' etc.? I will not recapitulate Chomsky's argument, which I think as convincing as need be. His conclusion is that 'The properties of gerundive nominals follow directly from the assumption that there is a transformational process of gerundive nominalization. The very different cluster of properties of derived nominals follows directly from the assumption that they are not transformationally derived' (p. 160). So 'John's refusing the offer' can be transformationally related to 'John refused the offer' but 'John's refusal of the offer' cannot. This, if it is convincing, is a further refinement of definition of the domain of transformational grammar, a drawing of one of its boundaries.

The domain is simply S, the sentence. Chomsky's phrase-structure and transformational 'components' are two ways of analysing sentences. S→NP+VP defines every sentence as having a noun phrase and a verb phrase. (If it hasn't, the missing phrase is represented as *deleted*, i.e. originally present in the analysis.) This is, of course, another system-dependent definition. The keystone of Chomsky's arch *must* be S; Koestler can help me make the point. His version of a Chomskyan tree puts at the top not S but I (idea). This is the linguist's dream but is *syntactically* impossible—and we are discussing syntax. 'Every sentence has a main verb' would be a grammatical definition, not an observation.

Chomsky's work is none the worse for being grammar, but if so it is not science. There is no way of testing a tree diagram experimentally.

I don't mean that grammatical analysis cannot be true or false; I am commenting on its status, which is not that of an hypothesis in science. If one *denies* that 'hit the ball' in 'the man hit the ball' is a VP one will be wrong or crazy: but one can only use TG analysis to say as much to people who already know. This is not experimental proof of hypothesis; moreover TG analysis cannot be conducted like a properly defined experiment.

TG grammar is usable in syntactic analysis. But it has no rules for applying the rules. The transformations apply in a fixed order;[7] some must come after others if sentences are to be correctly generated. But there is no rule beyond the sense made, i.e. one's pre-existent sense of language, for whether to apply a transformation at all. Chomsky begins his grammars 'assuming the set of grammatical sentences of English to be given' (*Syntactic Structures*, p. 18). The teacher analyses sentences and the learner imitates him and is eventually able to analyse sentences for himself; and that's all. Traditional grammars, says Chomsky, 'provide only examples and hints concerning the regular and productive syntactic process' (*Aspects*, p. 5). So does TG grammar, and is none the worse for that.

Grammar merely expresses one kind of regularity we sense in language, but outside our sense of language, to which grammar has to make its appeal, grammar can explain nothing. A computer programmed to analyse written sentences transformationally would always run the risk of being thrown by things like 'the memory was shaken by midnight' and generally by all the places where the rules of language are, as Hockett says, 'rubbery'. (And Hockett thinks that *all* grammatical rules are rubbery.) The only safeguard against such mistakes is familiarity with the language; i.e. experience of it in use, a sense of how far the elastic of language can stretch, which cannot be a property of a TG grammar. (Below, pp. 47, 173.)

Even if a computer did its analyses correctly, the correctness would be in the judgement of the grammarian following the machine with understanding. And his judgement that the computer was right or wrong could not finally be governed by the rules of grammar, though it would certainly use them.

The transformational part of Chomsky's grammars codifies, then, the relations between simple declarative sentences and all the other forms of sentence. 'Generative' is therefore *prima facie*

---

[7] The completest account of English tranformational processes to have received Chomsky's blessing is Marina K. Burt, *From Deep to Surface Structure, An Introduction to Transformational Syntax* (New York, 1971).

misleading, for Chomsky's grammars cannot *actually* generate sentences or give instructions about how to do so, and he is quite scrupulously clear on this point. Traditional grammars will in competent hands generate sentences (most obviously in course of translation), in the application to the lexicon of the rules of the grammar by someone who knows what he wants to say (i.e. is translating); TG grammar is a purer study and will only describe. As Chomsky says,

Actually, grammars of the form that we have been discussing are quite neutral as between speaker and hearer, between synthesis and analysis of utterances. A grammar does not tell us how to synthesize a specific utterance; it does not tell us how to analyze a particular given utterance. In fact, these two tasks which the speaker and hearer must perform are essentially the same, and are both outside the scope of grammars of the form (35). Each such grammar is simply a description of a certain set of utterances, namely, those which it generates. (*Syntactic Structures*, p. 48)

If I say that Chomsky has attained the goal of complete use-lessness I don't at all intend a sneer. At best Chomsky is quite clear that, like our blackboard analyses at school but unlike the paradigms of the French or German or Latin lessons, his grammar is pure 'description'. His troubles start, as we shall see, when he becomes dissatisfied with 'description' and attributes the tasks it does to 'speaker and hearer'. TG grammar is not meant to be a useful science, but this is no objection to it.

Within their limits traditional grammar and Chomsky's transformations are both solid and informative. Derwing, who takes to an extreme Chomsky's dissatisfaction with pure grammatical description, asks 'Of what significance is a "generative explanation", for which no psychological reality is even claimed?' (p. 287). The answer to that one is: Of grammatical significance. It may not tell us everything, it may even not tell us much, to say that some sounds are or are not a sentence, but it is something. Traditional grammar is not what Derwing earlier calls it, 'arbitrary descriptive devices for a corpus of sentences and structural descriptions which are of no psychological significance' (p. 285). It is true that grammar has no psychological significance of the kind Derwing demands, but not that its descriptions are 'arbitrary'. TG grammar, like any other, has one quality of an intellectual discipline: that is, by following its own self-contained rules it makes the sense it is.

This is why, also, Robert A. Hall Jr is unconvincing when in the course of an argument about 'deep and surface structure' with which I am in general sympathy (below, Chapter 4) he calls the Chomskyan kernel sentences 'nothing but a paraphrase of a given construction concocted *ad hoc. . .*' (*An Essay on Language* (Philadelphia, 1968), p. 53). They are paraphrases, but by the rules of the grammar, making grammatical sense and therefore not 'nothing but' and not '*ad hoc*'. Hall seems to me to concede the point when he goes on to give two alternative kernels underlying a phrase and to say that one is chosen only because 'it is easier to perform grammatical operations on'. What better reason could there be for choice in grammar?

Chomsky's contribution is small by comparison with the advances made in Athens and Alexandria and represented in the security, the commonplaceness of words like our *verb, noun, sentence, word*; but that is the common fate of genuine contributors to an established discipline. His transformations are an elegant addition to it: they do work and they do allow us to understand one aspect of the regularities of language. The sense made by traditional grammar and Chomsky's refinement of it is, as I shall go on to show, very restricted; but linguists (as I shall also go on to show) are not so fortunately situated as to be able to turn up their noses at *any* genuine sense about language.

3

The Limits of Transformational-Generative Grammar

The transformational part of Chomsky's grammar relates all the other forms of sentence it can define to simple declarative sentences. There is an obvious implausibility in trying to make this genuine achievement the basis for a scientific explanation of the whole of language.

Right at the beginning of *Syntactic Structures* Chomsky says, 'From now on I will consider a *language* to be a set (finite or infinite) of sentences...' (p. 13). But there is a lot more to language than the set of sentences which is all that TG grammar, as a form of traditional syntax, can study. Chomsky is unclear about this vital matter. Later in the same paragraph 'sentences' have slid into 'sequences', and by page 15 he is talking instead of 'grammatical utterances'. With this last and very important class TG grammar has nothing to do. 'Let us...assume tentatively that the primary linguistic data consist of signals classified as sentences and nonsentences' (*Aspects*, p. 52). No, signals so classified are the primary grammatical data subject to Chomskyan analysis; but the equation of what TG grammar can describe with language is here merely arbitrary.[1]

A TG grammar tells us that a group of words does or does not follow its rules for the well-formed sentences of a language, but the 'not' has to include *everything* not representable by a tree with S at the apex. Its only way of distinguishing (i) my breaking in mid-sentence of English into French, (ii) my beginning in

---

[1] Chomsky's equation of sentences and language is one of his entrances to the fallacy of the Acquisition Device, which I shall discuss in the next chapter; for instance when he writes, 'Primary linguistic data [consist] of a finite amount of information about sentences...Certain signals might be accepted as properly formed sentences, while others are classed as non-sentences, as a result of correction of the learner's attempts on the part of the linguistic community' (*Aspects*, p. 31). No, there is no need for the concept of the sentence to enter into corrections of children either on the adult's or the child's part, before the child goes to school and begins writing essays and is drilled to end sentences with a full stop. Sentences arrive with grammatical description, and that with grammarians.

mid-sentence to swear in English, (iii) my interrupting a sentence
in order to shriek, is by way of the notion 'degrees of grammaticalness', which plainly offers complete sentences as criteria.
Yet (i) 'The man hit——trois cents mille bleus diables!' is a
mixture of English and French, (ii) 'The man hit——f**k off,
damn it all!' is certainly all fluent English and 'The man hit——
AAARGH!' is half English and half not analysable language at all.
TG grammar cannot distinguish the cases. But are not the non-
sentences *of a language* an important part of a language which a
grammar ought to distinguish from other languages and from
non-language?

Some nonsentences are far from being degenerate or ill-
formed. At the head of this page or the next you will observe the
words '*The New Grammarians' Funeral*'. They are not a sentence (though had I been writing a hundred years ago they would
most likely have begun with a capital letter and ended with a
full stop) but are not objectionable on grammatical grounds.
'The Hon. Mrs Cholmondeley *At Home* Monday 23 August
7.30 p.m. *RSVP*' ditto. On an envelope 'Professor Noam
Chomsky, Massachusetts Institute of Technology, U.S.A.' could
not well be replaced by a sentence; 'Bear this letter right speedily
to...' before the name would be a joke in modern English. 'Ah,
but this is *writing*', says the linguist, 'and our subject is *speech.*'
My own belief is that our subject is language (see below, pp.
174 ff.); but in any case it is not hard to give examples of non-
sentences from what is spoken.

Chomsky will call things like the following utterances
'degenerate':

'What was it you were saying about...?'
'Hm...?'
'What, I mean——?'
'Oh yes, that was...no, I know...'
'It was her you mean and not...?'
'Well well!'

Is this not more like English than such hardly imaginable gems
as 'the old men come' and 'the man hit the ball'? (J. R. Firth
somewhere observes that linguists habitually work with examples
that would only be uttered by idiots.) This 'degeneracy' is far
from being confined to casual or second-rate uses of the language.
When Othello cries, 'Lie with her? lie on her? We say lie on

her, when they belie her. Lie with her: 'zounds, that 's fulsome: Handkerchief: Confessions: Handkerchief...' he is not speaking well-formed sentences. But not only is what he says English, it has been found by generations of hearers to be quite unusually clear and expressive English. Othello is judged ungrammatical only by the arbitrary rule that only sentences are grammatical.

If one says instead that the problem of analysing Othello grammatically is the ancient one of ellipsis, TG grammar's performance is not much improved.

At the beginning of the *Philosophical Investigations*, Wittgenstein imagines a number of 'primitive languages', one of which is a finite-state language consisting of a number of 'elliptical' utterances by a group of builders:

> Let us imagine a language for which the description given by Augustine is right. The language is meant to serve for communication between a builder A and an assistant B. A is building with building-stones: there are blocks, pillars, slabs and beams. B has to pass the stones, and that in the order in which A needs them. For this purpose they use a language consisting of the words 'block', 'pillar', 'slab', 'beam'. A calls them out;—B brings the stone which he has learnt to bring at such-and-such a call. ——Conceive this as a complete primitive language. (p. 3e)

There are difficulties about obeying the last instruction: it is difficult to conceive any such system as a language, for reasons that Chomsky often offers. He would say that its grammar is not a finite device for generating an infinite number of sentences and therefore does not qualify as the grammar of a natural language, whose creativity is infinite. A more Wittgensteinian objection might be to say that if a language is the form of a life, the life whose form this language is could not be recognized as human. But there are sentences to be found in English rather like Wittgenstein's 'Slab', 'Beam' etc., if either are to be called sentences.

I do not mean the language of two-year-old children, which might reasonably be thought of as primitive and does often consist of what we may be tempted to call 'one-word sentences'. Max Black says that these are ' "telegraphic" simplifications of adult sentences' (*The Labyrinth of Language*, paperback reprint (1972), p. 16) which, by unfortunately suggesting that the child is saying the 'adult sentence' to itself before shortening it, may show that this way into our problem is not enlightening. Collingwood's example 'Hattiaw' (below, p. 64) would then really mean 'I am throwing my hat off'. But what would 'really mean' mean? Again, I do not mean J. L. Austin's odd (quite unsubstantiable) belief that languages developed historically out of one-word utterances, and the consequent difficulty of wondering whether the later development is somehow expressed in the original word.

My examples are perfectly ordinary parts of our language. In some families when the children forget to shut the door the parents just say or shout 'Door!' They could say other things, of course, but they don't. Some people, too, if you stand in their light when they are reading will just say 'Light!' Are these to be expanded to 'Shut the door!' or to Claudius's cry 'Give me some light!'? And, to raise the different question of categories, are these single words nouns, verbs or what?

Or take the perhaps extreme case of the bus conductor who rings the bell once to stop the bus and twice to make it go. One is inclined to call what he does a kind of signal or code, which the driver decodes as 'stop' or 'go' in English. The bell can indeed be so paraphrased—to do so is to make a kind of grammar—and notices to that effect may be put up in the bus. But I know of no evidence that conductors and drivers do say 'go' or 'stop' to themselves at any stage when they ring or hear the bell, and it seems rather improbable. What is more, it is not necessary that conductors and drivers should ever have been taught the English meanings of the bell: they may be just picked up as common knowledge or even learned by induction. And we are discussing language, not conditioned reflex, because the driver understands and sometimes questions the instruction. We seem in fact here to have a Wittgensteinian primitive language—which, to be sure, could only be used by people who also have the other parts of a natural language, but which nevertheless is not easy to describe by a grammar of English sentences.

All TG grammar can do with these one-word or one-sound utterances is to relate them to the kernels it *can* deal with, by large numbers of 'deletion transformations'. But does this mean that, according to TG grammar, the longer unspoken sentences are somehow more real, or only that TG grammar cannot handle these cases without extreme clumsiness?[2] Either way, these

---

[2] Cf. 'The sentence is "elliptical", not because it leaves out something that we think when we utter it, but because it is shortened—in comparison with

examples demolish Katz's contention that common nouns 'cannot by themselves express full messages in linguistic communication, as do sentences'.[3]

Moreover with 'ellipsis' the limits of TG grammar are more severe than those of traditional grammar, for adjectives have to be treated in TG grammar as cases of ellipsis and derived from kernels by deletion transformations and relativization. 'Thus, *The gay red hat* can be thought of as involving two strings in deep structure: *The hat is red* and *The hat is gay*. Intermediate stages would be *The hat which is red is gay* and *The red hat is gay*' (Judith Greene, *Psycholinguistics* (1972), p. 161). This is clumsier than the older grammar, which would just say that 'gay' and 'red' are adjectives qualifying and governed by 'hat'. This could more or less be done by TG grammar if it included the adjective in the kernel sentence or base string, within whatever NP dominates it, i.e. by making the adjective categorial not part of syntactic structure. I suspect the Chomskyans prefer derivation from separate underlying strings not for any good grammatical reason but because it better fits their notions of logic (below, Chapter 6). The upshot, anyway, is that rather simple-looking sentences have to be derived from large numbers of kernels. The one I intend to play with later, 'she was wearing her old blue coat', will have to generate its adjectives by a series of deletions and relativizations from 'the coat was hers', 'the coat was old' and 'the coat was blue'. (The rest of the sentence will come from other strings.)

At another extreme, since TG grammar can only analyse sentences, if faced with a parenthesis it can only disentangle it from the sentence into which it is inserted and then analyse both separately; for a parenthesis is just one sentence placed in another but not related syntactically except by the insertion. TG analysis would miss the point of the particular relation of the two sentences. The relevant grammatical analysis is merely the layout on the page, with the parenthesis distinguished by means of commas, em rules or round brackets.

What is TG grammar to say of sentences that successfully break its rules? All it can do is to declare them ill-formed; but

---

a particular paradigm of our grammar' (*Investigations*, p. 10e; cf. also the preceding, extremely funny discussion of 'Slab!').

[3] Jerrold J. Katz, *Semantic Theory* (New York, 1972), p. 35.

what if people say them nevertheless? In reaction against the nineteenth-century tradition most modern linguistics looks to me excessively synchronic, and a relapse into prescriptivism is one result. A sentence that grammar will correctly call ungrammatical at one time may well be grammatical at another; and the two times may be contemporary in literature: 'It am I' in Chaucer as we read him now is grammatical, but would not be grammatical if I said it. On the other hand 'It's me' is now all right. TG grammar has no way of accommodating changes in the rules. In Shakespeare's day there must have been a sort of pressure towards that very useful word *its*: but the word was just not good English—until, rather suddenly, it just was. When such changes occur, TG grammar's rules for present English must be revised to allow for the change; but they can give no account of how, why, or indeed *if* the change happens.

A more central case is the poet who breaks the rules. There is no past imperative in English and, many philosophers would say, there could not be in any language because it makes no sense to order someone to have done something in the past. 'I hope Betty scrubbed the floor yesterday' but not 'Have scrubbed the floor yesterday, O Betty!' Yet one knows what form would be used for a past imperative, and in fact it is a form used by Hopkins:

> Have fair fallen, O fair, fair have fallen, so dear
> To me, so arch-especial a spirit as heaves in Henry Purcell.

Much of the rest of that sentence is equally ill-formed. The indirect object of the command is 'a spirit', not 'Henry Purcell'; further, spirits cannot 'heave', and the adjectives 'dear' and 'arch-especial' are wrongly placed. In well-formed English the sentence would have to be something like 'I hope good has come to the spirit of Henry Purcell, a spirit that still lives and is dear and especial to me.' Myself, I prefer Hopkins, even when he writes what Chomsky might well take as an example of a non-sentence: 'hold them cheap may who ne'er hung there'.

All that Chomsky's grammar could say about these is that they are, in particular ways, ill-formed. The same would have to be said of Roy Kerridge's innovation, in the mind of a character whom a mysterious 'They' persecute: 'The trouble was that They had forced him, by remote control, into a betting shop, where he had lost most of his poor workingman's dole money. From They it had come, and to They it had returned' (*Beside the Seaside* (Swansea, 1974), p. 19). And what could TG grammar make of Macbeth's profoundly expressive utterance, not to be explained as only a Freudian slip, 'My thought/Whose murther yet is but fantastical'?

Even within its proper limits, Chomsky's grammar has notable weaknesses. The rigid confinement of meaning to the lexicon as manipulated by the transformations, and of 'surface structure' to the ordering of sound, leads to difficulties about such a common part of language—securely within the province of the traditional grammarian—as stress and intonation.

Tone, of course, sometimes means something quite idiosyncratic, though even there it would seem to me to be part of the proper concern of the linguist, however far beyond TG grammar. Some tones, too, are part of the common language without being within the range of traditional syntax.

He had been quite certain from Lady Monogram's manner and words, and also from his daughter's face, that Mr Brehgert was mentioned as an accepted lover. Lady Monogram had meant that it should be so, and any father would have understood her tone. (Trollope, *The Way We Live Now*, Chap. 65)

There could, presumably, be some formal account of such tones, though it could hardly codify anything recognizable as 'rules', and would certainly not be explaining tone as the particular manifestations of some linguistic universal. Such examples also raise the problem we shall discuss later, of *what* it is that Lady Monogram says by her tone. 'She said *that* Mr Brehgert was Georgiana's lover' would hardly be an untendentious account, though what her speech does is to assure Mr Longestaffe of that fact.

Again, one can in spoken English use a tone to indicate that the words uttered are not one's own, to talk in inverted commas. What is the TG grammar of that?

The tones that Chomsky should have brought within TG grammar are, however, rather different. To go back to the example I have been using since well before Chomsky became interested in the question: however one stresses or phrases the sentence 'she was wearing her old blue coat' a grammar of the *Syntactic Structures* type will call it the same sentence and analyse it the same way into the same underlying strings. But with different stresses it can answer yes or no to about fourteen different questions, i.e. make about fourteen different propositions. Who was wearing her old blue coat? *She* was. . .Surely she wasn't wearing her old blue coat? She *was*. . .What was she doing with it? She was *wearing* her old blue coat. And so on.

Further, some stressings will alter the grammar even in Chomsky's terms. '*She* was wearing *her*. . .' can make the sentence refer to two women, and Chomsky would then have to derive the sentence from a different set of base strings. And what of Pope's line

> Sir Balaam now, he lives like other folk?

If we do not stress 'Sir' we misunderstand the line. Now he has been knighted, Sir Balaam has ceased to live eccentrically: or, in more traditional terms, 'Sir' is predicative. The information conveyed is given by the stress, a feature of the 'surface structure' that Chomsky thinks cannot affect syntactic analysis. He would have to judge '*Sir* Balaam now. . .' (='now that he is Sir Balaam') the same sentence as 'Sir Balaam *now*. . .' (= 'at this point in time Sir Balaam').

There is as far as I know nothing wrong with Chomsky's account of the interrogative transformation, and our sentence will go through it regularly to become 'Was she wearing her old blue coat?' Any declarative sentence, however, can be transformed into an interrogative more economically by the mere addition of a question mark: 'She was wearing her old blue coat?' In speech the interrogativeness will be expressed by intonation. But this too, Chomsky would have to say, is part of the surface structure and cannot affect the deep structure of the sentence.

Yet these stresses are different from Lady Monogram's meaning tone, and different again from the personal idiosyncrasies of tone which are hardly available for grammatical discussion, in that they do follow context-free rules of a kind enough like the rules of syntax to be brought within it. Chomsky, having come across these problems in more recent work, and faithful to his principle of avoiding the trivial and the vacuous, declines to modify his grammar in any of the possible ways that could include these last stresses within it. He very honestly refuses to save the phenomena at the expense of loosening the coherence of the transformational-generative system:

The gravest defect of the theory of transformational grammar is its enormous latitude and descriptive power. Virtually anything can be expressed as a phrase marker, i.e., a properly parenthesized expression with parenthesized segments assigned to categories. Virtually any imaginable rule can be described in transformational terms. Therefore a critical problem in making transformational grammar a substantive theory with explanatory force is to restrict the category of admissible phrase markers, admissible transformations, and admissible derivations...The 'most conservative' theory is one that has no more theoretical apparatus than what was described: phrase markers and transformations. The descriptive power of such a system is enormous. Hence this is a rather uninteresting theory. It can be made still more uninteresting by permitting still further latitude, for example, by allowing rules other than transformations that can be used to constrain derivations. (*Studies on Semantics*, pp. 124–5, 126)

But in this case the TG system just fails to account for these indisputable facts about language. 'The real hazards of language', as I. A. Richards says in a suggestive brief discussion, 'are conspicuously *not* represented' ('Why Generative Grammar Does Not Help', *English Language Teaching*, XXII, nos. 1–2 (1967–8); no. 2, p. 101).

TG grammar, even if it had attained such perfection as is possible to it, even if it were able to equate language with sentences and describe all sentences, would still not get very far with understanding sentences. No grammar can ever guarantee a sentence as belonging to the language. A computer could be programmed to generate well-formed sentences by the application of base-structure and transformational rules to a lexicon, but it would not follow that these were sentences of the language. All that could be said of them would be that they obey the grammatical rules of a language. But (in a wider sense of grammar) it is, for instance, a *grammatical* absurdity to suppose that computers can compose poems. To be part of the language a sentence has to be used, and the only people capable of doing that are human beings. (Below, p. 114.)

I postpone the discussion of competence *vs* performance and am not suggesting that grammar must formulate all the rules for being human. I do think, though, that any real linguist is interested in what sentences *do*, in language. Though what TG grammar can say is true, it can say little about what role sentences play.

The sentence must be used in language: hence Chomsky's effort to describe sentences by rules which are those of the whole language. But Chomsky's concentration on isolated sentences is itself a kind of atomism, for the sentence, to be a sentence, needs a home in language as well as in the rules of syntax; it needs a situation which will allow it to do what it does as a sentence. The Chomskyan syntactician, seeing language as a set of sentences, can only see the situation of any sentence as all the other competent sentences (just as a phonologist can only surround one phoneme by others). But this is not the situation (at widest the whole language) where the sentence does something in language.

Sentences are a rather small part of language. Chomsky never gives any account of paragraphs, chapters, books, or any other of the larger units of which sentences are a kind of atom. But it is the larger unit which decides what the sentence is doing in language, not vice versa. 'The waves broke on the shore' is a good Chomsky atomic sentence, capable of going through a number of transformations. But is it the same sentence as just used and as the last sentence of *The Waves*? Only by the rules of syntax, which are not, here, those of the real existence of sentences in language.

Borges's famous demonstration that 'the same' pages of a book have a quite different sense if they are part of Cervantes's *Don Quixote* from when they are part of Pierre Menard's is relevant here ('Pierre Menard, author of the *Quixote*', *Labyrinths*, transl. Donald A. Yates and James E. Irby, 1970), and so is thought about the fading of life from Restoration comedy in the early years of the eighteenth century. Characters in Wycherley or Congreve are in deadly, maniacal earnest in their hunt for women (or, if husbands, in their desperate determination not to be cuckolded). In Farquhar it has all somehow turned sweet, and by the time we get to Vanbrugh, although exactly the same things are said—imaginably the same sentences—as in the Restoration's disgusting prime, they are said as a romp, the desperation has departed, and 'the same' sentences would mean something quite different. The differences are controlled by the differences of whole plays: the sentences do different things in different plays.

Or take Browning's line 'Oh! to be in England, now that

April 's there'. The last time I heard that spoken was in tones of withering contempt by an old miner, climbing aboard a bus in Nottinghamshire as the grey light of dawn was breaking on All Fools' Day in the middle of a snowstorm. Do the circumstances not affect the sentence? Not its syntax, and not its status in Browning's poem. But it is not being used now as the first line of a poem, and if we say firmly that in any case it must be the same sentence what is that but an assertion that the only proper observation of language is syntax but that syntax is unfortunately unable to observe what really happens in language?

Chomsky always discusses one sentence at a time, but as Richards observes (p. 103) we rarely meet sentences in isolation—certainly not in Chomsky's works. In books of grammar the place of isolated sentences is as examples on the grammarian's specimen-slide, and that decides what they are and do. Elsewhere in language the specimens might be quite different. (I have seen Chomsky's example of nonsense, 'Colourless green ideas sleep furiously', as a line of a poem, where part of its sense is its allusion to the work of Chomsky.)

Similarly I don't believe there can be a TG account of sentence repetition. If we repeat a sentence TG grammar will just have to say that second time it is the same sentence. But does not our repetition make a difference? Think of a repeated phrase in music: second time it has just the same musical grammar as first time, but will make a different musical sense just because of the relations between 'the same' phrases made by repetition.

In short, Chomsky's syntactic abstraction—which is his respectability as an old-fashioned sentence-analyser—ensures that his grammar shall not describe what sentences really do in language.

I will begin to introduce this theme, the idea that what sentences are is what they do in language, by a preliminary discussion of what I will call 'aspect'. I take the term from the grammar of Greek tenses but want to use it much more widely for whatever we take any use of language *as*. For instance a grammatical negative can affirm something (below, p. 50). If a sentence has undergone the negative transformation, Chomsky must simply say that it is a negative, but if it is used to affirm something, if it plays an affirmative role, I will say that its 'aspect' is affirmative.

'Used' will also introduce my crucial disagreement with Chomsky, whose great aim is to state the rules of language as opposed to observing uses of language. I have heartily agreed with Chomsky that the grammar of a language cannot arise from the objective observation of a corpus; but I have not thereby abandoned the position that sentences, like words, are, and mean, what we use them to do, and that these uses, these things done, are the real subject of the linguist. If I use a negative to affirm something, the affirmative aspect is obviously closer to what is being done in language than the true identification by traditional grammar of the form as negative. Traditional grammatical analyses of sentences, or TG analyses, cannot themselves give any direct access to 'aspect'.[4]

By 'what an utterance does' I do not mean its effects on the hearer. The achieving of effects is important, and an utterance may certainly be intended to have an effect (an order to be obeyed, etc.—Austin's 'perlocutionary acts') but a hearer's reaction to an utterance may be quirky and beyond the reach of the linguist. An order may be given and received whether it is obeyed, disobeyed or ignored: the giving of the order is something done within language, whatever its effect. My discussion is of what utterances do in language. This includes some of what people often mean by the 'effects' of poetry—the workings of its images, rhythms, figures—but not our responses to them. Chomsky confuses what sentences do with the response to a stimulus which, as we saw, he firmly (and rightly) denies language to be, and in this way he makes it too easy for himself to evade serious consideration of the matter. (Cf. *Current Issues*, p. 10.) Donne's elegies may indeed have been intended as stimuli to which he wanted his girls to respond, and if we ask 'Did Donne's girls succumb?' we are not asking a question about language. But 'Do we read them as seduction poems?' is surely a question relevant to the linguist, and his answer will be an account of what the poems are in language.

I know that the phrase 'what utterances do' will—contrary to my intention—perform the perlocutionary act of arousing gloom in the heart of any orthodox linguist who accidentally chances upon it, for how can there be *rules* for what utterances do? If there can't, the linguist must lump it and stop looking for rules.

---

4 We shall return to this matter from a different direction in Chapters 5–6. J. L. Austin, for instance, distinguished 'how a sentence is to be taken' (which I think is almost 'aspect', i.e. what a sentence does in language), from what it means (*How to do things with Words* (Oxford, 1962), p. 73). This is inevitable if one thinks all meaning is propositional, but unnecessary if not.

I don't believe it would do the subject any harm if linguists were to meditate upon particular pieces of language for a decade or two, instead—they could read a few poems, for instance. But utterances have observable likenesses in what they do, limits of being able to do things, failures to do things that can be contemplated and discussed in a variety of ways, which for instance I wouldn't want to limit to Austin's lists of 'illocutionary forces'. One of the useful ways of saying that in some cases a sentence cannot do so-and-so is an appeal to the rules of traditional grammar. But that way is not always usable, and whether it is must depend on what can be got away with, not on the mere existence of the syntax of sentences.

The appeal to 'use' or 'aspect' is of course conceptually tricky. If you correct somebody by saying 'That just isn't done in English' he can always retort, 'Well, I've just done it!' Sometimes the discussion can be continued by an orthodox appeal to syntax or lexis, but is not this to be paraphrased 'You can't get away with it. . . ?' The only test is whether a speaker makes sense in what another speaker recognizes as the language: 'makes sense' being what grammar and syntax have to appeal to. (Below, pp. 173 ff.) 'To say "This combination of words makes no sense" excludes it from the sphere of language and thereby bounds the domain of language. But when one draws a boundary it may be for various kinds of reason' (Wittgenstein, *Investigations*, p. 138e).

'Aspect' is usefully elastic. Remove the adjectives from 'she was wearing her old blue coat' and we seem to have a Chomskyan kernel sentence, 'declarative' as he calls them. One attraction of the kernel sentences, as we shall see, is that they make propositions, and 'she was wearing her old blue coat' appears to be making a factual, verifiable statement. But what if it is the opening sentence of a novel? It is not then verifiable, but does that make it extraordinary? On the contrary it would be extraordinary for a story to begin with something verifiable. 'Once upon a time there was a very wicked old witch who lived in the dismal depths of a dank dark forest——' If you interrupt and say 'But that can't be so! for there are no such people as witches' you are falling into 'aspect-blindness', for nobody has asserted that there *are* witches. (Below, pp. 129 ff.) Reading the opening words, and with no further notation, one naturally takes them *as* a story, i.e. in the aspect of fiction.

Take the related case of irony. At one moment of Joseph Heller's *Catch-22* rather important consequences flow from an inability to detect irony:

> 'I *want* someone to tell me,' Lieutenant Scheisskopf beseeched them all prayerfully. 'If any of it is my fault, I *want* to be told.'
>
> 'He *wants* someone to tell him,' Clevinger said.
>
> 'He wants everyone to keep still, idiot,' Yossarian answered.
>
> 'Didn't you hear him?' Clevinger argued.
>
> 'I heard him,' Yossarian replied. 'I heard him say very loudly and very distinctly that he wants every one of us to keep our mouths shut if we know what's good for us.' (chap. 8)

TG grammar has no way of showing (although it is implied by common parlance) that saying something ironically is less basic to language than saying something straight. One linguistic universal I do believe in: I cannot imagine a language in which it would be impossible to say something ironically.[5] The difference between ironical and straight is one of aspect or use: any statement can be used, or seen, ironically. To recognize irony we need to possess the relevant language, and that is to have had some experience of the life of a speaker of the language; but this possession, these judgements, are not to be described by traditional grammar. 'Why should he say one thing so positively, and mean another all the while, was most unaccountable! How were people, at that rate, to be understood? Who but Henry could have been aware of what his father was at?' (Austen, *Northanger Abbey*, vol. II, chap. 11). People are understood, irony (or in this case self-deception) identified, in that experience of life which is the same as a deepening sense of language—not, that is, in TG grammar.

A failure to detect that somebody is *not* being ironical can be equally destructive of sense or understanding:

> 'Really, Mr Collins,' cried Elizabeth with some warmth, 'you puzzle me exceedingly. If what I have hitherto said can appear to you in the form of encouragement, I know not how to express my refusal in such a way as may convince you of its being one.' (*Pride and Prejudice*, vol. I, chap. 19)

She couldn't do it by an appeal to ordinary grammar: 'When I

---

[5] And a language in which it is impossible to lie?—Swift's Houyhnhnms'? The claim could only be made by incorrigible liars. 'I cannot tell a lie' can only be said by someone who, in another sense, could.

use these forms I am in earnest.' The 'rules' for saying that someone is being ironical are very unlike the rules for relating active and passive. But it doesn't follow that irony is no concern of the student of language: on the contrary my examples show that it is one of the points where language, one's sense of life and of oneself intersect. So it *is* possible to use the word 'no' to say what in my expository prose is meant by 'yes', 'Play the maid's part, still answer Nay, and take it.'

Here TG grammar's blankness about aspect combines with the insecurity of its treatment of intonation, for tone is often an indication of aspect.

I want to get away from any remnant of the idea that tone is a dead carrier of live substance. Tone is part of substance; it can make the same words carry wholly opposed meanings. If you know your contexts it's simple to make 'Goodbye' mean '...and I hope I never see you again' or '...and I can't wait to get back to you' or many points between. (Richard Hoggart, *Only Connect* (1972), p. 14)

I too want to get rid of the idea of tone the carrier, so much, in fact, that I must object that it is still there in Hoggart's passage. His two construings of 'Goodbye' seem to be meant to be tonally neutral, i.e. what *they* mean is independent of tone. To make his point he needed some qualification such as 'what in unironically intended prose we could express as...' before each. For '...and I hope I never see you again' can itself do the same thing in language as is done in unironic expository prose by '...and I can't wait to get back to you' and (more easily imaginable) vice versa. In those cases aspect would depend on tone.

I think that any student trying to observe language ought to be interested in what it is to use words or to take them as so-and-so (a story, a statement, a command, a question...). I think in their very different ways J. R. Firth and Wittgenstein would have agreed, and J. L. Austin nearly does so with his 'illocutionary forces'; but Chomsky can't. Hence some of the problems about 'Light!', 'Slab!' and the conductor's bell. The first two are called nouns in the dictionary (I assume 'Light!' is somehow connected with the noun not the verb) but they are taken *as* imperatives, though the imperative is supposed to be one of the functions of the verb. There is no TG way of transforming a noun into an imperative.

I am not suggesting that 'aspect' describes a real language

underlying what we say, that in 'Slab!' a real imperative underlies the surface noun. We do not ordinarily see something first
then later see it as what it is. It is quite basic to language that a
sentence or utterance should be what we take it as when we
understand its aspect. (Cf. below, p. 174.) In saying so we are not
going outside or below language. I believe on the contrary that
we are going further *into* language than Chomsky can take us.

It follows that TG grammar can say nothing about metaphor,
an obviously central case of aspect because in metaphor we speak
of something in terms expository prose uses for something else:
we take one thing as another.

> his virtues
> Will plead like angels, trumpet-tongued, against
> The deep damnation of his taking off:
> And Pity, like a naked new-born babe
> Striding the blast, or Heaven's cherubin, hors'd
> Upon the sightless couriers of the air,
> Shall blow the horrid deed in every eye,
> That tears shall drown the wind.

Is it merely carping to say that what TG grammar can do with
this is not very informative—that it doesn't in fact tell us much
about Shakespeare's language to know that these sentences are
or (more likely) are not well-formed?

It will be retorted that metaphor is parasitic upon propositions,
but even if that were so, how would linguistics demonstrate it?
Not that it is so. Metaphor is quite basic to language. My point
of view is not close to Roman Jakobson's, in general, and so I am
glad to refer to his discussion of aphasia and his recognition, not
the less important for being something all the medical men take
for granted, that a patient's failure to understand metaphoric
uses of language is an unmistakable symptom of illness and deep
disintegration of language.[6]

Chomsky is dissatisfied with what TG grammar can at present
do, but not along any of the lines I have mentioned. He does
yearn to make TG grammar the basis of a scientific account of
all language.

Chomsky frequently distinguishes three levels of ambition for

---

[6] Roman Jakobson and Morris Halle, *Fundamentals of Language* (The
Hague, 1956), p. 83.

grammars,[7] 'observational adequacy' (= only looking hard at a corpus), 'descriptive adequacy', and finally 'explanatory adequacy'. At its best the transformational system seems to me an adequate description of syntax. Chomsky is not satisfied with this and always hankers also after explanatory adequacy which will 'provide a principled basis, independent of any particular language, for the selection of the descriptively adequate grammar of each language' (Householder's citation of a work I have not seen). If there can be this adequate explanation it will appeal to universal rules and will also corroborate grammar with language-independent evidence. If this can be done, TG grammar will become scientific, for it will explain language in language-independent terms. Unless 'formatives and category symbols used in Phrase-markers have some language-independent characterization' they 'are just convenient mnemonic tags', says Chomsky (*Aspects*, p. 65); and as early as *Logical Structure* he had demanded that the grammarian 'be concerned with the problem of justifying and validating the results of his inquiries' (1). The justification and validation will prove the existence of 'competence' outside grammar and will record its rules in some language-independent way. TG grammar, that is to say, must become an hypothesis, and can then explain language scientifically.

[7] Cf. F. W. Householder Jr, 'On some Recent Claims in Phonological Theory', *Journal of Linguistics* 1 (1965), 14.

4

Chomsky's Temptations and Falls,
or
the Strange Tale of the Acquisition Device, Code, and the Linguistic Universals

(i)

THE ACQUISITION DEVICE: GRAMMAR IN YOUR HEAD

As long as Professor Chomsky remains a grammarian he is, odd mistakes apart, generally unassailable. Chomsky goes astray when he denies that a grammar is 'descriptively adequate' unless 'the set of procedures can be regarded as constituting a hypothesis about the innate language-acquisition system' (*Aspects*, p. 76). For in trying so to regard grammar Chomsky, just like Carroll and the structuralists before him, contents himself with 'explanations' which get any sense they may have from their unconscious dependence on ordinary grammatical knowledge. And to the extent that 'hypothesis' is used seriously Chomsky destroys the only safe base he has.

The fallacy I am trying to define is made possible to Chomsky by certain ambiguities in the terminology of TG grammar which have permitted him to take it on the one hand as grammar but on the other as a scientific explanation of language which can ultimately include linguistics within the science of psychology or even within the physiology of the brain.

To begin with the best-known of Chomsky's distinctions we have not yet discussed, let us ask some questions about the *deep structure* and *surface structure* of sentences, phrases Chomsky has depended heavily upon since *Aspects of the Theory of Syntax*.

Chomsky's doctrine is that 'transformations applied in sequence to deep structures [i.e. base strings]...ultimately generate the surface structures of the sentences of the language' (*Language and Mind*, p. 162). Deep structures are represented only indirectly or unclearly in the 'immediate constituent

53

analysis' or 'surface structure' of a sentence (though in the first example Chomsky gives at the cited place the deep and surface structures happen to be the same!).

One much-discussed example, which Chomsky has been using ever since *The Logical Structure of Linguistic Theory*, is 'flying planes can be dangerous'. How is grammar to account for the ambiguity of the sentence? Lyons concedes more than Chomsky when he says it would be possible to generate the sentence 'within a phrase structure grammar and to assign to it two different phrase markers' (*Chomsky*, p. 77: i.e. in traditional grammar we would merely say that in both senses 'flying planes' is the subject of the sentence but that in one case 'flying' is the verbal noun taking 'planes' as object, in the other the verbal adjective qualifying 'planes'). But 'under both interpretations, the immediate constituent analysis is, presumably, (((*flying*) (*planes*)) (((*can*) (*be*)) (*dangerous*)))' (*ibid.*).

What makes Lyons's unlabelled bracketing an account of any sort of structure? 'Surface structure' here seems to invite us to take 'flying planes can be dangerous' as a sentence (for of what else is either deep or surface structure supposed to be the structure?) yet without attributing to it either of the senses described by the two deep structures. How can this be done? And if it can't, how can there be a surface structure without a deep structure? Chomsky concedes that 'in an appropriately constructed context' 'the listener will interpret it immediately in a unique way, and will fail to detect the ambiguity' (*Aspects*, p. 21). But then the sentence will not be ambiguous, and will have only one structure, whether one calls that 'deep' or 'surface'. Chomsky also says that 'John is easy to please' and 'John is eager to please' are of similar surface structure. I can understand this as meaning that they have an obvious though superficial similarity, but how it can be supposed to be a syntactic similarity I do not know. Traditional grammar would say that John, if he is easy to please, is the subject of 'is' and the object of 'please', but if John is eager he is the subject of the whole sentence. After giving a similar account Chomsky merely asserts that there is 'no trace' of this structure on the surface (*Language and Mind*, p. 36). Can these words then somehow be analysed grammatically as a sentence (what else is any bracketing supposed to do?) but without being analysed into the components of the structure of the sentence? 'Deep structure' turns out to be *any* syntactic analysis and 'surface structure' functions in the system as something of an aunt sally or a ghost.[1]

I do not intend this as a very serious objection. 'Deep structure' can be a useful grammatical tool, part of a way of seeing clearly the syntactic structure of sentences. One has to object seriously, though, if the grammarian forgets that 'deep structure' is an instrument he has created.

'Competence', the set of rules which will generate all and only the well-formed sentences of a language, is identically a useful concept in grammar as long as it is so understood. Chomsky at first glance seems to make 'competence' even more of a grammatical abstraction than he should, for one difficulty of his grammar is to know how to connect this 'competence', the grammarian's set of rules, with 'performance', i.e. what people actually say.

Much of the actual speech observed [by the child] consists of fragments and deviant expressions of a variety of sorts. Thus it seems that a child must have the ability to 'invent' a generative grammar that defines well-formedness...even though the primary linguistic data...may...be deficient in various respects. (*Aspects*, p. 201)

The troubles here are the subject of this chapter: the immediate point is that if the child's invention of a grammar enables him only to produce the fragments and deviant expressions to be heard by the next generation, the need for 'competence' in an account of the spoken language is not obvious.

Chomsky says, 'the notion "acceptable" is not to be confused with "grammatical". Acceptability is a concept that belongs to the study of performance, whereas grammaticalness belongs to the study of competence' (*Aspects*, p. 11). So the sentence I generated above on p. 19 would be 'competent' though, for reasons connected with its syntax, quite 'unacceptable'. I suggested instead that Chomsky's rules are incomplete, i.e. not the

---

[1] But the bracketing of the example of 'surface structure' on p. 8 of *The Sound Pattern of English* is carefully and fully labelled: the transformations could operate without ambiguity on the parts of the string so defined. Here surface structure has taken over deep structure. But this lands Chomsky in another dilemma, for *this* 'surface structure' could not define the 'phonological component' unless it became more surface-like, i.e. bore some closer resemblance to the words of the sentence as spoken. I suggest that the real motivation for 'surface structure' in the Chomsky system is to give a place in grammar for phonology, otherwise left homeless.

rules of the language, if they permit such an unacceptable sentence.

In such later formulations Chomsky has gone back on a much more ordinary and sensible position as for instance when he said, 'One way to test the adequacy of a grammar. . .is to determine whether or not the sequences that it generates are actually grammatical, i.e. acceptable to a native speaker' (*Syntactic Structures*, p. 13), and when he goes on to gloss grammar as the explication of the intuitive. Even here I would prefer 'the only' to 'one' way, otherwise grammar cannot refer to language.

I am not here trying to reopen the old debate about whether grammar is 'prescriptive'[2] or 'descriptive'—whether, for example, a grammarian should say that split infinitives in English are incorrect. A prescriptivist would appeal to his notion of what is acceptable, which he would think a finer notion than some other people's; but this is different from Chomsky's 'competence' which is found in *nobody*'s performance. I take this as an instance of Chomsky's not very good habit of using ordinary words extraordinarily without saying so. Think of a pianist whose competence was not reflected in performance! Perhaps he has no hands or is permanently unable to concentrate because of the noise of passing traffic? But isn't competence in the end just being able to do something?

Although Chomsky's useful notion 'degrees of grammaticalness' is not the same as 'degrees of acceptability', since the former refers to the grammarian's system, not direct to language, I do not believe that 'degrees of grammaticalness' could make sense without 'degrees of acceptability', for it would not be referring to language. When a language changes, for instance, what was both unacceptable and ungrammatical will become acceptable and then the grammarian must alter his grammar accordingly.

My disagreement with Chomsky here is a quite basic one about where language is found. He wants to locate language in 'competence', the set of rules that will describe the sentences of the language. I believe on the contrary that language is found (always and only) in use by human beings. Chomsky's reaction against the observation of corpora has been taken to the point of refusing to study actual uses of language at all: which, in a

[2] Like A. S. C. Ross, Chomsky confuses the prescriptivist position with 'the effort to teach better manners to a rising middle class' (*Language and Mind*, p. 15).

linguist, is absurd. 'Grammaticality and meaningfulness, separable or not, must be sought within actual performance' (Hockett, p. 73; cf. p. 66). But:

A central idea in much of structural linguistics was that the formal devices of language should be studied independently of their use. The earliest work in transformational-generative grammar took over a version of this thesis, as a working hypothesis. I think it has been a fruitful hypothesis. (*Studies*, p. 198)

I think on the contrary it is impossible to study anything of language except in use, and I even regard this as a truism.[3]

'Competence' is, however, like deep structure, underlying strings and kernel sentences, useful as a concept in grammar, provided only that it is recognized to be so and not suffered to go on the rampage disguised as physical reality—provided, that is, that the grammarian is content to remain a grammarian.

The denial that performance is the test of competence, however, is Chomsky's fatal moment of weakness, for it forces him, if his grammar is to have any reference to language, to attribute to his unduly abstract competence just the kind of physical reality which his 'abstract' if used carefully would deny. Sometimes he is careful and gets the matter clear, as in the passage of *Syntactic Structures* already quoted where he says that a grammar is 'simply a description of a certain set of utterances, namely, those which it generates' (p. 48). But elsewhere Chomsky thinks of competence as really present not in 'performance' but in the brain, a device permitting the speaker to speak. It is this device which must give grammar a reference to the real, viz the brain, and the grammarian his chance of language-independent explanation.

[3] Like other truisms it is easily forgotten: Oswald Hanfling forgets it in the very act of defending meaning-as-use. In some cases, he says, 'the question about meaning can only be treated as a question about use', but goes on next paragraph to say that 'the meaning is *there*, in the dictionary, regardless of whether anyone looks it up, and uses the word, or not' (*Philosophy of Language* 2 (Milton Keynes, 1973), p. 8). This is Sir Karl Popper's position in *Objective Knowledge* (Oxford, 1972) and is open to an objection that I hope would have been congenial to Bishop Berkeley: to catch the word there in the dictionary without looking it up can't be done. It would be possible for an illiterate to see in the dictionary the marks that for the literate constitute the word (below, p. 171), without, for him, the word being there. To look a word up in a dictionary is one use of a word; but if the dictionary is not being consulted the words in it, whatever may be the case with regard to the marks on paper, are not being used, i.e. don't exist.

At the beginning of his career Chomsky seems to have been clearer about the attendant problems and dangers than he was later. The following seems to me, though sometimes close to danger, unexceptionable:

A speaker of a language has observed a certain limited set of utterances in his language. On the basis of this finite linguistic experience he can produce an indefinite number of new utterances which are immediately acceptable to other members of his speech community. He can also distinguish a certain set of 'grammatical' utterances, among utterances that he has never heard and would never produce. Can we reconstruct this ability in a general way? I.e., can we construct a formal model, a definition of 'grammatical sentence' in terms of 'observed sentence', thus, in one sense, providing an explanation for this ability? (*Logical Structure*, 115.1, p. 715)

Yes, the speaker does produce new utterances on the basis of his experience, and Chomsky is not offering here to say how, or how it is possible. And grammar can be seen as a formal reconstruction of this ability: the kind of 'explanation' grammar then provides is the only kind it can, namely, a grammatical explanation ('descriptive adequacy', in Chomsky's phraseology, not 'explanatory adequacy').

The first sign of trouble comes with this innocent-looking formulation from *Syntactic Structures* where, having described finite-state grammars, Chomsky says: 'This conception of language is an extremely powerful and general one. If we can adopt it, we can view the speaker as being essentially a machine of the type considered' (p. 20). *Non sequitur*, even allowing for Chomsky's specialized use of 'machine' as an abstraction in grammar. Even if the speaker is such a 'machine' it will not be the grammarian's business to say so, and if the speaker is a 'machine' but of a quite different sort from the grammar, the grammar will not thereby be invalidated. What the grammarian will have achieved if he can adopt the relevant grammar is to call the grammar such a machine. Then the grammarian can, if he feels so inclined, say that in grammar the speaker is such a machine, i.e. follows the rules of the grammar when he talks. But to make 'grammatically' the same as 'essentially' is grammarians' *hubris*.

This slip foretells Chomsky's large erroneous later development. The first major plunge is in *Aspects*, since which work

Chomsky has consistently spoken of grammar as 'internalized' by speakers.

> By a generative grammar I mean simply a system of rules that in some explicit and well-defined way assigns structural descriptions to sentences. Obviously, every speaker of a language has mastered and internalized a generative grammar that expresses his knowledge of his language. (*Aspects*, p. 8)

The first sentence is clear and, with the possible exception of 'well-defined' if it is meant to bring in mathematical precision, true. But the second sentence is not 'obvious' at all, and not necessarily connected with the first. The only evidence Chomsky ever brings in support of his belief that we have all internalized a grammar is that speakers *must have* done so or they couldn't speak.[4] (Chomsky at the same time consistently disdains the *a priori*.)

'Competence' *must be* present in the speaker's mind, something the speaker has 'acquired' and now 'puts to use' (*Studies*, p. 11); and the presence is physical:

> It has, I believe, become quite clear that if we are ever to understand how language is used or acquired, then we must abstract for separate and independent study a cognitive system, a system of knowledge and belief, that develops in early childhood and that interacts with many other factors to determine the kinds of behavior that we observe; to introduce a technical term, we must isolate and study the system of *linguistic competence* that underlies behavior but that is not realized in any direct or simple way in behavior. (*Language and Mind*, p. 4)

'Abstract' here should not be confused with the word in its grammatical sense. Chomsky is proposing to abstract the system in much the same way as he might abstract the digestive system or the gall-bladder, and 'isolate' also suggests the dissecting room. This must attribute a non-grammatical reality to the system. So grammar is 'a finite object, realized physically in a finite human brain' (*The Sound Pattern of English*, p. 6; cf. below, p. 165)—the brain being the speaker's not the grammarian's; 'the human mind' is 'a particular, biologically-given

---

[4] 'The child approaches the data with the presumption that they are drawn from a language of a certain antecedently well-defined type, his problem being to determine which of the (humanly) possible languages is that of the community in which he is placed. Language learning would be impossible unless this were the case' (*Aspects*, p. 27).

system' (*Problems of Knowledge and Freedom* (1972), p. 13); and '*Langue* [= "competence"], the system represented in the brain'[5] ('Formal Properties of Grammars', p. 326).

To use I. A. Richards's words, we must ask Chomsky here whether grammar is 'devised by the grammarian or by Nature' ('Why Generative Grammar does not Help', I, p. 7).

In these places Chomsky is confusing, as simply as can be, what the grammarian does with what the speaker does. With considerable excitement he then attributes to the entire human race the grammatical understanding worked out laboriously by Western scholars since the days of the Greeks. Thus fallaciously does 'competence' force its way back into 'performance', whence it should never have departed, and now with the additional fallacy that 'competence' must be a physical object.[6]

The final step in the development of this fallacy is to confuse language with grammar: 'For our purposes, we can think of a language as a set of structural descriptions of sentences. . .' ('Conditions on Transformations', p. 232). The recent essay I quote from takes further than ever before Chomsky's accounting for certain ways English sentences go: it is indeed a subtle work of grammar. One still has to make the basic objection that it is the grammar that is the set of structural descriptions, not the sentences described, and much less the language.

This drive to establish 'competence' as physically internalized comes from Chomsky's determination to provide a language-independent explanation of language. Unless 'competence' exists

---

[5] Deletion transformations (the obligatory inclusion of a feature in the base in order to explain its *absence* on the surface) are another place where the confusion of abstract and concrete is damaging. They may be all very well in grammar—though I suggested that, for instance, in handling adjectives the procedure is clumsy and unilluminating—but when it is asserted, as it sometimes is, that the things deleted have been present in the speaker's mind before deletion one can only wonder what kind of game we are playing, for *ex hypothesi* the existence is undemonstrable except by a circular argument working from and to the non-existence. Derwing has a good discussion (pp. 148–9) of a supposed deletion in the phonology of Russian, according to which sounds which dropped out of the language many years ago are thought to be present to the speaker's mind before being deleted in favour of the sounds actually used. Really this is saying nothing about mental operations, but including a bit of history in the transformational system.

[6] Hockett makes a similar objection to his own 'stratificational theory': it demands that 'all this machinery is not only in our description but also in the language and even, in some sense, *in the speaker*. For this there is no shred of evidence' (*The State of the Art*, pp. 32–3).

somewhere other than grammar there will be nothing outside language to corroborate grammar. Therefore competence *must* exist as physical endowment! But what if it doesn't?

Perhaps we could say that a general theory achieves 'explanatory adequacy' if it provides for the selection of grammars that are descriptively adequate...and, simply, that it is true to the extent that it approximates to the inner grammar-producing system, etc. (Chomsky, letter to Hockett quoted *The State of the Art* p. 42; Hockett chivalrously refuses to use this in evidence against Chomsky.)

But 'In fact we have no evidence about the innate grammar-producing mechanisms other than what we can determine by studying the linguistic problem of justifying grammars, so that in practice, the two problems collapse' (*ibid.*). 'Collapse', one might say unkindly, in more senses than one. The appeal to the internalized knowledge cannot give any independent evidence for grammar, because we only know of the internalized knowledge through and as grammar. Therefore language cannot be *explained* by this kind of argument. Why should that worry a scientist so much that it makes him take as explanation something not susceptible to experimental test and which adds nothing to what he knows?

Now it is not my case to establish that Chomsky is an utter idiot; I have been trying occasionally, on the contrary, to show that not all the games grammarians play are as childish as they may appear to the casual observer. Chomsky is a serious man, worth some attention, and here, it seems to me, in the Laocoon embrace of a deep fallacy. Not being a great fool, Chomsky does realize that there is something odd about the discussions I have just been mocking. Sometimes he denies flatly that he is attributing to grammar the kind of physical reality I say he does.

We have now discussed a certain model of competence. It would be tempting, but quite absurd, to regard it as a model of performance as well. Thus we might propose that to produce a sentence, the speaker goes through the successive steps of constructing a base-derivation, line by line from the initial symbol *S*, then inserting lexical items and applying grammatical transformations to form a surface structure, and finally applying the phonological rules in their given order, in accordance with the cyclic principle discussed earlier. There is not the slightest justification for any such assumption. In fact, in implying that the speaker selects the general properties of sentence structure before selecting lexical items (before deciding what he is going to talk about), such a proposal seems not only without justification but entirely counter to whatever vague intuitions one may have about the processes that underlie production. (*Language and Mind*, pp. 156–7)

This might look clear enough, but even here Chomsky's grasp of the essential distinctions is insecure. The 'model of competence' still means a picture of what is really in the language-user's head, and Chomsky next page is securely back within the assumptions he seemed to be attacking: 'The child must acquire a generative grammar of his language on the basis of a fairly restricted amount of evidence. To account for this achievement, we must postulate a sufficiently rich internal structure...'

There is another denial in *Language and Mind* that grammar is being taken as 'a description of the successive acts of a performance model' and 'in fact', says Chomsky, 'it would be quite absurd to do so' (p. 117). But he again continues, 'The grammatical rules that generate phonetic representations of signals with their semantic interpretations do not constitute a model for the production of sentences, *although any such model must incorporate the system of grammatical rules*' (my italics).

The point here seems to be that other matters (the 'other information' of the model) must be incorporated too, but 'incorporate' is used as simply as ever and still means that competence is made flesh, a necessary though not a sufficient condition of performance.[7]

Elsewhere Chomsky offers his running together of the grammarian's discussion with what the speaker does as 'systematic ambiguity': 'Using the term "grammar" with a systematic ambiguity (to refer, first, to the native speaker's internally represented "theory of his language" and, second, to the linguist's account of this)...' (*Aspects*, p. 25). But if the native speaker really possesses an internalized grammar there is no ambiguity: all the grammarian is doing is to describe the internal possession. If on the other hand there is no reason to attribute any theory of his language to the native speaker, what Chomsky is offering is not ambiguity, systematic or not, but confusion. 'We use the term "grammar" with a systematic ambiguity. On the one hand, the term refers to the explicit theory constructed by the linguist

---

[7] Cf. similar discussions where in agreeing that competence will not alone explain speech Chomsky still insists that the speaker must acquire it, in *Current Issues*, p. 10; *Topics*, p. 10.

and proposed as a description of the speaker's competence. On the other hand we use the term to refer to this competence itself' (*The Sound Pattern of English*, p. 3). Once again we have here either identity (for 'competence itself' is the 'theory' if the grammarian is taking the necessary care) or confusion. 'No confusion should result from this standard usage if the distinction is kept in mind' (*ibid.* p. 4). How can that be, when the effect of the ambiguity in common use can only be to blur the distinction? What light can be thrown by deliberately using the same word for things we are trying to keep apart?

Chomsky asks us to

Consider the fact that a speaker of English has acquired the concept 'sentence of English'. Suppose that we were to postulate an innate quality space with a structure so abstract that any two sentences of English are nearer to one another in terms of the postulated distance measure than a sentence of English and any sentence of another language. Then a learner could acquire the concept 'sentence of English'—he could, in other words, know that the language to which he is exposed is English and 'generalise' to any other sentence of English—from an exposure to one sentence. ('Some Empirical Assumptions in Modern Philosophy of Language', p. 265)

But there is no need to suppose that speakers of English have acquired a concept 'sentence of English' (whatever that proposition is, it isn't a fact) or in the case of toddlers of two that they possess any concepts at all, or that 'the true theory of each language' is 'in the head of every four-year-old' (*Language and Mind*, p. 91), or that we must assign to any mind other than Chomsky's 'as an innate property, the general theory of language that we have called "universal grammar"' (*ibid.* p. 88).

Chomsky should have paid some attention to the work of Professor Gilbert Ryle, which is, after all, pretty well known. Not only does *The Concept of Mind* make the distinction between 'knowing how' and 'knowing that' which ought at least to have made Chomsky think harder about what sort of knowledge he is attributing to young children; Ryle demonstrates, conclusively, I would have thought, that when we say we do things 'in our heads' we are speaking metaphorically: 'This special use of "mental" and "mind" in which they signify what is done "in one's head" cannot be used as evidence for the dogma of the ghost in the machine. It is nothing but a contagion from that dogma' (*The Concept of Mind*, reprint 1963, p. 35). Chomsky takes 'in the head' literally and thinks of the human mind as a machine in a machine, embodying knowledge, a variant on the ghost-in-the-machine image Ryle has made notorious.

Chomsky is in deep trouble with that (certainly troublesome) word *know*.

The child cannot know at birth which language he is to learn, but he must know that its grammar must be of a predetermined form that excludes many imaginable languages. Having selected a permissible hypothesis, he can use inductive evidence for corrective action, confirming or disconfirming his choice. Once the hypothesis is sufficiently well confirmed, the child knows the language defined by this hypothesis. (*Language and Mind*, p. 88)

I cannot hear intentional irony in these comic assertions. 'Know', 'choose', 'hypothesis' all attribute to the newborn child a quite advanced capacity for grammatical thought. If Chomsky were right 'the child' could at birth be made to pass an examination in linguistics before being countenanced as a child.[8] Objections along the lines of Ryle's 'knowing how/knowing that' distinction have been made, e.g. by Gilbert Harman.[9] But, replies Chomsky convincingly, this newborn child neither 'knows that. . .' about talking nor 'knows how' to talk, because it can't.[10] It follows for Chomsky that the innate knowledge his conception of grammar demands is rightly named but quite unconscious. 'Any interesting generative grammar will be dealing. . .with mental processes that are far beyond the level of actual or even potential consciousness' (*Aspects*, p. 8): but the rules of which the child is unaware and cannot become aware (*ibid.*) are still said to be 'what the speaker actually knows' (*ibid.*, repeated *Language and Mind*, p. 196), and at the latter place Chomsky claims that this actual but unconscious knowledge is 'a rather ordinary sense' of *know*.

The element of sense that makes this doctrine worth discussing is that knowledge is indeed something we rely on or trust, often unconsciously. Adding up my change I rely on my knowledge of how many pence there are in a pound without consciously repeating it. I also rely on my command of language and if words

[8] Contrast R. G. Collingwood, *The Principles of Art* (Oxford, 1938), pp. 227 ff., on a child's grammar when shouting 'Hatty off!'

[9] 'Psychological Aspects of the Theory of Syntax', *The Journal of Philosophy*, 64 (1967).

[10] 'Comments on Harman's Reply' and 'Linguistics and Philosophy', the latter reprinted in *Language and Mind*.

will not come I may be (in English) nonplussed and alarmed or, in a second language, French, driven to the reflection that after all I don't know the language well. Here knowing is the conceptual descendant of Middle English *can*. If I *can* do something in Middle English I either know how or just am able to. Chomsky's ideas of innate knowledge simply paraphrase the fact that we *can* talk, but very misleadingly.

For there is still a great difference between knowing in the wide sense of relying or trusting or being able, and knowing that one knows, i.e. consciously reflecting on what we *can* do. Chomsky is sliding from the one sense to the other.

But what *knowledge* can it be that is not taught—for no child is ever taught language, only how to improve when it is already talking—which cannot be made conscious (except, let us remember, by the grammarian) and which is demonstrated in no skill, for the newborn child cannot talk? Even intuitions and hypotheses have in Chomsky's doctrine to be unconscious. 'To acquire language, a child must devise a hypothesis' but this 'does not refer to conscious formulation' (*Aspects*, pp. 36, 46). I do not know what an unconscious hypothesis is supposed to be. If Chomsky is stretching the word for the sake of new thought, what light does his stretching shed? 'The child who acquires a language. . .knows a great deal more than he has "learned" ' (*Aspects*, pp. 32–3). There we first remove the inverted commas from 'learned' to 'knows', then ask what sense Chomsky's special use has conferred on the latter word. I regret that the answer is 'none'.

If, as Wittgenstein believed, our use of language is our criterion of certainty,[11] we do rely on language before we know anything else, for all we know is measured by our uses of language. But language is a necessary condition of academic knowledge, not a result of it: language must give the possibility of knowledge before it can itself be known.

Surely the time is overdue for Occam's razor. Abandon unconscious knowledge and nothing in the observed facts or in Chomsky's grammar need change. The newborn child simply has no knowledge of language or of grammar within the range of our word *knowledge*.[12]

---

[11] My crude reference to hard and difficult work is accurate enough for my present purpose only. Cf. the whole of *On Certainty* (Oxford, 1969).

[12] Since writing this chapter I find that a comparable argument against the vacuity of Chomsky's idea of innate knowledge has been elegantly con-

The talk of 'predisposition' adds nothing, either, and it can go too. The child's beginning to talk is not, as Zeno Vendler argues (*Res Cogitans* (Ithaca, 1972), pp. 174–6), like the middle-aged man's beginning to grow gouty if his heredity is wrong. The latter is indeed a predisposition that can be not only forecast but controlled and treated; whereas all children just do begin to understand and talk. To that prime fact of human nature neither Chomsky's doctrine of internalized competence nor Vendler's discussion of predisposition adds anything whatever.

Granting Chomsky's case that innate competence is not 'knowing how' or 'knowing that' we merely say that it is not knowledge at all and retire to our first objection that Chomsky is confusing what the grammarian does with what the speaker does. 'The systems of grammatical knowledge that must be attributed to the speaker of a language' (*Aspects*, p. 54) must on the contrary be attributed to the grammarian. 'Language acquisition is based on the child's discovery of what from a formal point of view is a deep and abstract theory' (*ibid.* p. 58). It is a 'theory' only from the formal point of view and is 'discovered' by the grammarian not the child. The only people to whom 'grammars that are in fact constructed by people' (*Aspects*, p. 38) applies are grammarians.

Linguistics finds this hard to grasp.

[Grammar] describes what people do when they speak their language; it is not something that has to be found in books, written down or learnt by heart. As investigators, of course, we *do* want to write down, i.e. write about the grammar of a language; but writing it down does not bring it into existence any more than writing about biology creates living cells. (F. R. Palmer, *Grammar* (1971), p. 13)

But descriptions do have to be written down; and writing about grammar is what I am doing, not what grammarians do. Gram-

---

ducted by Stephen P. Stich ('What Every Speaker Knows', *Philosophical Review*, 80 (1971), 476–96). 'Now in those passages where Chomsky does attribute knowledge of linguistic theory to the child, he is careful to deny that the knowledge is anything more than tacit or implicit. But, having agreed that a linguistic theory is a theory about certain predispositions of the child, what does it add to say the child knows the theory?' (p. 486). I dissent only from the belief that 'linguistic theory' is a theory about predispositions. I believe it is a mode of contemplating language. Cf. also Hockett, *The State of the Art*, pp. 62–3.

marians write grammar, in books. Biologists don't write about biology, they write biology and about living cells (etc.). Without biologists there would be living creatures but not biology; to say a creature is composed of cells is a statement only to be made in biology. Writing about living cells creates not the cells but a way of seeing and understanding, i.e. biology; but biology does bring the cells into existence in the sense that it provides the way of seeing and making sense of living creatures known as biology and without which they would not have that sense. Similarly without grammar we would all talk, but would lack the grammarian's understanding of language. (This does not make grammar a science.) Yes, grammar does describe 'what people do when they speak', but from the grammarian's point of view.

I know that this crucial point is not easy and so I think it not a waste of time to try an analogy.

Everybody who enjoys a Mozart piano concerto, we may say, hears certain sounds as music, in the same way that everybody reading takes certain marks as written language. The listener hears what a musicologist will call first and second subjects, development section, recapitulation, cadenza, coda, and so on; the listener recognizes the musical relations, the parts of the music that are the same, similar or different. If a movement is what the grammarian of music calls theme and variations the listener will hear, if he hears the music at all, the similarities and differences that are so described. Chomsky's line of argument is then to utter exclamations of astonishment that untutored listeners can understand anything as technical as sonata form or theme and variations, and to offer as an explanation that they must be born with the innate capacity to develop, when exposed to music, a perfect knowledge of the grammar of Western music (although they are quite unaware of this knowledge) and to select from the set of possible musical forms sonata form or theme and variations, binary form, minuet and trio, bourrée, sarabande, gigue, loure, siciliana etc. while rejecting the forms of Indian raga, Chinese tsin music etc. The case is just that naive listeners hear the music and musicologists talk about it in their true way without saying anything about how naive listeners manage to hear what musicologists describe. Some passages, said Mozart of three of his piano concerti, could be appreciated only by connoisseurs, but 'the less learned cannot fail to be pleased, though without knowing why' (Mozart's Letters, translated by Emily Anderson (1956), p. 204).[13]

This is true at the more elementary level of scales and modes. The intervals of the major and minor scales are not dictated by nature, but many people quite formally ignorant of music can sing a major scale. Two hundred years, also, after the triumph of the key system, folksingers were still accurately singing in some of the modes, and some musicologists fell into precisely Chomsky's muddle of thinking that they could not have done so unless they had academic understanding of the modes; though I do not know that anybody offered as an explanation that the modes are innate:

The fact [of traditional singers who 'could not read music—perhaps could not read at all—but could sing spontaneously in what the theorists explain as the Dorian or Mixolydian mode'] seems to have surprised some pioneers of the folk song movement. Dr Vaughan Williams had a story of one scholar who, confronted with some notations newly taken down from a folk singer, declared: 'These must be wrong. Nobody's going to tell me that an uneducated villager sings correctly in the Dorian mode when, as often as not, even our trained musicians don't know what the Dorian is!' (*The Penguin Book of English Folk Songs*, p. 10)

Or take maps. My fellow-citizens and I know our way about Swansea. Do we then carry maps of Swansea in our heads? Not all of us could draw one, anyway. What would talk of an internalized map add to saying that we know our way about the place and that mapmakers could make maps of what we know?

The matter of grammar is a little more complicated, because some grammatical ideas are part of our language and therefore all speakers of English have some grammatical notions. We talk of 'saying' 'things', and we can all say things like 'I didn't say "this", I said "that"', and 'Will you say that again slower, please?' There are all the locutions involving 'saying that' which link our language's ideas of saying and knowing. English has also the words *language* and *English*—and I doubt whether formal grammar could get anywhere if it hadn't. We all, even, have some formal mastery of grammar for we all possess the word *word* and anybody who can write (see below, pp. 174–6) demon-

---

[13] The analogy works, too, in that music's 'grammar' notoriously misses the real thing in the music: so little is said about music by 'here he modulates into G minor' or 'the second variation is a canon', though what is said may be true and useful. No work of musicology, either, can tell us that a piece is or is not music.

strates knowledge of what words are in separating them by spaces. With much of grammar, however, we are in a position analogous to discussing a language which has no word for 'word'. We do not know what the imperfect subjunctive passive is unless we are taught, nor conjunction and relativization, though we use the latter frequently. It does not follow that a language without a word for 'word' has no words—if the grammarian can see words he can say so if he chooses—but its naive speakers will then be incapable of discussing words until they are shown how. In this case it would be plain that even 'word' is a grammatical abstraction rather than a self-evident natural category.

The final sign that Chomsky does think of grammar as a real physical box of tricks is his talk of the 'Acquisition Device' (AD) on the observation of which depends all hope of progress at that frontier of grammatical knowledge, psycholinguistics. The road to the Acquisition Device is straight enough, given the determination to corroborate grammar by observing something outside language. The crucial slide is from the abstract and unexceptionable 'acquisition *model*'[14] of *Aspects* p. 30 to this 'acquisition *device*' in the following pages (my italics). If even stupid children's speech comes to follow the rules of grammar although they cannot formulate these rules, we all MUST, thinks Chomsky, have some special anatomical equipment which gets to work on the degenerate linguistic phenomena around us and from them develops the internalized competence that allows us to form and understand sentences. It doesn't follow though that because the AD must exist it does exist. That would seem to be an empirical matter. Where is it?

Chomsky's path into what I think is the crucial fallacy is perfectly clear as early as the first Skinner review. 'One would naturally expect that prediction of the behavior of a complex organism (or machine) would require, in addition to information about external stimulation, knowledge of the internal structure of the organism, the ways in which it processes input information and organizes its own behavior' (p. 27). This is not true. If I turn

---

14 I don't wish to imply that Chomsky's use of models or the word *model* is illuminating. He shares his predecessors' ambition to make diagrams of language and grammar, but they are always obscure because there is never any way of testing them against actual uses of language. Cf., for example, *Language and Mind*, p. 117, and below, p. 150.

the radio on I can predict that in the overwhelming majority of cases it will come on whether I know anything of its works or not. The prediction of the behaviour of a horse, in the cases where we really do predict it (expecting the horse to stop when we say 'Whoa!' etc.) requires no knowledge whatever of the horse's in'ards.

More importantly, it does not automatically follow that if we have the knowledge Chomsky demands we have explained what we are trying to explain. 'Were we able to develop the specifications for a language-acquisition device of this sort, we could realistically claim to be able to provide an explanation for the linguistic intuition—the tacit competence—of the speaker of a language'[15] (*Topics*, p. 21). But what sort of explanation?

Has Othello got a jealousy-acquisition device, and if so would we have explained his jealousy by describing the device? What we know is that Othello rapidly becomes ragingly jealous. It might be worth saying that in his jealous love Othello discovers what he really is. But we know he had it within him to become jealous just because he does become jealous; nothing *explanatory* would be added to the story by saying he was predisposed to jealousy. And if Othello *had* a jealousy-acquisition device, it would be 'explained' by jealousy, not vice versa, as follows.

Imagine that Chomsky, Derwing, Greene and the rest are right and that there is a part of the human anatomy correctly labelled 'the language-acquisition device'; ignore for a moment that no evidence for such a device is forthcoming, any more than it is for a special organ to be called 'the human soul'. Imagine the grammarian of the future observing on some screen repre-

---

[15] Derwing's book is an effort to take the idea of the Acquisition Device with scientific seriousness. He shows that not much progress has been made towards investigating the AD and proposes that we should try harder. The same programme might have been offered to disgruntled alchemists: if at first you don't succeed in finding the Philosopher's Stone ... 'Obviously *some* relevant innate endowment exists in human beings; this point is not open to serious question. It is sufficient support for this general assertion that genuine "language" is an apparent species-specific trait of the human race alone' (p. 51). No, his second sentence is not supporting evidence for the first, it is paraphrase. All that needs to be said from Derwing's point of view of the empirical searcher is that there is no evidence for the existence of an Acquisition Device. All I have tried to do is go a little further and identify the whole quest as conceptual confusion. Derwing and Chomsky say there must be an AD; the first step in intellectual progress (cf. 'There *must* be a philosopher's stone') will be to get over the shock of doing without one.

sentations of our brainwaves and being able to say 'that one's a noun!', 'there goes a verb!' or 'look at that indirect object!' If this brain activity were somehow seen to be the same shape as TG grammar (though I find it hard to imagine what kind of grammatical prediction could be fulfilled here) that would be some kind of corroboration of Chomsky. But would it be the sort of explanation he is seeking? Would it be like explaining an appetite by the emptiness of the stomach? Wouldn't it be more like trying to explain love by the physiology of sex? In our hypo-thetical situation it would be our grammatical notions that made sense of the physical movements; brain activity could only cor-roborate what we already know. Language, in this sense, would constitute the explanation of the language-acquisition device; our understanding of language would allow us to interpret these brain currents.[16]

But the AD could no more constitute an explanation of language than a minute examination of a tenor's vocal cords could in principle constitute an explanation of how 'La ci darem la Mano' is music. The question for music would still be 'How do these movements become music?' and it would have to be dis-cussed as music is usually discussed, not in the ear-nose-and-throat department of a medical research institute. For linguists the question still is 'How do we understand these patterns as language?' Only grammar can so identify them. Cf. Palmer's odd statement, 'Speech is normally located in the left hemisphere of the brain' (*Grammar*, p. 10). No, whatever you might find if you look in the left hemisphere, it won't be speech—unless the linguist manages so to interpret it.

It is true that neurology becomes of interest to linguistics in cases where grammatical mistakes or partial or complete inability to speak are associated with brain damage, and that in such cases certain areas of the brain can be identified as the seat of the capacity for speaking. It may even be true, as studies of aphasia suggest, that different brain areas can be distinguished as seats of what Saussure distinguished as the syntagmatic and para-digmatic relations of words.

Even if this is so, for the linguist the centre of interest

---

[16] Cf. 'The question whether or not a given individual has a certain capacity —e.g. to understand higher mathematics—can only be asked within the context of the problems of higher mathematics' (Peter Winch, *Ethics and Action* (1972), p. 86).

remains language, and only within the linguist's understanding of language can information about the brain make *linguistic* sense. As Jakobson rightly says, 'To study adequately any breakdown in communications we must first understand the nature and structure of the particular mode of communication that has ceased to function' (*Fundamentals of Language*, p. 69). So Chomsky is quite right to talk of 'degrees of grammaticalness' not 'degrees of brain malfunction': the latter is not the grammarian's business except as the former.

The existence of the organs of speech and the brain is a necessary but not sufficient condition for language. So is the existence of the heart, the digestive-urinary tract and the bloodstream, and one would have about as much chance of understanding language by minutely examining the blood as by poring over the electro-encephalograph.

'I do not see how Occam's razor figures in this discussion. In investigating acquisition of language...' (Reply to Black, p. 467). The grammarian investigates not acquisition of language but language; so Occam's razor cuts out *all* the talk of 'a system of unknown properties which gives as "output" . . . a generative grammar . . . given sufficient data as input' (*ibid.*).

In my view language is not acquired by the AD but by the whole human being—or rather, the acquisition of language makes or defines the person who acquires it.

The search for the Acquisition Device is, then, strictly on a par with the search for the historical origins of language—the bow-wow theory, the ding-dong theory and all those other comical efforts to give a historical account of what logically antedates history. They all beg the essential question of what turns 'ding dong!' 'bow wow!' etc. into language.[17]

Chomsky was lured into these fallacies of grammar as a black box in the brain, the product of the Acquisition Device, by the

---

[17] For all we *know*, if knowledge is to be based on evidence, language may be a quite recent development. (By 'recent' I suggest something like 4004 B.C. as the starting date.) Perhaps, once those revelations began that gave us humanity, history, and speech, all went quickly. The development of language could hardly, anyway, be explained as Darwinian evolution, noises gradually step by step becoming speech. (And is not language positively counter-productive, survivalwise, inclining us as it does to speculate and to make and read poetry?) 'Just such a wonderful moment may have come by a happy or unhappy chance to a beast, and that was the moment that made the beast into a man' (T. F. Powys, *Soliloquies of a Hermit* (1918), p. 116). We are in the realm, that is, of mythology not history; which isn't a bad thing provided we know.

true observation that language is not physical sound and not a S–R system. Language does exist only in our inner possession as we use it. What does not follow is that to consider language we must get the neurologist to look inside our heads. The inner possession may indeed be discussed (among other ways) by the grammarian—but *as* grammar. The inner possession is language, and our ways of discussing it can only be our ways of discussing language.

The real status of the Acquisition Device in the study of language is as an exclamation of wonder at human nature. Children begin to understand what is said to them and to talk. All children. That is a wonder of the world—of the specifically human world. What children say does indeed quickly come to follow the 'rules', even the most complicated the grammarian can define; and talking is something, certainly, that we do, not something that happens to us. As we talk we are in command of language, which to us is a simple matter, though to the grammarian almost unimaginably complex (the imagination of the complexity being the grammarian's utmost achievement). Yes, how wonderful! But Chomsky's exclamation of wonder is vitiated by trying to see itself as something else, namely language-independent explanation, intended to subject linguistics to psychology. A real psychologist, however, makes my point clearly:

I want to say that the existence of language, and the development of the ability to speak in a child is a miracle, something that the notion of explanation as to how it came, and comes to be, does not make sense. It is something indeed for us to wonder at and be thankful for. (M. O'C. Drury, *The Danger of Words* (1973), p. 76)

(ii)

CODE

The new grammarians talk as freely as their predecessors of language's being the *encoding* of messages; and to understand what anyone says is for new and old alike *decoding*. Language as code follows naturally enough from the picture of competence as a physical attribute, and can be rejected with that picture.

If language is ultimately electric impulses in the brain the words we read or hear are only a kind of stimulant to ensure that the same activity shall occur in the brain of the reader (or hearer) as of the writer (or speaker). If these two sets of brain activity could somehow be placed side by side we could judge whether the 'message' had been received, and if there were some more direct method of ensuring the same activity the clumsy methods of sound or written marks could be superseded. 'Decoding' is thus the resolution of sound or writing into the brain activity which is the 'information' that language 'encodes'.

The ordinary pre-Chomsky position was this:

Presumably the speaker has some information to transmit, and he has some excitatory tendency to transmit it. From his own subjective point of view, his 'information' may consist of sensations, perceptions, memories, thoughts, concepts, or even images, but if we desire to rule out subjective events as evidence for our description, we can infer the existence of some kind of 'information', prior to its being linguistically coded, from the overt behavior—usually verbal behavior—that ensues, basing our inference on our knowledge of the general properties of stimulus-response systems. (Carroll, *The Study of Language*, p. 89)

As usual though, one may ask what the presumed prior existence of the information is adding to what we can observe, and in this case we can also show the whole position as bare assertion merely by asking for the evidence that human beings are stimulus-response systems. People are talking and we can understand them if we share their language: what more is being said? But the determination to demonstrate the existence of information previous to its 'encoding' in language goes deep into linguistics. Saussure's similar picture was this:

A given concept unlocks a corresponding sound-image in the brain; this purely *psychological* phenomenon is followed in turn by a *physiological* process: the brain transmits an impulse corresponding to the image to the organs used in producing sounds. Then the sound waves travel from the mouth of A to the ear of B: a purely *physical* process. Next, the circuit continues in B, but the order is reversed: from the ear to the brain, the physiological transmission of the sound-image; in the brain, the psychological association of the image with the corresponding concept. If B then speaks, the new act will follow—from his brain to A's—exactly the same course as the first act and pass through the same successive phases. [There follows a diagram.][18]

[18] Ferdinand de Saussure, *Course in General Linguistics*, transl. Wade Baskin (1960), pp. 11–12. Chomsky is, of course, deeply influenced by Saussure and derives his competence/performance distinction from Saussure's

The position has hardly changed in the seventy years between Saussure and Katz. The latter says,

The encoding, by which a thought is transformed into instructions for the muscles of the articulatory tract and then into a syntactically structured and acoustically realized pattern of sound, proceeds in part by the same principles as the decoding, by which such sound patterns are transformed back into a thought. (*Semantic Theory*, p. 24)[19]

What could be more reasonable than to put Saussure's account to experimental proof by catching the sound waves *en route* between brain and brain and agreeing that they are indeed physical and must therefore turn into concepts somewhere else? And 'The status of the message between the bodily pathways of the speaker and listener, the transmitted vibrations in the air, are being ever more adequately mastered, owing especially to the rapid advance of modern acoustics', say Jakobson and Halle, truly (*Fundamentals of Language*, p. 44). Unfortunately, as the same authorities put it, with notable mildness, 'The initial stage in any speech event—the intention of the sender—is not yet open to a precise analysis' (*ibid.*).[20] Unless, of course, one takes the

equally dangerous *langue/parole*. Baskin's Introduction shows Saussure's career as a remarkable prefiguring of Chomsky's leap from the atomistic frying pan into the universal fire. To Saussure's predecessors, 'language was simply an inventory or mechanical sum of the units used in speaking. Piecemeal studies precluded the development of an insight of the structure (*Gestalteinheit*, pattern or whole) into which the fragmentary facts fit' (p. xii). This seems very unfair to the great nineteenth-century achievement of Indo-European scholarship, which is pre-eminently the perception that certain fragments *are* fragments of a whole; but if Saussure did feel hemmed in by a linguistic inventory one understands his own descent into psychology. It ought, however, to have been a warning to Chomsky. In the quoted passage 'psychological', 'physiological' and 'physical' have ousted language completely.

[19] Surely, by the way, it is the thought that is supposed to be syntactically structured (as the TG grammar operates on the lexicon) not the sound? This structure is then invisible on the surface, i.e. in the sound.

[20] This did not prevent Jakobson comparing with a straight face the code of language and that of the DNA molecules of contemporary genetics. 'The title of the book by George and Muriel Beadle, *The Language of Life*, is not a mere figurative expression, and the extraordinary degree of analogy between the systems of genetic and verbal information fully justifies the guiding statement of this volume: "The deciphering of the DNA code has revealed our possession of a language much older than hieroglyphics, a language as old as life itself, a language that is the most living language of all" ' (Roman Jakobson, *Main Trends in the Science of Language* (1973), p. 49). We proud possessors of this primal language are, of course,

intention to be realized in the utterance; in which case it remains possible that the sounds of the utterance are themselves the 'message' when they are properly understood, that is when they are taken as language. I regret that Koestler embraces the same fallacy. He discusses 'the basic issue of how thought is parcelled out into language, how the shapeless rocks of ideas are cunningly split into crystalline fragments of distinctive form, and put on the moving belt to be carried from left to right along the single dimension of time' (*The Ghost in the Machine, ed. cit.,* p. 48). How pleasingly substantial 'rocks' sounds! But where are these rocks? One can make Johnson's objection to Berkeley in reverse: the trouble with these rocks is that nobody can kick them: they exist only in language—and there not as crystalline fragments, but as utterances. Concepts are only 'given' in language.

To substantiate Saussure's 'model' we would need to check it by some science-fiction device such as the helmet that transmits thoughts directly into any language or translates any language into thoughts: 'Inoltre, i nostri elmetti traducono i nostri pensieri direttamente nella vostra lingua.'[21] This is, alas, despite its resemblance to the AD and competence, not at present available outside the pages of a Mickey Mouse comic.

Professor F. H. George gives away the game of language as code when he writes, of the use of a code in wartime, 'The original ideas are really thrice encoded and therefore thrice decoded. They start as ideas with the general and he encodes them as sentences in English and then into cipher and then into morse code' (*Semantics* (1964), p. 135). The general's message certainly is decoded from morse into cipher and from cipher into English. But then. . . ? Where is the analogy between decoding code and understanding English? Where is the decoded English for us to inspect? Code always presupposes a language in which the decoded message is understood, but we have no reason yet for saying that language presupposes code.

Even if language were to be decoded by the hearer, where would the code be? It bears a suspicious resemblance to the Acquisition Device. 'The addressee of a coded message is assumed

quite unaware of it until the geneticist explains the code to us. We are aware of being alive, but that is another matter. We do, though, manage to speak and understand what is ordinarily called language whether anybody starts talking about code or not.

[21] *Topolino,* no. 890 (17 December 1972), 890.

to be in possession of the code and through it interprets the message.' Yes indeed. But if we continue, 'A native speaker responds to any text in his language as a regular decoder' (*Fundamentals of Language*, p. 28), one can always demand that the code be produced. And it takes a grammarian to do that— and he, according to Jakobson and Halle, is a kind of crypt-analyst, i.e. somebody who *breaks* a code he begins by not possessing.

The rigorously scientific Derwing quotes one 'model' of 'encoding' from communications engineering, in which the first steps in the 'communication event' are:

(1) S_1 represents an original *message* (an 'idea' or 'meaning') conceived in the mind of the speaker. Whatever the nature of this message, its existence is presumably manifested in the central nervous system (CNS) of the *speaker*.

(2) This message is next 'encoded'. . .into the form of a time-sequenced series of speech articulations. (p. 303)

How are the events of the central nervous system part of com-munications engineering? *Why* does the engineer presume any such manifestation? Linguistics ought merely to ignore these speculations. But if we take them seriously the conclusion is that 'the language *process*. . .is almost exclusively a psychological (and ultimately physiological) phenomenon, in that almost everything of real interest takes place. . .during the so-called "encoding" and "decoding" phases' (Derwing, p. 304). I would have thought the real interest was confined to before and after coding, but in either case Derwing is merely admitting defeat, for these phases, if they exist, cannot be observed for just the same reasons that the Acquisition Device cannot be observed. If the case were as Derwing says, linguistics would be impossible in principle.

We are saved from this unfortunate conclusion by the coinci-dence that the real grammar of the mental events, the shape of that which is encoded, turns out to be exactly the same as the grammar of the language we observe in use. I shall therefore merely ignore the 'coding' jargon as meaningless, and shall assume that when linguists write of words or sentences they mean the ones that enter our minds as our perceptions of sound, not ones that have a mysterious existence in the mind which it is impossible to observe.

The attempt to locate the reality of grammar outside language is none other than the elderly notion of language as the 'dress' of separately existing thought: first you have your thought then you search for the *mots justes* (found in the best dictionaries) to clothe it in. In Locke's well-known sentence, 'The Comfort and Advantage of Society, not being to be had without Communication of Thoughts, it was necessary, that Man should find out some external sensible Signs, whereof those invisible *Ideas*, which his Thoughts are made up of, might be made known to others.'[22] Katz makes the necessary link of clothes and code: 'One reason for us to believe we can penetrate phonetic or orthographic clothing is that speakers...do exactly this when other speakers successfully communicate with them' (*Linguistic Philosophy* (1972), p. 15). No, this isn't a reason. What if this emperor is naked? Discredited in literary criticism and in the philosophy of Wittgenstein, the notion of language as dress has thus retreated to a last redoubt in, of all places, 'the science of language'. To make the idea collapse all one has to do, as in the case of language-as-code, is to demand *any* evidence for the existence of the ideas in their natural nudity.

Psycholinguistics, however, is still thoroughly Lockean. Dr Greene writes of 'every intuition that people start with "what they want to say"' (*Psycholinguistics*, p. 108), and of the speaker's choosing a particular string to express his meaning (p. 141), which suggests a comparison of a stock of strings with the meaning that unfortunately and in principle cannot be observed. She explicitly uses the hopeless old distinction of content and form:

Undoubtedly, the notion that a speaker goes about expressing 'what he wants to say' by first generating an abstract NP, VP syntactic structure and only then choosing words has always seemed inherently implausible. What might be claimed, however, is that the distinction between deep and surface structure made in transformational grammar has led to recognition of a new and possibly more manageable problem: assuming that the *content* of a response is already given, what factors determine the *form* in which it is expressed? (pp. 178–179)

But we *can't* assume that content is given, and I plead innocent

[22] John Locke, *An Essay Concerning Human Understanding*, Book III, chap. ii, sec. 1.

to these intuitions. They are not intuitions but part of our language, and a misleading part that linguistics needs to straighten out. If I want to say something (how do I know I want to say something?) I may, or may not, have any one of a variety of vague feelings, impressions or images, but I discover the 'content' I want to express only by expressing it, i.e. at the same time as I use (not, often, choose) a form. This is saying no more than that our ordinary uses of 'meaning' and 'intention' make sense. (Try, by the way, distinguishing what one means from what one wants to say *in French.*) So we can sometimes tell someone else what he means, i.e. what he wants to say ('No, Sir, you do not mean tardiness of locomotion; you mean, that sluggishness of mind which comes upon a man in solitude'),[23] but only if we can say it. What we want to say, when we speak well, is what we do say and can be found nowhere else.

The one place where one does know what one wants to say in advance of saying it is translation or paraphrase. What one wants to say is then what is to be translated or paraphrased, and the task is to say 'the same thing' in the other language or the 'other words' of the paraphrase. Translation is also the situation in which traditional grammars are most commonly used. But this is not on a par with wanting to say something that is not yet language, and it suggests both that paraphrase is not the central case of meaning which the empiricists want to make it, and that paraphrasing is not like 'encoding' thought into language.

(iii)

LINGUISTIC UNIVERSALS

We can now try to draw out the links between the solidified 'competence' of internalized grammar, the 'coding' of non-linguistic ideas, and Chomsky's other *fata morgana*, linguistic universals, as we discuss this last. All are products of the desire to view language externally, linked principally by the desire for language-independent explanation. 'Notice that if the notions "noun phrase", "verb phrase", "sentence", "verb", can receive a language-independent characterization within universal grammar, then the grammatical relations defined above...will also

[23] Johnson telling Goldsmith the meaning of 'slow' in the first line of *The Traveller*; Boswell, 9 April 1778.

receive a universal characterization' (*Language and Mind,* p. 139). If wishes were horses beggars would ride. The wish in this case is for an objective universal grammar that will be *the same* as the innate Acquisition Device. One sentence quoted earlier about the child's acquisition of TG grammar ends 'we must postulate a sufficiently rich internal structure—a sufficiently restricted theory of universal grammar that constitutes his contribution to language acquisition' (*ibid.* p. 159).[24] This would have all the advantages, if it could be shown to work, of making the rules of grammar exact and language a well-defined set of systems, of corroborating TG analysis, and of proving the existence of the AD. It fails because it does not touch actual uses of language at any point.

Hall makes the point that 'we are now witnessing the forcing of all languages into the mould of English, just as in earlier periods they were forced into that of classical Latin' (*An Essay on Language,* p. 53). I do not believe that our 'noun', 'verb', 'active', 'passive' and so on, widespread as is their application, refer to any general or necessary parts of language. I will mention here only a few of the confusions the belief in linguistic universals entails.

The first is shown by reflection on a series of investigations into the language of deaf-mutes reported by I. M. Schlesinger.[25] The essay is worth attention and I can only give the most summary account of it here. Schlesinger's experiments were designed to make people sign (i.e. express in sign language) descriptions of pictures of men giving monkeys to bears, bears giving monkeys to men, monkeys giving men to bears, and so on; the intention was to demonstrate that sign language has subjects, verbs, direct and indirect objects. The results varied a good deal, but, especially in communications between signers without knowledge of any other natural language, there was a very large percentage of failures to transmit the message. Things were signed which are representable in English by locutions like 'man bear give', 'man

---

[24] Chomsky's accompanying belief that, because grammar is universal, generalizations about language can be safely based on observation of one language seems to me on about the same level as his idea that the AD could get to work and develop a grammar of English after experiencing one sentence (above, p. 63). Both are too feeble to need further comment.

[25] 'The Grammar of Sign Language and the Problems of Language Universals', in John Morton, (ed.), *Biological and Social Factors in Psycholinguistics* (1971).

I bear give present', 'man; monkey give', 'I bear; monkey; man', 'bear give man you; bear give; bear man give monkey', 'I man give monkey bear' (p. 110). These naturally often baffled the recipients. The conclusion would seem to be that sign language has nothing much like the grammatical relations of English.

Perhaps it will be objected that a language unable to transmit these messages is not a language at all, and that Chomsky's point is made because if on the other hand the language *could* say all these things about the pictured men, bears and monkeys it would have verbs and direct and indirect objects. But then, in Schlesinger's experiments the messages sometimes did get across. If subsequent communication shows that somebody understands 'man; monkey give' in the sense intended the grammarian might say that somehow the work of subject–verb–direct object–indirect object was being done; but he has observed nothing about what did the work and how, or whether there is any point in translating the grammar of these afflicted people into the grammar of English. One might also say, more to the point, that the reason so few communications in these experiments were successful is that men handing bears to monkeys, monkeys handing men to bears etc. is probably not a favourite topic of conversation among deaf-mutes. But if for any reason these matters became of interest to them they would no doubt work out some way of signing them more reliably. The linguistic universal would just be that we could understand them and could describe what they were doing in terms of our grammar. The universal is that the grammarian, if he is determined enough, can apply his grammar to anything he calls language.

But think of the case of languages like Anglo-Saxon which have no future tense but express the sense of the future by the present. (The use survives in modern English: I am going to Florence tomorrow, thank God, and can forget Chomsky for a bit.) Must we say here that the universal future is deleted and transformed into the present? Will we have said much if we do?

What paroxysm of deletions and transformations from the universal categories could explain deponent verbs in Latin which, I was taught lucidly enough, are passive in form but active in meaning? And is the middle voice deleted from the huge majority of languages in which it does not occur? Here universal grammar is just logomachy.

My other example of linguistic universals as principal chimera is from one of the strongholds of Chomsky's despised predecessors. 'The theory of universal phonetics attempts to establish a universal phonetic alphabet and a system of laws. The alphabet defines the set of possible signals from which the signals of a particular language are drawn' (*Language and Mind*, p. 121). Chomsky's effort to put the theory into practice is *The Sound Pattern of English*, the method of which is to represent every sound of speech as 'a matrix with rows labeled by features of universal phonetics' (p. 5). He also says in the same work, of his appeal to the universal:

> A phonetic feature specification consists of a 'phonetic scale' (called a 'phonetic feature') and an integer indicating the position of the phonetic segment in question along this scale. The phonetic scales form a predetermined universal set, namely the '(phonetic) distinctive features'...they must be determined absolutely, within general linguistic theory, and independently of the grammar of any particular language. (p. 164)[26]

Chomsky's idea of a universal repertoire of possible sounds from which natural languages select some descends from the work of Roman Jakobson and, through him, *via* Saussure, of the Neogrammarians whose contribution to Indo-European philology was the insistence that sound changes must without exception obey exact general laws.

Jakobson's work on the sounds possible to the human vocal apparatus, and on our principles of distinguishing them by way of 'opposition' and 'contrast' is interesting.[27] The difficulty comes when we proceed from the set of possible sounds to the sounds actually used by languages. The crucial question is whether the sounds used by languages (phonemes, as they used to be called) differ from one another like Jakobson's, Halle's and Chomsky's discrete particles—whether, that is, phonemics is separable from universal phonetics.

[26] The *Language and Mind* formulation is a more aggressive development, therefore easier to discuss, from long discussions in *Current Issues* (pp. 65–111) and *Topics* which I shall neglect.

[27] On the workings of prosodic stress Jakobson seems to me excellent, and I wish I had known his work when I was working on *Chaucer's Prosody*. See for instance *Fundamentals of Language*, pp. 36–7.

This, even as it stands, may not look straightforward, and the problems it leads to are sure to be less straightforward still.[28] It may well be that Chomsky's real contribution to phonology is to challenge the structuralist belief that we know most of what there is to be known about the sounds of language. I can only skate over this surface as quickly and gingerly as possible.

[28] I will list a few of the other problems in phonology which Jakobson–Halle–Chomsky have not settled.

(1) It is unclear what sort of reality Chomsky's 'set of possible signals' can have, determined absolutely though they be. The vocal sounds we are capable of perceiving seem at first hearing to be an infinite set but not to be differentiated into Chomsky's discrete units. This must lead to the question:

(2) *Who* defines or predetermines the universal sounds, and by what criteria? 'The hearer', answers Jakobson. 'In order to decode the message, its receiver extracts the distinctive features from the perceptual data' (*Fundamentals of Language*, p. 46). This raises on the one hand the difficulties about phonetic/phonemic I discuss in the text (for will not the 'receiver' extract the sounds of his particular language rather than those of the universal catalogue?) and on the other the speaker/grammarian confusion we discussed. 'If the listener receives a message in a language he knows, he correlates it with the code at hand' (p. 15). At whose hand if not the grammarian's?

(3) Are the universal sounds realized in actual utterances? Chomsky is inclined to say not, despite Jakobson's talk of 'extracting' them: but if not we face a variety of the competence/performance difficulty.

(4) How is the Chomskyan phonologist to treat sounds grossly different from his paradigms (whether phonemic or phonetic) but which a hearer can take *as* such-and-such a sound? We can sometimes take a sneeze or a silence as a phoneme.

(5) Take the case of dialect boundaries. When these are lines between different sounds Chomsky will have to say that they can only be drawn between sounds that differ in the universal catalogue. But in fact dialect boundaries are drawn according to what questions are being asked. Sometimes we note gross differences, but there is no obvious limit to the fineness of the distinctions we can make if we choose, other than that of the fineness of our ear.

(6) Jakobson and Halle except from their discussion certain abnormal, distorting conditions of sound production or recognition: whispering, shouting, singing, stammering; distance, filtering, noise; auditory fatigue (p. 25). But is 'normal' normal, and who decides? Do not stammerers normally stammer and singers sing? and at what point is the distance between two conversers abnormal? Have we not, here, a set of non-discrete oppositions which might suggest that the sounds of speech belong on an infinitely gradable spectrum, not in a catalogue of discrete alternatives?

(7) Isn't the whole business of defining the sounds of language, in fact, rather mysterious? I mention in the last chapter the little question of how to join up discrete sounds into anything recognizable as language, and I would guess that Firth's approach via 'prosodies' is more illuminating than the suspiciously atomistic-looking analysis of Jakobson and Halle and Chomsky.

Chomsky wants to get rid of phonemics as unnecessary to grammar. He shunts off the work that used to be done by phonemics into his universal features, classificatory matrix and formatives, so that in a Chomsky grammar the surface structure will generate phonetic representation direct, without the interposition of any phonemic level (*Current Issues*, p. 66; *Topics*, pp. 76 ff.). Phonemics used to deal with the level of language it supposed to exist between idiolect (the individual's own oddity of sound) and something like Chomsky's set of the sounds we might possibly make. Chomsky knows, of course, that languages differ in what they will treat as the same sound and in what sounds they will differentiate, but his bent is nevertheless to minimize the fact. But is not the question *for the study of language* not what necessary physical steps go to producing such-and-such a sound, nor the ways it is necessarily modified in certain contexts, but what a given language will agree to treat as the same sound?[29]

I will just mention a few of the facts which may suggest that each language does, as traditionally supposed, have its own sound system which is better studied as such than by way of the universal.

Accent does exist, after all. Talking a foreign language we notoriously do so 'with an accent', i.e. by pronouncing words of one language with an approximation to the sounds of another. Sound is here distinguishable from all other aspects of language. It is possible to have a good French accent without knowing a word of French—possible, that is, to know of French only what is covered by 'accent'.[30] A colleague examining oral French for

[29] If I had devoted a chapter to phonology I think I would have been able to show both Chomsky and Jakobson having both ways the essential question whether the sounds of speech can be objectively discriminated, i.e. by criteria other than those of particular languages. Jakobson and Halle claim on the one hand that 'the sameness of a distinctive feature throughout all its variable implementations is now objectively discriminable' (*Fundamentals of Language*, p. 25), as against the 'vague and subjective search for resemblance' (p. 24) of earlier investigators: but on the other they sometimes seem to recognize that these distinctive features are not the sounds used by languages: 'To find out what motor, acoustic, and perceptual elements of sounds are utilized in a given language, we must be guided by its coding rules; an efficacious physiological, physical and psychological analysis of speech sounds presupposes their linguistic interpretation' (p. 46). Yes. How then can the system of universal features, supposing it to exist, define the sounds of language?

[30] A related example is to twiddle the medium wave-band tuning knob of the radio set and hear languages without being able to understand a word of

'A' level reported the rather eerie experience of being forced to judge a voluble outpouring of genuinely French sounds and gestures which had nothing else in common with French. (He awarded a distinction for accent and a failure for everything else, which seems to me quite correct.) Secondly there are sound-games and spelling-games. In Henry Green's *Loving* the characters in one scene all speak with affected lisps so that 's' comes out as 'th'. (The game lapses when Raunce's blasphemous 'Jethuth Chritht' is frowned upon.) Does not the possibility of such games show the existence of a phonemic level in natural languages?[31]

Chomsky therefore seems to me to concede much more than he realizes here:

If the theory is correct, each signal of a language can be represented as a sequence of symbols of the phonetic alphabet. Suppose that two physical events are represented as the same sequence. Then in any language they must be repetitions of one another. On the other hand, two physical events might be regarded by speakers of one language as repetitions and by speakers of another language as non-repetitions. In this case, the universal alphabet must provide the means for distinguishing them. (*Language and Mind*, p. 121)

Yes, it might provide the means: but it can't provide the rules. Only the sound systems of the respective languages can do that.

The sounds of language can be recorded in a universal alphabet (such as after all linguists have possessed for a long time) but not explained by it. The possible use of Chomskyan phonetics to linguists is to give them a tool of notation. But the universal alphabet is, like all other tools in grammar, an abstraction that is useful in referring to language, not in explaining it in a language-independent way.

The only linguistic universal is language. If we call something 'language' we do so not because it fits some language-independent definition of language but because it falls within the range of what we recognize as language—because, that is, we can use the word of it. There might sometimes be point even for the linguist

them. One may be able to say *only* 'That's Chinese', 'That's Urdu', and so on.

[31] I chose this example to show again that what I am saying is *inter alia* an observation about spelling. In the case in point I know little about the sounds used by the characters in Chomsky's universal phonetics (perhaps Raunce has a Peterborough accent) but I do know that different phonemes are employed just because the novelist spells words with 'th' instead of 's'. (Cf. below, p. 175.)

in thinking about language as a universal (I shall suggest in the last chapter that this is the same as the linguist's thought about human nature) but not if it leads him to think of uses of language, the only places where language is found, as inaccurate reflections of the universal. This idea does damage to phonetics, but not so much as to semantics when it appears as the belief that the meanings of words are also drawn from a universal catalogue. We must now trace Chomsky into the latter fallacy.

5

The Wild Goose Chase of Meaning out of Language:
Chomskyan Semantics I: Universal Concepts

When I think in language, there aren't 'meanings' going through my mind in addition to the verbal expressions. (Wittgenstein, *Philosophical Investigations*, p. 107e)

Chomsky offers a series of 'models' of language, and of linguistics, and of grammar, in all of which meaning is found in some other *place* than sound or syntax, so that meaning is a 'component' of language—syntax and phonology being others. This is a deep misconception and the rest of this monograph will largely be devoted to saying why. Words, in Chomsky's grammars, flank syntax on one side, 'surface structure' on the other—the function of the latter, I suggested, being to admit phonology into a grammar from which it is otherwise excluded. The other end of the model, the 'semantic component', is the upshot of Chomsky's belief that if meaning is not in phrase structure or sound it must belong to words as an inherent property of them. The study of meaning in this view becomes an effort to define (and, as usual, to explain) 'lexical entries', leaving syntax to do certain definite logical things with the intrinsic meanings of words, and sound as nothing to do with meaning at all.

Words, therefore, are thought to have meanings, and semantics is going to try to study these meanings in ways closely analogous to TG grammar's analytic study of sentences. But in the case of semantics we are offered the bum's rush into the universal without any such preceding observations about the patterns of language as are the strength of the transformational system.

As in the case of universal phonetics, we might hope to establish general principles regarding the possible systems of concepts that can be represented in a human language and the intrinsic connections that may exist among them. With the discovery of such principles, universal semantics would become a substantive discipline. (*Language and Mind*, p. 124)

In the regrettable but total absence, however, either of any such principles or of any principles for discovering them, universal semantics is vacuous. Chomsky here is revelling, though he doesn't say so, in his realm of speculation; but why he thinks the speculations of any value is not clear.

The central speculation is that the meanings of words can be explained in a language-independent way by reference to a universal system of concepts underlying all linguistic meaning. Chomsky's disciple Katz writes, 'Since the meanings of words are not indivisible entities but, rather, are composed of concepts in certain relations to one another, the job of the dictionary is to represent the conceptual structure in the meanings of words.'[1] Chomsky talks in much the same way of a word's meaning being composed, like its sound, of a set of features: 'The lexicon is a set of lexical entries; each lexical entry, in turn, can be regarded as a set of features of various sorts' (*Language and Mind*, p. 140). If Katz's formulation were to mean only that the task of a dictionary is to mark in its way the varying boundaries between words, it would be true; but both Katz and Chomsky demand that the 'language-independent semantic absolutes' (*Aspects*, p. 77) that make up a word should belong to some universal non-linguistic reality.

In this way the Chomskyans fall plumb into the old atomism they began by attacking; the difference being that these features of meaning, unlike the parts of sound, in no sense exist. Yet both Katz and Chomsky feel themselves on safe ground here. Katz in the quoted essay feels no need either to provide evidence for supposing that words have meanings and are composed of concepts, or for suggesting what such evidence could be.

Chomsky's own analysis of 'sincerity' and 'boy' is found on page 85 of *Aspects*, where he tries to get at the meaning by a process analogous to his 'rewrite' syntactic analysis of a sentence:

(24) (i) N → [+N, ±Common]
    (ii) [+Common] → [±Count]
    (iii) [+Count] → [±Animate]
    (iv) [−Common] → [±Animate]
    (v) [+Animate] → [±Human]
    (vi) [−Count] → [±Abstract]

[1] Jerrold J. Katz, 'Semantic Theory', reprinted in Danny D. Steinberg and Leon A. Jakobovits (eds.), *Semantics* (Cambridge, 1971), p. 298.

(25) (*sincerity*, [+N, −Count, +Abstract])
(*boy*, [+N, −Count, +Common, +Animate, +Human])

The effect on the tree diagrams is to cause another level of shoots to sprout:

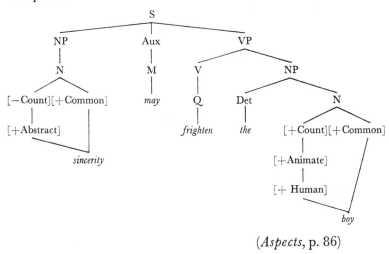

(*Aspects*, p. 86)

How words are composed of concepts remains problematic. Katz claims that the definitions given by his conceptual analysis ask empirical questions and are capable therefore of being proved true as their predictions are verified (*Semantics*, p. 306), and he offers an analogy between the conceptual structure of a word and the molecular structure of a compound in organic chemistry. What the experiments with words can be that will analyse them as if they were a paraffin or an alcohol we are not told.

Katz's first example is *bachelor*, which he defines in four senses, in each case offering the concepts he takes to underlie the word. The first and fourth are: '(i) (Physical Object), (Living), (Human), (Male), (Adult), (Never Married)...(iv) (Physical Object), (Living), (Animal), (Male), (Seal), (Without a mate at breeding time).'[2] There are some obvious objections, for instance that though out of context we might assume bachelors to be living

---

[2] This is not, of course, a new game. Hobbes (to go back no further) plays it in chapter 6 of *Leviathan*:

'For *Appetite* with an opinion of attaining, is called HOPE.
The same without such opinion, DESPAIR.
Aversion, with opinion of *Hurt* from the object, FEARE.
The same, with hope of avoiding that Hurt by resistance, COURAGE.

and 'a dead bachelor' at least an oddish phrase Chaucer's Squire
is a lusty bachelor without being either a physical object or living
and Bishop Berkeley did defend the taxation of 'dead bachelors'.
But the main question we have to ask is, since *living* (not to mention the other 'components') seems to the naked eye to be no more
and no less a word than the word it is analysing, why *living* should
be more elemental than *bachelor* and how the one could underlie
or explain the other. Why is *bachelor* less explanatory than
the universal equipment that must include 'without-a-mate-at-
breeding-time'?

The same objection has to be made to McCawley's profound
analysis of *kill* into 'cause be (or become) not alive'.[3] Perhaps if
one had to explain *kill* to a thick-witted member of a pacifist
vegetarian tribe to whom killing was unknown, one might come
up with some such words. But to claim that they are the conceptual structure of *kill* doesn't *explain* anything. Chomsky takes
the discussion a step further without meeting the objection. He
goes one better than *kill* and offers a conceptual analysis of
murder: '*cause-to-die-by-unlawful-means-and-with-malice-afore-
thought*' (*Studies*, p. 72). Chomsky also offers as the conceptual
structure of *uncle* '*brother of (father or mother)*' (*ibid.*). There it
ought to be plain even to generative semanticists that what we
are being offered as conceptual structure is simply dictionary
definition or paraphrase.

Katz calls the other words he uses to define a word 'concepts',
but doesn't define the conceptual structure of the concepts—

Sudden *Courage*, ANGER.
Constant *Hope*, CONFIDENCE of our selves.
Anger for great hurt done to another, when we conceive the same to be
done by Injury, INDIGNATION...'

The difference here is that Hobbes, though he has earlier talked of 'simple
passions', can be taken to be philosophizing in the manner of J. L. Austin.
He doesn't go to the length of asserting that these qualities are composed
of each other as molecules are composed of atoms; he may be doing no
more than define these words *vis-à-vis* each other.

[3] As Derwing remarks, 'cause be not alive' is not even an accurate paraphrase of *kill*. Derwing instances king David, who causes Uriah to become
not alive without actually killing him—though in that instance the Lord,
through the mouth of Nathan, appears to agree with McCawley: 'Thou
hast killed Uriah the Hittite with the sword...and hast slain him with the
sword of the children of Ammon' (2 Samuel xii. 9). Shakespeare, however,
makes the relevant distinction:
> And, though I kill him not, I am the cause
> His death was so effected.
>   *All's Well that Ends Well*, III. ii. 118–19

which he could only do by the use of yet other words, and other words by other words, and so *ad infinitum.* 'Without a mate at breeding time' as an element of 'bachelor' is surely a plunge into infinite regression. It would nevertheless be interesting to see what the conceptual structure of *cause, become, not, alive* is supposed to be, and of words like *by* and *and* and *word*, not to speak of *concept.*

John Lyons is aware of the difficulty of making more of the universal concepts than the old phrase 'in other words':

According to an analysis proposed by a number of linguists, including James McCawley and Bierwisch...the meaning of *kill* can be described roughly as follows: (CAUSE (BECOME (NOT (ALIVE)))). Two points should be noticed about this analysis: (i) CAUSE, BECOME, NOT and ALIVE are not to be directly identified with words of English or any other language—they are 'elements' of meaning, as it were, which can be combined in various ways to form the meanings of many different words (and ALIVE is perhaps susceptible to further semantic analysis)...(*TLS* 23 July 1970, p. 797)

What can be made of this instruction? These items in capital letters can all be looked up in dictionaries, which Chomsky agrees to be the test of what is a word. I see these English words there on the page, but am told not to identify them as words. If I do, the semantics in question collapses—but how is it *possible* not to see *cause, become, not* and *alive* as the English words we know them to be?[4] And alas! there is no test for the existence of a universal concept analogous to looking a word up in a dictionary: the catalogue of universal concepts is not to be found on the library shelves (nor, as we shall discuss, in the world at large).

Attempts have been made to provide experimental proof of the existence of some of the elemental concepts supposed to underlie words. Chomsky offers as a 'formal universal' 'that the color words of any language must subdivide the color spectrum into continuous segments' (*Aspects*, p. 29); and one reported

---

[4] Cf. 'I will adopt, for the purposes of this paper, English words in small capitals as a notation for "semantic" representation. Such representation is understood to refer to (some of) the meaning of the English words in abstraction from their idiosyncratic and language-specific lexical properties' (George Bedell, 'The Arguments about Deep Structure', *Language* 50 (1974), 425). If we deny that English words have any meaning except in English we are left in this essay with what we see on the page, namely English words in small capitals.

discovery is of a natural order in the development of colour terms.

The work that has made an impact here is Brent Berlin and Paul Kay, *Basic Color Terms, their Universality and Evolution* (Berkeley and Los Angeles, 1969). The very bold-looking thesis of this work is that

although different languages encode in their vocabularies different *numbers* of basic color categories, a total universal inventory of exactly eleven basic color categories exists from which the eleven or fewer basic color terms of any given language are always drawn. The eleven basic color categories are *white, black, red, green, yellow, blue, brown, purple, pink, orange*, and *grey*.

A second and totally unexpected finding is the following. If a language encodes fewer than eleven basic color categories, then there are strict limitations on which categories it may encode. (p. 2)

The limitation is that (with some refinements) the basic colour terms in any language appear in the order given: all languages have terms for *black* and *white*, all languages with only three basic colour terms add *red*, and so on. The other part of Berlin and Kay's argument is that this is an evolutionary development represented in the history of all languages. 'Basic' is defined to answer some obvious objections; the signification of a basic colour term 'must not be included in that of any other color term', it 'must be psychologically salient for informants' and so on (p. 6).

I note a few possible scientific shortcomings of the work which I do not, however, wish to make the centre of my comment.[5]

---

[5] (1) The strikingly determinate results would seem to depend on a large amount of consistent evidence, but Berlin and Kay report that the boundaries between colours vary greatly for different speakers of the same language, as well as for speakers of different languages (pp. 12–13; and cf. the huge range covered by RED, the category out of which *red* is later defined, on p. 18 and pp. 28–9: '"RED". . .includes maroon, red, orange, yellow, and mixtures in which these qualities are seen to predominate; "GREEN". . .covers light green and mixtures of green, yellow and light brown. . .').

(2) Berlin and Kay therefore lay great emphasis on the points marked by people on colour charts as the *centre* of colours—the *real* red, green etc., so to speak. But have colours such centres in languages? Aren't we more likely to use colour terms to distinguish hues, and if so aren't boundaries more linguistically real than centres?

(3) I am unable to judge the sufficiency of Berlin and Kay's evidence. They relied on forty informants for one language, one bilingual inhabitant of San Francisco per language for nineteen further languages, and sundry

Let us grant for the sake of argument that a case has been made about our innate apparatus for observing colour, that something in our make-up does make us differentiate colours in this order. Something would then have been said about human perceptual universals. Some of our perceptions can indeed be discussed as an effect of our constitution; we have a different field of vision from horses, for instance, and see quite differently from spiders. But this is not to say anything, so far, about *linguistic* universals.[6]

The difficulty for linguistics, granting that Berlin and Kay's evidence supports their definition of basic colours as areas of the colour chart, is that the meaning of the colour terms is not easily equatable with these references. I shall postpone until the next

written evidence for about seventy more. (There are over 3,000 languages currently spoken in the world, mostly by monoglots.)

(4) All the information Berlin and Kay collected took the form of answers to questions about a standard colour chart that presents 'hue' (defined on p. 105 as wavelength) on one axis, brightness along the other. The chart entails difficulties about *grey*; for although *grey* is one of the basic eleven terms it is not a hue and not representable on the chart. Why did Berlin and Kay assume that hue and brightness define colour rather than, say, dimensions representing warm/cold, pure/mixed or nice/nasty? Why are we to assume that the axes are the universally right ones? In point of fact they constitute in themselves a kind of translation into English. 'The ancient Greeks and Romans classified colours not as we classify them, by the qualitative differences they show according to the places they occupy in the spectrum, but by reference to something quite different from this, something connected with dazzlingness or glintingness or gleamingness or their opposites, so that a Greek will find it as natural to call the sea "wine-looking" as we to call it blue, and a Roman will find it as natural to call a swan "scarlet"—or the word we conventionally translate scarlet— as we to call it white' (R. G. Collingwood, *An Essay on Metaphysics* (Oxford, 1940), p. 195).

(5) The relations between the areas of the colour charts referred to by Berlin and Kay's capitals and our colour words remains obscure. It is remarkable that all Stage 1 languages have BLACK and WHITE rather than one term and a negative construction; but how could our *hue* be translated into such a language? and if it can't how are BLACK and WHITE hues? The languages that have only the four terms BLACK, WHITE, RED and GREEN will have numbers of shades that will have to be translated into English by the hardly grammatical *reddish green* or *greenish red*.

(6) The second half of the argument, that there has been a development of basic colour terms in a uniform predictable order in all languages, is based on *no* evidence of change and on prejudice about industrial advance (thought to be the same as general cultural advance, pp. 4, 15–16, 104) and can hardly be taken seriously.

[6] Berlin and Kay see the likeness of their work to Jakobson's in phonetics (pp. 105 ff.). The difficulties are similar too: the problem in both cases is how to bring observations about perceptual universals into linguistics.

chapter the general questions raised by attempts to treat meaning
as reference. Grant that, given a knowledge of the relevant
language and a bit of common sense, we can be taught the names
of colours from a colour chart,[7] it is by no means a straightforward deduction to say that the right areas of the chart are the
meaning of the colour words. Colour words, like any others,
mean what we use them to do in language, and we do many other
things as well as comparing objects with colour charts.

This is only to say that in our perceptions and in our language
(where colour and colour terms are found) the definition of
colour terms by reference to colour charts has no particular
centrality.

It would be hard to imagine, too, a language without terms for
day and *night* or distinctions between light and darkness, and
perhaps these are just the distinctions made by the Berlin and
Kay Stage I languages. But could *light* and *darkness* in English
be explained by reference to a colour chart? How is the linguist
to be sure that references to colour charts precede religion either
logically or historically in the use of colour terms? Are sin and
socialism both scarlet in languages that have words for all
three?

Berlin and Kay report that the term completing the basic
colour vocabulary of Stage II languages, RED, is derivable in
many languages from the word for *blood* and the fourth,
GREEN, from words to do with vegetation (cf. pp. 26–7, 38, 40).
This may be more of a linguistic explanation than the perceptual
universals can be, because it takes us into language. It may be
that Berlin and Kay's RED is better rendered *bloody* and that
many primitive peoples uninterested in colour charts wanted a
word to associate objects with blood. (That in turn might explain
how a RED derived from *blood* comes to qualify objects nowhere
near the position of normal blood in the colour charts.)

'Like the Ndembu the Gusii have three primary words. . .*-ráb-*,
Be bright, shining, clean; *-mwam-*, Be dark, dirty, cluttered;
-bariir-, Ripen and change colour, redden. In the appropriate
contexts they may be translated as white, black and red respec-

---

[7] 'The ostensive definition explains the use—the meaning—of the word
when the overall role of the word in language is clear' (Wittgenstein,
Investigations, p. 14e). None of the modern linguists writing about colour
terminology seems acquainted with Wittgenstein's discussions. They are
not hard to find: all one has to do is leaf through the *Investigations* until
one comes to a colour chart.

tively.'[8] Yes indeed—in the appropriate contexts. But why should a linguist think that *red* is here a more primary sense than *ripen?* In Middle English *falw* is a colour term used, presumably, of the part of the spectrum occupied by fallow deer; but it applies so consistently to dying or dead objects and to the autumn, and is so ordinarily used when feelings of the sadness of decay are being expressed, that *dead-looking* is often a better modern English rendering than *brown*.

One of the language-games we[9] can play with colours is Berlin and Kay's mappings. But there are plenty of others, and we have no reason to suppose that theirs is more central *in language* than the rest. 'What looks as if it *had* to exist, is part of the language. It is a paradigm in our language-game, something with which comparison is made. And this may be an important observation; but it is none the less an observation concerning our language-game—our method of representation.'[10]

'But "green" *must* refer to something universal and physical', a linguist might say, retreating to what he can be sure of. 'Green ideas' are part of Chomsky's famous nonsense-sentence; ideas, we presume, cannot be green because they cannot be referred to any part of the spectrum. Not even if they are the young ideas that are taught how to shoot? or the ideas of a girl looking but greensickly upon a matter? And what if someone annihilates

> all that's made
> To a green thought in a green shade?

What part of the spectrum does Marvell's green thought occupy? Is it a glossy, matt or gleaming green? transparent or opaque? and how can what is annihilated have a colour?

There is no evidence that we would be able to pick 'green' out on a colour chart if we were unable to understand phrases like 'green thought': both what we do with a colour chart and what we do in poetry belong to our language and have their sense there. And the sense may well be different from any sense possible to other languages.

The other commonly-offered conceptual universal is human kinship. Leech has a discussion (*Semantics* (1974), pp. 237–62)

---

8 W. H. Whiteley, 'Colour-words and Colour-values: the Evidence from Gusii', in Robin Horton and Ruth Finnegan (eds.), *Modes of Thought* (1973), p. 149.

9 I am not convinced that this is a linguistic universal.

10 Wittgenstein, *Investigations*, p. 25e.

ending in the remarkably cautious conclusion that 'those that are philosophically inclined to the universalist position will find that an assumption of weak universals enables them to see a common basis in obviously similar conceptualizations of kinship that arise in geographically and linguistically diverse environments'. Well, yes, it would be hard to imagine a human society without words for father, mother, brother, mother-in-law. . .though perchance this may be easier in the brave new world of the year 2000. But is this because of the underlying biological relationships so differently reflected on the surface of languages? Can any child say 'mother' without defining his relation to her in the terms of his particular language? Does he always mean the woman who has borne him? Even if he couldn't define *woman*? What the child means by *mother* must be within a range of what the word can mean in a particular language. *Marriage*, too, is a well-nigh universal institution which notoriously varies with different cultures; if the word is a universal concept that is because one definition of humanity is that we do always make a human sense of the facts of nature, not because it is always, if you go deep enough, the same sense. (It is interesting, for instance, that in English our terminology of the marriage and kinship of human beings is applied to animals only as baby-talk or a kind of joke, though the biological relationships may be identical.)

An Englishman will read '80' as 'eighty' and a Frenchman as 'quatre-vingts'. Isn't the '80' then the direct representation of a universal concept which different languages express in different words (and even through different concepts, for '80' needn't make us think of four twenties)? It *is* possible to do mathematics in many languages, though by no means all, using number systems very like ours: many languages are close enough here to make translation very easy. It can also be said that all the uses of numbers are a kind of language, broadly, 'the language of mathematics', which is found in many natural languages. (Below, p. 177.) Call this a 'metalanguage' if you wish. Whether 'quatre-vingts' can do quite the same things as 'eighty' remains an open question. *In mathematics* it can, given that French and English are languages in which maths is done. But is '13' unlucky in all languages and if not how is it our 'thirteen'? Is Hopkins's 'Five!' automatically translatable into a cardinal number? When D. G. Rossetti informs us that the stars on the breast of the Blessed Damozel were seven, is that translatable into a language where '7' happens to represent the number of the important infernal powers?

One of Chomsky's own examples of an innate idea, a universal concept underlying whatever languages do with it, is the triangle. He quotes Descartes: 'But because we already possess within us the idea of a true triangle, and it can be more easily conceived by our mind than the more complex figure of the triangle drawn on paper, we, therefore, when we see the composite figure, apprehend not it itself, but rather the authentic triangle', and begins his comment: 'In this sense the idea of a triangle is innate' (*Language and Mind*, pp. 83–4). *Triangle* here is not quite a Platonic Idea, the true form of all triangles, but something determined by the lay-out of our brains, which ensures that there is this universal concept underlying all words for *triangle*. If a language has no such word the concept will nevertheless be lying dormant, ready to throw up a word when required.

I will take Chomsky's word for it that some of our perceptions of length, shape etc. (I would add, rhythm) precede language. What nonetheless invalidates the notion of *triangle* as underlying all languages is that to understand the suggestion we need to know some geometry (cf. Winch, above, p. 71). The perfect triangle, represented only crudely in the degenerate triangles people actually draw, is a concept comprehensible only in geometry. It is not within anybody's power to notice 'that triangle is isosceles!' unless he has learned the meaning of the phrase. (Is the innate triangle, by the way, going to be right-angled, acute-angled, or what?) We might without any mathematical knowledge observe in a variety of ways the similarity of shape between what geometry calls *triangles*; but to know them *as* triangles, to know the kinds of things that are done to figures called *triangles*, is to develop a terminology (in this case that of geometry) and to make a 'grammar' of triangles. Inside or outside geometry what a triangle is depends not on any innate idea of the triangle but on what we do with these lines.

Take as an example the aspects of a triangle. This triangle [diagram follows] can be seen as a triangular hole, as a solid, as a geometrical drawing; as standing on its base, as hanging from its apex; as a mountain, as a wedge, as an arrow or pointer, as an overturned object which is meant to stand on the shorter side of the right angle, as a half parallelogram, and as various other things. (Wittgenstein, *Philosophical Investigations*, p. 200e)

The categories of universal semantics are supposed to be the real ones underlying all the meanings of natural languages, but in fact every language has its own conceptual system—which is only one way of saying that different languages use different words. The point may come clearer in a brief look at R. M. W. Dixon's fascinating Mother-in-Law language. Dixon found an aboriginal Australian tribe speaking a language (or perhaps two languages) which he thinks offers an unusually clear example of the real conceptual structure of a language, though that is not his phrase.[11]

The tribe discussed might almost have been one of Wittgenstein's legendary ones and the case does illustrate, if nothing else, that if you search far enough you can find almost any imaginable linguistic oddity. This tribe used to speak, as far as vocabulary goes, within its language Dyirbal, two quite different languages, the ordinary one, Guwal, and Dyalŋuy, used only to mothers-in-law and on connected occasions. The latter has a much smaller vocabulary than the former but no actual overlap of words. Mr Dixon wants to argue that if one word in Dyalŋuy covers five in Guwal, then the one word must show the system of classes of the larger vocabulary. The smaller vocabulary would thus give somehow the essential categorizations of the larger vocabulary. Interesting as the discussion is, it will not do; for one might equally say, on the one hand, that the larger vocabulary is the necessary explication of the smaller or (more relevantly) that the classes made by the smaller are simply the classes *it* makes, rather than the ones *naturally* belonging to the larger. Each language makes its own classes.

Universal semantics falls into the plotting of 'meanings' (as universal phonetics plots sounds) on arbitrary graphs, followed by the bland assertion that the graphs are the true reality. In this way Chomsky's semantics is in the true tradition of *The Measurement of Meaning*, a volume politely reviewed in the same issue of *Language* that carried Chomsky's first devastation of Skinner. Another expert semanticist wrote of what he elsewhere called this 'major book':

The method expounded in this book is based on a simple device, called the 'semantic differential'. This consists of a number of scales, each with seven divisions, whose poles are formed by pairs of oppo-

---

[11] 'A Method of Semantic Description', in Steinberg and Jakobovits, *Semantics*, pp. 436–82.

site adjectives, and the subjects are asked to enter each concept in the division which they find most appropriate. (Stephen Ullmann, *Language and Style* (Oxford, 1964), pp. 20–1)

Is this a science or a party-game?

Infinite translatability need not be implied by the belief in the universal catalogue of concepts. Chomsky says that a 'fixed class of items' 'does not imply. . .that there must be some reasonable procedure for translating between languages' (*Aspects*, pp. 28, 30). But it does mean that the same universals are always there underlying all languages, that all languages are 'after the same pattern' and, as Chomsky reports with approval from the Port-Royal Grammar, 'the same deep structure may be realized differently in different languages' (*Cartesian Linguistics*, p. 34).

But does knowledge of different languages in mere experience support the belief in universal concepts? The French, that nation of breakfasters upon toast, have no one word for toast (*une rôtie* seems to be being replaced by *du pain grillé*). *Pain grillé* does look like a conceptual analysis and one might think that 'grilled bread' underlies our 'toast': at least it is an accurate description of toast by the rules of cooking. But if I don't know what a grill is am I debarred from understanding toast? And if I have something with my toast will it be *marmalade* or, more really because closer to a universal concept, *confiture d'orange*?

Or consider the more serious problem well known to many missionary societies, translating the Bible into languages without the essential Christian concepts. What has often to be done is virtually the conversion of the pagan language, without which the idea of converting the heathens is meaningless. The language has to be made to transcend its heathen meanings but in its own vocabulary. One can see something of the process at work in Anglo-Saxon. But is it illuminating to see this as the releasing in a language of universal concepts? To graft something quite alien on to a language requires an effort of perhaps hundreds of years and a corresponding change in the lives of the people who speak the language. Languages certainly change and develop, but that might suggest their differences more strongly than any under-lying sameness. Was Anglo-Saxon the same as a heathen and a Christian language?

Could there be (to use one of David Sims's examples) a trans-lation of the medieval poetry of courtly love into the language of bushmen? and if so would their language be the same after as before the translation? and if not were the concepts of courtly love in the universal catalogue before the poetry was written?

Leech too offers in support of the belief in universal concepts that 'it is possible to translate correctly from one language to another' (*Semantics*, p. 35). Well, sometimes it's possible (mathematics can be done in any European language) and sometimes it isn't (much poetry is untranslatable) and that, I think, is that.

Once more Occam's razor seems called for. What is added to our discussions of words by talk of an underlying universal conceptual structure? Does 'living' *add* anything to Katz's *bachelor*? Chomsky, interested in the problems raised for his system by uses of syntax which do what he thinks should only be done by the intrinsic meanings of words, observes that in certain contexts the use of the preterite tells that the subject is dead, whereas the perfect is used of the living. 'Julius Caesar lived at Rome' but 'President Nixon has lived at the White House for five years.' (Actually the perfect in this use describes a continuing state; in 1974 'Mr Nixon lived for five years at the White House' does not imply his death. A better example would be 'Britten has written many operas.') This is interesting, but do we add anything to the observation by saying that the perfect can carry a component 'living'? Are we not merely paraphrasing our observation pompously? Or take the case of what I will call the 'plot-recounting present'. We say, 'David Copperfield marries Dora then after her death marries Agnes' not 'David Copperfield married Dora then after her death married Agnes.' The latter is incorrect; it suggests that the events could be looked up in official documents, whereas with the former we know we are referring to a work of fiction. But is anything more said, is anything explanatory added, if we begin talking of a 'plot-recounting component'? On the other hand we could not discuss the matter unless it were something we commonly *do* in our language; and I again conclude that the linguist must contemplate what is done within language.

Dictionaries do define words as literally as can be, by setting their bounds as words, and often much more finely than Katz's examples. But defining a word in a dictionary is giving, for the immediate purposes of the dictionary, certain other words as in certain contexts the equivalent of the word defined. Dictionary definition is not the quasi-chemical analysis Katz is pursuing and it makes no attempt to relate words to anything universal or to explain (except in the case of etymological dictionaries, which make etymological explanations) why words mean what they do. Moreover a good dictionary (Johnson's was the first) will do most of its work by quotation, giving a reader the sense of what words mean by seeing them used.

Semantics must indeed ask where words really come in language, and if it chooses to call the words concepts I don't mind. But these conceptual analysts are prevented from asking good questions about words by their paraphernalia of the universal. What they are fumbling for is something like J. L. Austin's detailed discussions of actual words. For example in the often reprinted 'Plea for Excuses' Austin really is talking about the conceptual structure of our language—but all the time by looking carefully at the ways we actually do use our words, at their boundaries, contexts, moments of appropriateness and so forth. Even in *How to do things with Words* (Oxford, 1962), where I shall suggest Austin misses one of his own points, he is so careful to distinguish the differences within his 'performatives', so attentive to the way these words actually go, to what we actually do with them, that he is a standing rebuke to Katz and Chomsky.[12]

The linguistic scientist will retort that Austin's account of *excuses* is just arbitrary, that he is failing to explain why words are as they are. In one sense this is true. Why does *game* have the range it does and not any other? Why are chess, cricket and patience all games but battles, going to the theatre and swimming not games? There is, Wittgenstein argues in a famous passage of the *Investigations*, no central core of meaning, no one definable quality of 'gameness'—in Chomsky's terminology no underlying

---

[12] I think of things like Austin's demonstration in 'A Plea for Excuses' that 'voluntary'/'involuntary' are not necessarily usable in the same contexts, 'until we even doubt whether there is *any* verb with which both adverbs are equally in place'. One context where his principle 'no modification without aberration' is very useful is in discussing productions of Shakespeare. If one protests about the gimmicky or crooked productions of recent years, in which the producer's vanity is displayed at the expense of the play, the standard retort is 'But what is a *straight* Shakespeare production?' The retort is based on a grammatical mistake: the opposite of a crooked production is not a straight production but just a production. A *straight* production might be a peculiar kind, but the questions about crookedness only arise when one feels the need of that word.

universal concept—that all games have in common. A game is a game just because we so use the word, the 'because' there obviously not being an offer of language-independent explanation. But if 'arbitrary' implies 'senseless' I deny it. And if our language is misleading, if we think it needs reform, the reform must be seen as something new but belonging to language. (It is not even clear how this would differ from ordinary uses of language, which are always new.) If all our uses of language are misleading and confused we are in irretrievable chaos and madness with no chance of escape. But if that were so could we say so? The limits of our language are the sense we manage to make in it recognizable as sense to others; the reason in *game* is just the sense made, just that we can and do talk of games knowing what we mean and without reducing the world or language to chaos. *Game* links all the different activities we call 'game'. Hence Wittgenstein's emphasis on 'intermediate examples'—and Chomsky's disdain for analogy (below, p. 137). *Game* is a way of seeing that some activities are like others in some ways: in the ways, that is, created by our uses of the term. This kind of observation of the language from within is what Wittgenstein calls 'grammar': it may be a better idea of grammar than Chomsky's.

Imagine again that Chomsky is right and that nouns *are* composed of concepts selected from a universal catalogue—what then? This would be a curious fact about the structure of language, but would it explain what words mean? This conceptual analysis, if successful, might do for the lexicon something similar to what the transformational system does for syntax, but it would no more explain the uses of words than TG grammar explains the aspect of syntactic structures. Words—which, after all, have no existence other than in use—would still mean what we use them to do; and it is not apparent that conceptual structure can give *any* information about how we use words.

In the end it must be a kind of philistinism in a linguist to think, as Chomsky does with his doctrine of universals, of all languages as pretty much alike. It means he has lost that wonder at the splendid multiplicity of language and languages which is the other side of the wondering at language as a common human possession. Chomsky's semantic universals are as if a critic were to try to explain great poems (as is not unknown) by looking for an underlying Great Poetry that they share. To do so would inevitably be to have lost interest in poems, as well as in the possibility of discussing poetry in general. Can a linguist hope to get anywhere unless he is fascinated by languages?[13]

What would follow from the picture of nouns as universal concepts would be a 'model' of language in which the rest of deep structure, syntax, would make predications about concepts. I do not think this makes the Chomskyan 'model' more illuminating, but it does allow the Chomskyans the chance to revive the old ambition of seeing language as a calculus of propositions and grammar as identical with logic.

[13] The modern universalists have never to my knowledge made any serious effort to refute the so-called Whorf–Sapir hypothesis—the series of observations showing, for instance, that several Amerindian languages structure time and space quite differently from ours (and from each other) and that some languages have nothing like our notion of causation and can therefore have no science. Even the most bizarre language can sometimes, in some of its uses, be translated into English; the universalist can if he wishes go on talking of an underlying unity. But won't the striking thing still often be the differences between languages? Is translatability and the fact that we can discuss linguistic differences in English enough to justify linguistics in concentrating all its energies on universals and in neglecting linguistic diversity?

6

Chomskyan Semantics II: Making Propositions

Grammar recognizes a form of discourse called the sentence, and among sentences, as well as other kinds which serve as the verbal expressions of questions, commands, &c., one kind which express statements. In grammatical phraseology, these are indicative sentences; and logicians have almost always tried to conceive the 'unit of thought', or that which is either true or false, as a kind of logical 'soul' whose linguistic 'body' is the indicative sentence.

R. G. Collingwood

(i)

SENSE AND LOGIC

Chomsky's semantics is an offshoot of the empirical tradition of philosophy. Chomsky frequently denies that he is an empiricist, but 'by their fruits ye shall know them' and, as Quine observes, of one of Chomsky's pronouncements about the need to postulate an 'Acquisition Device' with innate properties, 'This indisputable point about language is in no conflict with latter-day attitudes which are associated with the name of empiricism, or behaviorism.'[1]

One centre of the group of ideas I have in mind when I say that Chomsky is an empiricist is the notion that language is a *mirror* of nature. The world is everything that is the case because the conceptual elements or atomic facts of language reflect the corresponding elements of the external world.

There is no *necessity* for the belief that language reflects the world to cohabit with Chomsky's doctrines of the acquisition device and/or the linguistic universals; but they do all fall together easily enough in the work of all the Chomskyans who have paid any attention to them, and these ideas have in fact been close philosophical associates for a very long time. 'For Aristotle. . .certainty is given us both in the physiological root of our knowledge, in sense-perception, and in the direct intellectual apprehension of the essential natures of kinds of things which is the highest power of mind' (Marjorie Grene, *The Knower and the Known* (1966), p. 64). The 'kinds of things' are the Chom-

---

[1] W. V. O. Quine, 'Linguistics and Philosophy', in Sidney Hook (ed.), *Language and Philosophy* (New York, 1969), p. 95.

skyan universal concepts as they define the external world; substitute 'innate ideas' for 'sense-perception' and you could read
'Chomsky' for 'Aristotle'.

The Chomskyan psycholinguist will say that our brains determine the way we talk about the world, the empiricist philosopher
that the nature of the world determines what we can truly say of
it; the psycholinguist will concentrate on our innate capacities,
the empiricist on how the external world controls knowledge,
but they will unite in looking for a true form of language free
from or underlying the vagueness of natural languages and will
agree that truth and meaning cannot well be found *in* language.
For truth, both will say, we have to go to the world as perceptible
by our innate capacities.

The two positions fully coalesce in the work of Chomsky's
philosophical ally Zeno Vendler:

Facts and possibilities do depend upon the conceptual framework of
the human mind, which. . .must transcend the idiosyncrasies manifested in particular languages or language groups. Once the world is
given, and the human mind is given, the facts and possibilities arise
as something objective, that is, as transcending the limitations of
individual humans and their tribes. (*Res Cogitans* (Ithaca, 1972),
p. 88)

The means of reflection of reality by language, in the empiricist
view, is the proposition, and one great empiricist quest is for the
(definite article) true form of propositions. It is not easy for me to
say what propositions are without either joining the quest,
making the question formally grammatical (proposition = what
is predicated of a subject) or lapsing into the ineffable or the
circular (propositions are that which is asserted, questioned,
denied etc.); and I have certainly no thoughts to offer about
propositions. I mean by 'proposition' any expression which says
something 'analytically' true or false or something true or false
about objects. (This would be objectionable in various ways if
offered as philosophy, but I hope it can pass as a hint about how
the word is often used in English.) A proposition if asserted is a
statement, but it can also be questioned, negated, and generally
made to do all the tricks of algebraic logic. Nouns, in this sketch,
get their meaning by reference either to things or to the universal
concepts we tried in vain to meet in the last chapter; verbs introduce the sense that, being predicated of the subject of a sentence,

constitutes the proposition made. Thus propositions are represented in sentences as, in a traditional phrase still used by Austin, the sum of the sense and reference of the sentence.

This sketch is aimed, I repeat, not at saying anything about propositions, but at suggesting how the word is often used. The sense I propose seems to me to be Chomsky's when he quotes the Port-Royal Grammar in support of his beliefs in deep structure: 'The principal form of thought is the judgment, in which something is affirmed of something else. Its linguistic expression is the proposition' (*Cartesian Linguistics*, p. 33).

Now empiricism is an ancient and distinguished tradition within philosophy, which is much more than can be said for 'the science of language', and I have neither the capacity nor the desire to make a frontal assault upon empiricism—though I will not go so far as pretending to like it. What I do want to show is that when modern linguists accept empirical doctrines as self-evident truths they are led away from their proper work, the contemplation of language, and that the effect of the introduction of uncriticized empiricism into linguistics is much like that of the introduction of an uncontrolled bull into a china shop.

The pursuit of the true form of propositions, a pure example of devotion to reason, has had in the history of philosophy all the force of a great passion. When linguists are converted to the faith I have to show that it becomes positively unintellectual.

The great attraction of propositions for philosophers is that they are supposed to be that which is true or false. '$2+2=6\frac{1}{3}$', 'Napoleon died at Paris in 1842 at the height of his power', 'hydrogen burns in oxygen to make potassium permanganate' are all excellent propositions because demonstrably false—within their respective modes of discourse. But '$2+2=$yellow' would be not false but senseless (cf. Hockett, p. 72). So philosophers naturally proceed from propositions as what can be true or false, to an emphasis on verification.

In the influential popular statement of the position, A. J. Ayer's *Language, Truth and Logic*, what is meaningful is what can be verified.

The principle of verification is supposed to furnish a criterion by which it can be determined whether or not a sentence is literally meaningful. A simple way to formulate it would be to say that a sentence had literal meaning if and only if the proposition it expressed was either analytic or empirically verifiable.[2]

Everything not so verifiable is pronounced senseless.

This immediately links empiricism with the dominant school of contemporary semantics. Geoffrey Leech, having given a list of types of 'basic statement' and having asked the good question 'Why choose these as basic statements?' gives as his first reason that everybody else does. 'A second reason...is that they are statements easily translatable into terms of truth and falsehood. This in turn means that they lend themselves to tests of validity' (*Semantics*, p. 85).

'The verification principle' in Ayer differs from the doctrine Wittgenstein is said to have been propagating a few years earlier, 'The meaning of a proposition is the method by which it might be verified', for Wittgenstein places no immediate restriction on what can count as method of verification, and therefore allows the possibility of different 'rules', e.g. that a proposition about a work of art might be 'verified' differently from a proposition in physics; whereas Ayer as a true empiricist will only admit as verifiable those propositions which are 'analytic' or physical. He holds, for instance, that there is 'no possibility of arguing about questions of value in aesthetics, but only about questions of fact' (p. 113).

Contingent propositions, then, at their simple centre, say something about something which can be judged true or false by the comparison of what is said with reality, reality supplying the criteria of truth. This is indeed, in a very refined way, what happens in the physical sciences; and the drive of the philosophical school in question has always been to take the physical sciences as models of the proper use of language.

To the linguist the first lure of propositions is that they claim to be the content of language, the 'what' of what is said. I do not believe that the claim is always substantiable.

It is no accident that Chomsky's base strings and kernel sentences are 'simple, declarative, active' and that the great majority of his examples are in the third person of the preterite—the ordinary form of contingent propositions saying something about something: 'The man hit the ball' etc. Chomsky never discusses

[2] A. J. Ayer, *Language, Truth and Logic*, second edition (1946), p. 5; Ayer is sketching the position simply in order to modify it a little.

forms like 'I bet £20 on Also Ran', 'I promise to pay you $5.00 next Tuesday', 'I grant you a *decree nisi*', in chess '*j'adoube*' or in a marriage service 'I will'. These are all examples of J. L. Austin's 'performatives':

If I utter the words 'I bet. . .', I do not state that I utter the words 'I bet', or any other words, but I perform the act of betting; and similarly, if he says he bets, i.e. says the words 'I bet', he *bets*. But if I utter the words 'he bets', I only state that he utters (or rather has uttered) the words 'I bet': I do not perform his act of betting, which only he can perform: I describe his performances of the act of betting, but I do my own betting, and he must do his own.[3]

Performatives

have on the face of them the look—or at least the grammatical make-up—of 'statements'; but nevertheless they are seen, when more closely inspected, to be, quite plainly, *not* utterances which could be 'true' or 'false'. Yet to be 'true' or 'false' is traditionally the characteristic mark of a statement. (*ibid.* p. 12)

'I hereby promise. . .' is not true or false in the way that either '2+2=4' or 'hydrogen burns in oxygen to produce water' or 'Napoleon died on St Helena' are, though 'I promise. . .' may be, in Austin's term, 'unhappy' (the circumstances may make it impossible to promise or to fulfil the promise; the promise may be made in bad faith; the words may be understood as in any of a variety of ways *not* performing a promise, etc.).

Performatives are one line of evidence in support of what I offered as a truism, though it is denied by all Chomskyans: that what utterances mean is what they do in language, not merely what is contained in the propositions they embody. An example where a slip of Austin's has not been corrected and helps to make the point: '*j'adoube*, said when I give check' is 'suiting the action to the word' (p. 65). Actually *j'adoube* is said not in giving check (where it is usual, though not necessary, to say 'Check!' as a kind of crow) but in adjusting the position of a piece without making a move. If a player touches a piece when it is his move he must make a move with the piece unless he says '*j'adoube*'. If he says '*j'adoube*' then makes a move with the piece he has adjusted the words are redundant; but when correctly used the words can

---

[3] *How to do things with Words*, p. 63. The last point needs a little modification: Henry Crawford does do Lady Bertram's betting for her in *Mansfield Park* with such forms as 'her ladyship bets. . .' Bookies' runners also exist.

distinguish two movements that are physically the same. If a player picks up a piece it may be *either* the beginning of his move in the game *or*, with *'j'adoube'* said, not a move in the game: what is *done* in the game depends here on whether the words are used.

Comic examples of accidentally performing something are the traditional interpretation of a chance nod at an auction as a bid (the nod being taken to do the same thing as 'I bid. . .') and the exclamation at cricket (in a Herbert Farjeon story?) of 'Well, I declare!' intended as a mere expletive but taken as declaring an innings closed.

The last-but-one example is a paraphrasable performative: there are many ways of bidding. But not all performatives can be paraphrased and still perform. When the Queen assents to a parliamentary bill, or when you or I sign a cheque, we are performing what only our respective signatures can perform. Or, to take one of Austin's favourite examples, in the marriage service only 'I will' will get the parties well and truly married. 'Yes!' looks like an effectively performative answer to 'Wilt thou have this woman to thy wedded wife. . . ?'—or even Petruchio's

> 'Ay, by gogs wouns,' quoth he, and swore so loud
> That, all amazed, the priest let fall the book.

But nowadays at least the priest would have to pick the book up again and insist on the correct form.

I don't think there is much more one need say about performatives. Chomsky's philosophical friends do say a great deal more because if they are to defend propositions as the real, true, central meaning of language they must subvert the apparently sensible view that performatives do something (i.e. mean something) not accounted for by the propositional calculus.

Austin himself, who did not live to prepare *How to do things with Words* for the press, has what seems to me a deep nostalgia for propositional truth/falsity which in the second part of the book leads him away from his insight about performatives. He tries hard to show that performatives themselves depend on propositions, and the effort has been taken up by Katz, Vendler and others.

The line of argument is to marry performatives to propositions by way of 'illocutionary force' and a discussion of reported speech.

Vendler distinguishes 'the message itself' from 'the illocutionary force with which this message is issued' (*Res Cogitans*, p. 63). He does so in order to enforce his contention that performatives 'belong to the genus of propositional verbs' (p. 14) and only 'denote' (rather than just *are*) speech acts (p. 28).

Performatives will usually be followed by a 'that. . .' or similar clause expressing a recognizable proposition, which is the 'message'. In 'You deny it? I say that Mount Everest *is* the highest mountain in the world', 'I say' is a kind of performative, and the 'that. . .' a proposition. Similarly we say 'I promise that. . .', 'I demand that. . .', 'I utterly deny that. . .' When these sentences are rendered into indirect speech, the 'I say that. . .', 'I promise that. . .' etc. become the propositional 'He said/promised that so and so. . .'; moreover, says Vendler, the verb before the 'that. . .' in indirect speech need not be the same as in the direct speech performative. What follows the 'that. . .' clause may change, too; but if the report is accurate whatever follows the 'that. . .' will be the real propositional content of the utterance. And the original performative, or the reported speech report, will be demoted to a label denoting the type of proposition. So 'I say that Mount Everest. . .' could well be reported as 'he asserted that. . .' or 'he declared that. . .' and the proposition asserted, declared etc. might appear in a great many other words.

As saying something consists in the performance of an illocutionary act, telling what somebody said will consist in specifying the illocutionary act that person performed. Consequently any such report will begin by indicating the illocutionary force: He *stated. . .suggested. . .promised. . .ordered. . .praised. . .*etc. (p. 55)

In this view there are as many types of proposition in a language as distinguishable performatives. In this way Vendler leads the discussion of performatives back onto the more familiar ground of the paraphrasability of propositions, where we will follow him soon.

One objection that needs to be made first is that if we specify an illocutionary act by 'he promised. . .', 'he threatened. . .', 'he urged. . .' we may be incorrect. Reported speech has, notoriously, many ways of being tendentious. I found myself retorting to the Director of Oxfam 'I didn't "concede" that. . .nor did I "admit" that. . .' On the other hand the BBC, reporting the latest terrorist murder in Northern Ireland, says 'The Protestant Action Group claims responsibility.' I think it should have been 'admits'.

For Vendler's argument to work there has to be one true illocutionary act underlying performative and reported speech. But even if this were so we would face our usual difficulties in getting it out from beneath. It is worth asking whether we are ever forced to identify an utterance as one kind of illocutionary act in particular: but if we do agree, we are merely specifying what the original words have done. *Insult* is an interesting performative because (Austin, p. 117) it can't be used in the ordinary performative way in the first person singular present indicative active, or with the word 'hereby': you can't insult me by saying 'I hereby insult you.' Whether someone has indeed been insulted may be a question that only close attention to the words or deeds supposed to constitute the insult can decide, and then only in our possibly disputable judgement. *Refute*, too, is not to be used as the BBC has just illiterately begun to do: 'I utterly refute it' does not constitute refutation. Whether someone has been refuted depends on the judgement, which may extend over centuries of printed matter, of what was said. I am happy to believe simply that performatives perform what they perform, and that we can characterize the performance, accurately or not, in many ways, without thereby being granted a specially privileged or dependable access to the 'what' of what has been performed.

Indirect speech is, of course, a kind of paraphrase, and Vendler's most important arguments from indirect speech are a variety of the traditional ones about the paraphrasability of propositions, used also by Katz.

In this view, essentially Russell's, '*Basic meaning* is roughly what two (or more) paraphrases of a sentence have in common' and this is 'equivalent in a very loose sense to "what you say" ' (Roderick A. Jacobs and Peter S. Rosenbaum, *Transformations, Style, and Meaning* (Waltham, Massachusetts, 1971), p. 2). But who decides why 'basic' is basic and by what rules two paraphrases are judged to share the same base?

(We have taken the term *meaning* to refer to the sum of the propositions expressed by a sentence or the sum of the concepts expressed by a subsentential constituent.) We also understand *proposition* to convey what synonymous sentences have in common by virtue of which they are synonymous. (Katz, *Semantic Theory*, p. 120)

It follows for Katz that the choice of one in particular from the set of synonymous sentences is merely a stylistic matter, viz, a question of surface decorativeness: he speaks of 'stylistic matters such as the factors underlying a speaker's choice of a particular sentence from a set of sentences that are the same in meaning' (*ibid.* p. 433).

Vendler takes up the argument about paraphrase and uses it as he is trying to show that thought, as in Chomsky's models, begins by being unexpressed in the mind. Vendler denies that 'what we say' is 'something constructed out of words' (*Res Cogitans*, p. 52) and continues:

What we say. . .is a thought expressed in words, couched in words; whereas the same thought, unexpressed and not coded in words, may be the object of a mental state or a mental act. . .I could use the word *thought* to denote this common object. . .In order to avoid a possible ambiguity, however, I shall use a familiar technical term, *proposition*, to refer to this common object, and I shall reserve the name *thought* for such an entity insofar as it is the object of a mental act or state only, that is, insofar as it remains unexpressed in words. Finally, I shall use the word *message* to denote propositions expressed in words. (*ibid.* pp. 52–3)

Here the position that propositions are the true meaning is seen to belong with, if not to depend on, the notion that language is only a code, a dress, of thought. So for Vendler 'no sentence, no noun-clauses, in fact no string of words whatever, can be what one says' (p. 58).[4] The *what* is the not necessarily expressed thought, the proposition that may take different words.

[4] One must distinguish between the unconscious and the non-existent. The 'that. . .' clause is supposed to represent our otherwise unconscious but certainly existing thought, but there are cases where surely nobody would say it represents a thought at all. Think of the common experiences of picking up an object and finding it unexpectedly light, or of finding that there is an extra step, going downstairs, or one less than we thought. We assumed, expected, thought that the object was heavier, that there was one step more or less. These thoughts were unconscious not because all thought is unconscious but because though 'I thought that. . .' I wasn't in fact in the sense Vendler demands thinking at all until 'I was surprised that. . .'

As Vendler amusingly observes, we wouldn't reply to the question 'What did the parrot say?' with indirect speech, 'The parrot said that. . .' Vendler rightly says that this is because we do not believe the parrot really said anything: it did not perform a full speech act. (Actually it didn't even, as Vendler thinks, speak words: it imitated sounds which we took as words.) But it is true that we sometimes use the locutions of indirect speech about animals. An animal can be said to know or realize, even to know or realize that. . . where the 'that. . .' introduces a proposition like

But the same proposition may *do* different things (above, Chapter 3, 'aspect'), as in Katz's example of rhetorical stresses which make changes in 'what the speaker finds surprising' without altering propositional content (p. 431), and different propositions may do the same thing.

Language notoriously means, sometimes, what it doesn't say (if 'say' refers to propositional content). Think of the fine sense of the state of political power in the Soviet Union expressed to Rusanov by the *size* of an article in a newspaper and the *absence* of a black border (Solzhenitsyn, *Cancer Ward*). One could hardly say that size or absence can make propositions; but in that context, at that moment of history and that habit of expectation, Rusanov's paper does indeed mean exactly what he takes it to mean, and it is the paper that means it, not anything else. Even silence can have an unambiguous expressive function dependent on its context in speech ('Good morning!' greeted by silence. . .) and then the expressiveness belongs to this particular silence, that

the ones important to Vendler's argument about indirect speech. The penguins know that it is feeding time. Foxhounds do not realize, 'as the house dog so readily does, that human beings have preoccupations in which dogs can be ignored'. A horse 'had had ideas about bucking on the road to testify his appreciation of these things. . .' (E. Œ. Somerville and Martin Ross, *The Silver Fox*, chapter 6). This shows not that animals can talk but that reported speech is itself something done in language by the reporter, and not a safe guide to unexpressed thought.

Again, it may be thought that if the 'that. . .' of indirect speech is the 'what' of 'what is said', we have explained why exclamations and interjections cannot go into reported speech. If you say 'Oh!' I can't report it as 'You said that. . .' anything; it has to be 'You said, "Oh!"' or an illocutionary/syntactic report, 'You made an exclamation.' The reason that 'Oh!' will not go into indirect speech is then supposed to be that the 'Oh!' is not saying anything. But this is just a repetition of the claim that only propositions are proper language, not evidence of the truth of the claim. 'Oh!' is not, out of context, propositionally paraphrasable. But when the argument is put to me I shall say 'Oh indeed!' in a certain tone, and I think I shall be saying something reportable as 'he rejected the argument' or even, if supported by the present sort of discussion, 'he refuted the argument'.

And when writers or speakers refer to their unspeakable feelings, apparently inviting us to share them. . . ? If the feelings genuinely are unspeakable they are not spoken; but if spoken they are in the language as usual. Language is still what the words do—expressing feeling, or not. 'He words me', says Cleopatra of Augustus, which is true. Augustus tries to persuade Cleopatra that he is not 'wording' her, but her sense of what his language is really doing is too acute. But if Augustus were genuine in his professions, that would be expressed in his words (in, of course, a context including deeds) at the places where now we hear his calculation.

is, to an intention it expresses in the right context, and not to anything else. But what is the propositional content of silence? Would Vendler offer as reported speech of a silence answering 'Speak or die!' 'He said that he agreed to die'? or just 'He agreed to die'? Yet 'Silences, backed by the power of speech, had as many shades of significance as uttered words in the way of assent, of doubt, of negation—even of simple comment' (Conrad, *Nostromo*, Part Second, chapter 5).

Conversely language can make one proposition while apparently expressing another. 'Will you marry me?' (a good yes/no question, easily to be replied to with one 'bit' of information, see below) can certainly be answered in the negative by 'NO!' but also by 'You are the most insulting man I ever met in my life' (which could also mean 'Yes') or 'To take is not to give' (ditto) or even 'It is starting to rain again.'

Searle gives as an example an American soldier captured by Italians who wants to use his one sentence of German to convince the Italians that he is a German, although he knows the sentence means 'Knowest thou the land where the lemon trees bloom?' (*Speech Acts*, pp. 44–5). One difficulty here is that the American is trying to do what he is very unlikely to be able to do with his one German sentence: his intention is unlikely to be successfully expressed. But I don't see why one rejects out of hand, as Searle does, offering no reason other than that 'he finds himself disinclined' to hold it, the view that what the American means with his German sentence is to pass himself off as a German; though it is also true that if he were instead sitting a German exam. and called on to translate the sentence he would offer the English words. The use of the German would then be different. But change the venue a little to that deep study of language, Molière's *Bourgeois Gentilhomme*, and can one not say that the rhyming *lingua franca* used in making M. Jourdain a *mamamouchi* means (*inter alia* and to M. Jourdain not to the audience) that the speakers are Turks? This, that they are supposed to be speaking Turkish, is the level of language operating (within language) in that case, but not in making anyone say in a true proposition 'I am speaking Turkish.'

Shakespeare's Prince Hal, when he so cruelly and snobbishly plays upon the drawer Francis, utters some sentences that are well-formed but in Chomskyan terms meaningless. Had they come at random from a computer they would not have been

English. Their meaning in context is merely to perplex and delude Francis: that is what they do in the language:

Prince: Why, then, your brown bastard is your only drink; for look you, Francis, your white canvas doublet will sully: in Barbary, sir, it cannot come to so much.
Francis: What, sir?

1 Henry IV II. iv

Meaning here is not explicable as propositional content.

'Walt Whitman does not seriously incite the eagle of liberty to soar' says Austin (*How to do things with Words*, p. 104), not intending the remark as literary criticism. Seriously = propositionally: Whitman is not issuing a command to a bird. But *of course* Whitman's incitement is as serious as he can make it given his limitations as poet.

If meaning is the set of acceptable paraphrases of propositions, what makes the paraphrases acceptable if not that they do the same thing in language? But what can do the same thing in language as *Macbeth*?[5] (And is *Macbeth* an eccentric, peripheral example of language? It would be just like linguists' cheek to say so.) 'You *could* select either of two poems to remind you of death, say. But supposing you had read a poem and admired it, could you say: "Oh, read the other, it will do the same"?' (Wittgenstein, *Lectures and Conversations on Aesthetics, Psychology and Religious Belief*, ed. C. Barrett (Oxford, 1966), p. 34). Yet the propositions in *Macbeth* are paraphrasable *qua* propositions like any others.

Music is generally recognized to be unparaphrasable. A composition can be rescored for different instruments or transposed into a different key, but to 'say Schubert's Unfinished in different notes' wouldn't mean anything. 'If I admire a minuet I can't say: "Take another. It does the same thing." What do you mean? It *is* not the same' (*ibid.*). (As music, that is. Of course if one just wants to dance a minuet, any other minuet will do.) Put this together with 'understanding a sentence is much more akin to understanding a theme in music than one may think'

---

[5] There are problems about what '*Macbeth*' refers to: the play can be performed in a variety of styles, read aloud or silently or even by a blind and deaf person in Braille. I will not discuss this and only propose that *Macbeth* is the infinite set of acceptable readings and performances. It is not in the mind apart from all these but is every one of them. The phrase 'reading *Macbeth*' is not misleading.

(*Philosophical Investigations*, p. 143e) and the linguist's faith that propositions are the only true meaning may be shaken. Or not, as the case may be.

All works of linguistics and even all works about linguistics are themselves strings of propositions. I am trying, for instance, to say what is the case with regard to the study of language. Linguists should beware of the natural temptation to regard what they do themselves as a specially central or important use of language.

If the philosopher wants to concentrate on propositions and physical verifiability, that is his affair, but how can the linguist deny that language does many other things? And by what *linguistic* criteria does he make propositions the only true centre of what utterances mean?

Vendler uses a similar argument from translatability:

People exposed to the diversity of languages are conscious of the possibility of discussing in their native tongue views expressed by speakers of other languages, of agreeing and disagreeing with them, and so forth. . .Now surely, if I can say in English what Descartes said in Latin, or if I can contradict in English what Descartes said in French, then what Descartes said, and what I say, cannot be a string of words, English, Latin or French. (p. 61)

Jakobson goes further and asserts that 'the meaning of any linguistic sign is its translation into some further, alternative sign' (cited Steiner, *After Babel*, p. 260), from which it follows that anything untranslatable is meaningless—a neatly circular way of affirming faith in semantic universals.

It is true that we all lapse into discussions of things like 'Descartes's ideas' whether we are acquainted with Descartes's words or not, and that this can be done after a fashion so long as our language is not too far from that of the unfortunate philosopher discussed. (I am not sure that one could similarly discuss the views of the Book of the Dead.) But translatability is surely dangerous ground for those who think that words are never thought. Where there is dispute about 'what is said' have we not merely, as with indirect speech, to go back to the original text—whether it be philosophy, poetry or mathematics?

'Everything is water' is not, on the face of it (as Bertrand Russell somewhere observes), a very inspiring start for Western philosophy *because*, I would say, the sentence is so straight-forwardly propositional that it must look to us like crazily mistaken chemistry. We can contradict in English 'what Thales said' all too easily. To know what he meant we would have to become as inward as possible about the questions he was asking, his presuppositions and problems, and his position relative to other thinkers. 'What Thales said' has, in other words, to be put in a context that at widest is that of his original language, if we are to understand what he meant by what he said.

I don't need to go to the original to see that Aristophanes's contribution to the *Symposium* is extremely funny. But what precise degree of irony is there about the myth in the *Timaeus* of love as a divine semen, entering a man's head from the celestial regions but, if it goes wrong, descending his spinal column? or about the means of causing the feathers of the wing of the soul to sprout in the *Phaedrus*? Is not the tone here to do with the seriousness?—does not the style of Plato's humour affect 'what is said' if the phrase is to mean anything? And how can I, who know so little Greek, then know what Plato said?

What is an acceptable paraphrase, what is the same in meaning, always depends on context: the idea is incomplete until we know by what rules two utterances are judged to mean the same. Sometimes a discreet cough can be an acceptable paraphrase. Katz seems to be looking for the absolute, some set of rules that will declare two meanings the same or different for all purposes and in all circumstances. When this unicorn is not forthcoming numbers of circumstances and rules are declared to be improper, and within the domain that is left to them (that, usually, of mathematical logic and/or physics) linguists are able to declare that certain utterances are acceptable substitutes for certain others. This is their contribution to the search for the true form of propositions. But then the domain within which the para-phrases are acceptable is not language, but whatever field within language the linguist has defined in order to make paraphrase acceptable.[6]

In its infatuation with propositions and logic linguistics has fallen into the vile durance of the information theory from which

---

[6] It is the same with analogy: the Chomskyans seem to think that unless there is *absolute* likeness, likeness not limited by 'in this way' or 'in that way', the idea is useless. But we always see likeness within some mode of seeing. A likeness implying a mode may well show something about language. Cf. above, p. 101; below, p. 137.

Chomsky began by offering to deliver it (above, p. 3). This is another place where insistence on propositional content, the belief that thought is a mental event distinct from the words that express it, and the idea of language as code, all fall together. In information theory, if 'an *encoded* message is accurately *decoded* by the intended receiver, the purpose of the communication system has been achieved' (Black, *The Labyrinth of Language*, p. 17). The linguist likes to believe that language is similarly messages (propositions) present to the mind and similarly encoded and decoded by language. But in fact communications theory always presupposes language in just the same way as we saw code doing, not in the same way as words presuppose language.

When linguists discuss information theory they always assure us, with a kind of mathematical smirk, that 'information' is highly technical and unlike the word we use in common speech— as indeed I can believe that it is, within mathematics. But information theory as it has made its way into linguistics is (like 'deep structure', 'underlying' etc.) all too well named. 'Information' is not restricted to the conveyance of facts, any more than the 'proposition' of the more sophisticated empiricist philosopher; but it *is* essential to information theory that messages convey 'bits' of information. A bit is anything that can be expressed as one of two alternatives, answering some question yes or no, an idea essential to the binary 'language' of digital computers. The 'yes' or 'no', however, depend for their sense on the question, the question on its mode of discourse, and the mode of discourse on a whole language. To try to build up to meaning, or to a whole language, from bits of information, is just atomism over again.

A pure instance of 'information' is the blue litmus paper that turns red in acid. Here there are only two states, acid or alkali, and the litmus paper informs us which. The different colours therefore make one of two possible propositions. But here it is obvious that the information answers our question only if we are capable of putting it, and in a certain context. If we don't know what an acid is, the paper will turn red in vain. The Davey lamp that burns differently in the presence of firedamp similarly conveys one bit of information—to those capable of asking a certain question in a certain area of knowledge. Ditto everything that can be done by a digital computer.

When we have decided what yes/no questions to ask we can

certainly express the answers as bits of information, i.e. proba-
bilistically, for here information content varies inversely with
probability and if the answer to a question is predictable it has
no information content. (So Malinowski's 'phatic communion' is
information theory's 'noise'.) But when Black says, 'It is hardly
surprising that natural languages are found to have a high degree
of "redundancy"—of the order of 50%' (*ibid.* p. 18) he is
judging redundancy by the standards of information theory,
which are just those of the measurement of yes/no propositional
content. When he goes on to note that 'we could remove half of
any written or printed communication and still be understood.
The surplus symbolization is a safeguard against carelessness,
inattention and confusion' he is asserting that the information
theorist's view of language is *the* central view. In fact one could
delete far more than half of *Macbeth* without damaging its
propositional content: therefore Shakespeare is mostly 'noise'
and the poetry of the play is a safeguard against carelessness etc.?

Information theory and code both bring us out into the same
philosophical arena, where propositions take on all comers as
the only proper uses of language. I believe still that they will there
be mauled by certain linguistic lions, and that when the linguist
rather than the empiricist philosopher is emperor, propositions-
as-the-only-meaning ought to get the thumbs-down signal.

George Lakoff, whose 'generative semantics' is based (in-
securely, I think) on Chomsky's generative grammar, says 'I
assume that a grammar of a language is a system of rules that
relates sounds in the language to their corresponding meanings,
and that both phonetic and semantic representations are provided
in some language-independent way' ('On Generative Semantics',
in Steinberg and Jakobovits, *Semantics*, p. 232). 'Language-
independent' is the usual announcement of a programme to take
meaning out of language and look at it free from that degenerate
environment; meanings only 'correspond' to sounds in language,
as usual. The new thing is that Lakoff is taking a step beyond
Chomsky in the direction of propositional analysis. Lakoff's
modification of Chomsky's system is that he permits lexical sub-
stitution in the base string before the transformations operate;
he has on his side the obvious sense in saying that 'the old man
comes' is a sentence very like 'the old woman comes' and also
very like 'the old man died' and 'the young man comes'. But TG

grammar has no way of accommodating such likenesses within its account of syntax, as Chomsky says rather convincingly (*Studies*, p. 135).

The more radical generative semanticists, who as I write are trying to seize the initiative in linguistics from Chomsky, want to derive all expressions of the same meaning from the same underlying string. Chomsky's counter-argument is that there are no rules for doing so analogous to the rules for deriving non-recursive transformations from the same syntactic strings, and it seems to me an unanswerable argument.

Propositions, however, and the logical hoops they can be made to go through, bear a family resemblance to kernel sentences and non-recursive transformations; this has proved an irresistible temptation to some disciples of Chomsky to resuscitate the old ambition of making linguistics the same as logic. The new twist is that Katz, for instance, believes that only linguists can uncover the true logic of language—not in the contemplation of uses of language, but in revealing its underlying structure. The logic of language, in this view, is as well hidden as 'deep structure' because the two are identical. 'The distinction between logical form and grammatical form, between the thought or meaning of a sentence and its overt phonetic or orthographic shape, is an appearance–reality distinction' (Katz, *Linguistic Philosophy*, p. 11). Katz elsewhere argues that 'the alternative to a philosophical theory about logical form is thus a linguistic theory about logical form'.[7]

Katz assimilates linguistic to logical forms as if they are indistinguishable. He puts questions like 'what is semantic truth (analyticity, metalinguistic truth, etc.)?' and 'what is entailment?', which are questions in logic, in the same list as 'what is a possible answer to a question?' (*Semantic Theory*, pp. 4–5).[8]

But are people when they talk always really, deep down, if they are talking at all, following the rules of formal logic?

We do say things, especially in academic contexts, like 'What you really mean is. . .', the sentence being completed by a modification of what was said in order to make it follow some logical rule more clearly. This is a good thing to do, in the right context,

---

[7] 'The Philosophical Relevance of Linguistic Theory', reprinted in J. R. Searle (ed.), *The Philosophy of Language* (Oxford, 1971), p. 108.

[8] Chomsky himself is more cautious about what linguistics can offer philosophy; *Language and Mind*, pp. 161 ff.

and academics couldn't get on without it. I am certainly not going to suggest that logic is somehow untrue. But not all languages insist on logicality like the surviving respectable academies of the West.

Peter Winch discusses some examples from Zande 'where what appear to us as obvious contradictions are left where they are, apparently unresolved' and comments on one of them, 'It is noteworthy. . .that the Azande, when this contradiction. . .is pointed out to them, do *not* come to regard their old beliefs about witchcraft as obsolete' (*Ethics and Action* (1972), pp. 24, 26). Perhaps our natural reaction, in English, is that they jolly well ought, and we may join with Lewis Carroll's Achilles when the Tortoise asks him what would happen if he didn't accept a logical conclusion: 'Logic would take you by the throat and *force* you to do it!' *Soit*; but we can't conclude that the Azande, however illogical, are either misusing their language or failing to make sense.

There are examples nearer home. People frequently do assert simultaneously *p* and not-*p*, as anyone will know who has studied public opinion surveys. People may be wrong to think it best both to retain and abolish hanging, to make marriage inviolable and divorce easier to obtain, to vote Labour and Conservative—but are they *ungrammatical*?

The point may come clearer if I can refute (as linguistics not as logic) two of Austin's examples on pages 47–8 of *How to do things with Words*. 'We cannot say. . ."The cat is under the mat and the cat is on top of the mat" or "the cat is on the mat and the cat is not on the mat".'

But what if we *do* say these things? There are surely problems about giving examples of the ineffable in English? What if these unsayable things are introduced by 'I dreamed that. . .'? The real sense seems to be 'we cannot say these things if we are making ordinary factual sense of the world'. But:

> I stared at the cat on the mat.
> The cat on the mat sat and sat.
> I stared at that cat
> Till my mind reeled, so that
> The cat was and was not on the mat.

That isn't very good, but why is it not grammatical English, and meaningful? We might also get drunk and see the cat as at once under and on the mat. (And is being drunk extraordinary? I am glad to hear it; but is that a proposition in grammar?) If we drunkenly asserted as much would what we said be senseless?

'My saying "the cat is on the mat" implies that I believe it is...We cannot say "the cat is on the mat but I do not believe it is".' Of course we can! If 'the cat is on the mat' were to be said on oath in court and perjury were not to be committed it would imply belief. But Austin himself has just said 'the cat is on the mat' without implying anything about his belief in the physical location of any cat, and in fact the sentence is said exclusively by parents teaching children to read and by philosophers desperate for examples, neither of which groups believe that the cat is on the mat.[9]

William Blake is a great poet and an important thinker, but for him consistency of thought is not important: on the contrary he believed that 'Without Contraries is no progression' (*The Marriage of Heaven and Hell*, Plate 3), contradicted himself shamelessly, and produced as his best work poetry in which there is indeed a clash of contraries, without resolution, whose point is in the contradiction itself. But even Blake didn't, like Shakespeare, go as far as to assert that he could believe what he knew to be a lie:

> When my love swears that she is made of truth
> I do believe her, though I know she lies.

Is Shakespeare writing either nonsense or an ill-formed sentence? Surely not. And if anybody tells me that Blake and Shakespeare are less English than (shall we say?) L. S. Stebbing, I shall merely give my best imitation of a Blakean laugh. This is *not* to say that grammar is unconnected with what sense we can make, but to

[9] Implication and presupposition as a genuine problem for the linguist are quite different. When we talk with something 'at the back of our mind' (even something as large as our life in this world) how is this expressed in what we say? When a speaker is under a strain which he effectively suppresses is the strain *in* what he says?

Antony has a conversation with Enobarbus in which Antony and the audience, but not Enobarbus, know that Antony has just learned of the death of Fulvia. This knowledge makes a difference to what he says—but we couldn't say he is saying *that* Fulvia is dead; he is not making a proposition. Perhaps we would tumble to the fact in the end: Antony is talking as if his wife is dead, or not inconsistently with her death—and it may well be that we pick up many essential facts from such takings for granted that are far short of logical implication. But this is very puzzling.

affirm that grammar is a study of the infinite creativity of language, not confinable to the rules of mathematical logic.

To say that certain logical forms really underlie what we say is to judge language from the point of view of the logician (the 'really' is no more than 'logically'), and from what other point of view could a logician judge anything?

What has not been established is the priority *in language* of the operations of formal logic; but that would be the only grounds on which they would occupy a privileged position for the linguist. There are no grounds, for instance, for supposing that the language of the garden of Eden consisted of propositions (presumably about the flora and fauna) in all their logical varieties; nor that when the child begins to speak he is demonstrating a mastery of formal logic. For the linguist the question about logic is the same as the question he asks about all language: what use do we make of logic in language? Unless we are logicians that question will not be answered by logic.

Katz's 'What is a possible answer to a question?' could only be answered by an infinite list of contexts, not by an introduction to formal logic. (The first answer to *his* question is: It all depends what question.) 'What do you mean?' is a question with *many* kinds of answer—as many as there are distinguishable styles of making sense in our language. 'What do you mean?' is not always paraphrasable as a demand for paraphrase. 'What, pray, do you mean by calling my wife a bitch, Sir?' is not answerable, except in terms of further insult, by 'I mean that she is a female dog, Sir!'

The question whether something is true or false can certainly be important, even *the* question, as Austin says, but it isn't an absolute question, any more than the meaning of a word is absolute. Questions about truth/falsity always imply contexts and rules in which we judge the question appropriate and by which we answer it; and rules and contexts vary. Katz, beginning a book by explaining that modern linguistics is a leap forward that explains the underlying reality of language in a new way, just as 'the atomic theory of matter' did for matter, asserts that 'continuity is only the surface appearance of matter and that in reality it is composed of incredibly many tiny particles with empty spaces between them' (*Linguistic Philosophy*, p. 2). This can *really* be refuted in the way Johnson offered to refute Berkeley, by kicking a stone. *Of course* matter is continuous, as we all know by the 'rules' of common experience (without which there would be no physics). This book will not slip away through the empty spaces between the particles of your knee or table— unless the latter happens to have holes big enough. But by the rules of atomic physics (which hold in atomic physics and no-where else) matter is discontinuous. 'In reality' is the assertion that one set of rules should judge the rest, especially if they are the rules of physics. The sun doesn't rise, says B. F. Skinner; to speak accurately we must say the earth revolves. What nonsense! I saw the sun rise the other day. But if I happen to be following the rules of elementary astronomy I will agree that the earth revolves.

Not everything that is true or false is verifiable by the same means. Physicists show that their hypotheses are not contradicted by experiment. But in literary criticism? Some propositions are true and others false, though the mode of verification (if we so call it) is quite different from physics, and leaves a large area for the necessarily indeterminable.

The guarantee of truth within any set of rules is the sense made. Physics makes physical sense; logic makes logical sense; it is even occasionally true that criticism makes critical sense. But if linguistics is a discipline it must make the sense that constitutes the discipline, not decide whether it is doing so by the rules of other disciplines. I began by saying that the only final test of linguistics is the depth of understanding of language it can offer: it is not a hopeful omen when linguists begin trying to measure the depth of linguistics by its closeness to physics or formal logic.

The Chomskyans' hankering after physics or mathematics does them harm even at their strong points. Chomsky's account of the passive transformation, I suggested, is an elegant and irrefutable restatement of traditional grammar; but he does it damage, in defiance of his own effort to separate syntax and semantics, when he drags in the logical status of the passive.

In the case of the other non-recursive transformations what they do, Chomsky assumes rather too easily, is self-explanatory: 'Transformations ought to introduce certain syntactic relations that are semantically significant', as Katz says (*Semantic Theory*, p. 439). The interrogative asks a question, the negative negates, and so on. But what does the passive do? Both Chomsky and Katz have produced examples, mainly using 'quantifiers', where active and passive have a different propositional content ('many men read few books'/'few books are read by many men') but both believe that generally active and passive mean exactly the same and are interchangeable (Katz, *Semantic Theory*, pp. 436–437; Chomsky, *Language and Mind*, p. 153).

Here Chomsky is getting the worst of both worlds. On the one hand, as pure syntactician, he need not raise the question how we use the passive: all he need do is give his syntactic account of it. But if on the other hand the grammarian does aspire to a fuller picture of language and does try to give an account of the role of the passive, Chomsky's doctrine is the worst possible, because it denies the passive any *raison d'être*.

The deep difference between the active and passive is the quite basic division we make between what we do (active) and what we experience or suffer (passive). If I say I do something, I take a certain responsibility for it; but when I suffer something I am only responsible for how I suffer, that is, for what I do with what is done to me. (If this doesn't matter neither does the freedom of the will.) And though there are plenty of uses of the passive for what we do and the active for what we suffer, and though Chomsky would not recognize these remarks as at all connected with grammar, they do explain some of the places where the passive means something different from the active.

To do something with words in Austin's sense one has to use the active: the performative 'I promise you £5.00' will not be acceptable in its passive form '£5.00 is promised to you by me', which rather suggests a memorandum of a previous agreement. Or take these active/passive pairs:

1 John is boiling the eggs
  The eggs are being boiled by John
2 John is growing oak trees
  Oak trees are being grown by John
3 John is growing a beard
  A beard is being grown by John
4 John has taken some hard knocks
  Some hard knocks have been taken by John
5 John has caught a cold
  A cold has been caught by John

Though these passives are all just about possible they are increasingly odd. 2–5 are all instances of verbs we use quite ordinarily in the active with a direct object but without implying that the object results from the deliberate action of the subject. Or if the subject is responsible for what happens (as in 'growing') it is not because he does anything to the oak trees except plant and nurture them or with his chin except refrain from shaving it. In example 1, although John does go through the actions of putting the eggs on to boil, it can also be said that the water or the stove is boiling the eggs. In all these cases the 'by' of the passive indicates agency more directly and unequivocally than the subject of the active, so that it seems a little odd to say that the eggs are boiled by John not by boiling water. The passive of 'John is growing a beard' makes the odd suggestion that the beard grown is not on John's chin—that he is taking some sort of deliberate action to grow a beard somewhere else; and the cold that was caught suggests some effort or a chase.

These observations explain, I think, at least one necessary passive. My physics master always used to mark it wrong when we reported experiments in the active. (Would one say that his reason for doing so was stylistic or grammatical, and what would the difference be?) It always had to be 'the bar was heated and temperature readings were taken and it was observed that. . .' For although physics was even for me certainly an instance of people doing something not suffering something, it is necessary to physics that observations should be as impersonal (repeatable by all persons in possession of their faculties) as possible. And those who emphasize that *objective* only means 'what everybody can perceive' and who therefore favour the alternative use of the first person of the active will still make it a plural, 'We did so and so' not 'I did so and so.'

Conversely if you ask a boy what he has been doing today and he replies 'At first my algebra homework was done by me then breakfast was eaten and the bus caught; then lessons were attended and at break Smith's head was punched by me. . .' you will sooner rather than later interrupt and ask why he is using all those passives. And you may well put it by saying you want to know what he *did*.

If one began with passives as kernels instead of actives, there would be no need to include the phrase 'by + NP$_1$'[10] of

[10] In Chomsky's account the passives without 'by + NP$_1$' 'are formed by a second "elliptical" transformation that converts, e.g., "the boy was seen by John" into "the boy was seen" ' (*Syntactic Structures*, p. 81). So we cannot analyse 'my grandfather was killed in the Boer War' without first deleting 'by someone' from 'my grandfather was killed in the Boer War by someone'.

Chomsky's transformation. Jespersen begins his discussion of the passive in his shorter grammar,[11] much more like a man really interested in saying what the passive does in our language, with examples that have no ordinary active equivalent. The active of 'my grandfather was killed in the Boer War' would be something like 'Someone killed my grandfather in the Boer War', which rather suggests a murder during the relevant period.

The expressiveness of the passive is obscured by the logical–propositional–referential fascination. What the passive does is simply not accounted for by its propositional similarity to the active.

Again, the transformations that do seem to have a logical function are not the less transformations if they don't. Take this version of the conditional (cf. Jespersen, *op. cit.*, section 35.3):

If you come by train there's one at 8.45.
If you're having dinner there's turkey on the menu.
The teacosy is for the little pot if it fits.

In these cases, which are all perfectly competent and acceptable, the *if* clause expresses what in syntax we shall still call the conditional though there is no logical dependence: the train will run whether you come or not, etc. From a logical point of view the sentences are misleading and need straightening out: but from a linguistic point of view they are *not* like 'O my Lord, if my Dutie be too bold, my love is too unmannerly', to which the retort 'I do not well understand that' is called for both in logic and common speech (*Hamlet*, III. ii). The point is relevant to our understanding of Vaughan's lines

> If thou canst get but thither
> There grows the flower of peace.

Which kind of conditional is that?

Geoffrey Leech is more cautious than semanticists a few years since, and includes several caveats:

Such is the complexity of the field that present efforts at reducing it to rule can be regarded as at best a promising beginning. . .It is generally assumed that the principles of such a natural logic must be largely universal to all languages; but at the present stage of investigation, this is no more than an attractive conjecture. (*Semantics*, 1974, p. 9)

[11] Otto Jespersen, *Essentials of English Grammar* (1933), pp. 120–1.

(I don't see why *complexity* of data makes the formulation of rules, in this age of computers, particularly difficult. It *is* difficult to explain data, though, when one's rules don't apply.) One still has to ask why Leech thinks the attempt to equate syntax and formal logic either a 'beginning' or 'promising' when it has produced no results but plenty of obscurity. Why are conjectures about universal logic so overwhelmingly 'attractive' to the linguist? I suspect the answer is that logic gives the linguist something to hang on to—when he has lost touch with language.

(ii)

REFERENCE

To continue the crude sketch I made at the beginning of this chapter: if the meaning of language is the sum of sense and reference, 'sense' is the propositional content of an utterance and 'reference' the things to which sense attaches itself and which anchor it in reality. Propositions may have no reference (mathematics is analytic, i.e. pure sense) but if they are contingent, as in physical or historical propositions, their sense will depend on their reference to whatever physics, history etc. judges capable of being referred to.

One need not, to hold Chomsky's position on innate ideas, also believe that the objects language refers to somehow guarantee the meaning at least of nouns, and certainly not that language is somehow caused by the objects it names.[12] But it is very significant that *reflect* should be a favourite Chomsky word rather than *express*. 'Language. . .would naturally be expected to reflect intrinsic human capacity in its internal organization' he says (*Aspects*, p. 59), and 'The central doctrine of Cartesian linguistics' (which Chomsky thinks true) 'is that the general features of grammatical structure are common to all languages and reflect

---

[12] This view is sometimes attributed to the Book of Genesis where if Adam names the creatures it is thought that the sense of the names must be controlled by the creatures he is naming. (This would be roughly equivalent to an Aristotelian recognition of natural categories existing before language.) Adam in fact begins with very wide classes, *cattle, fowl of the air*, and so forth, before giving the creatures the names that are further classifications (he doesn't descend to proper nouns at all); really in Genesis language precedes Adam's naming, for there are several conversations before Adam gets to work on the creatures, and naming precedes creation: 'And God said, Let there be light, and there was light.'

certain fundamental properties of the mind' (*Cartesian Linguistics*, p. 59).

Reflection of the external world is a different matter, of course, and one to which Chomsky has devoted less attention. But he does say 'Proper names, in any language, must designate objects meeting a condition of spatiotemporal contiguity' (*Aspects*, p. 29) and Vendler defends the opinion that any name which does not refer to a physical object is parasitic upon nouns that do: 'True, one can refer to Zeus or to Hamlet, but this is by a special dispensation, parasitic upon the basic framework. For, after all, the former is supposed to have lived on Mount Olympus and the latter in Denmark. In fact they did not live anywhere, at any time; therefore in fact they are nothing' (*Res Cogitans*, p. 76). Yes, in verifiable *fact* Hamlet and Zeus are no *things*. But who supposes that Hamlet did live in Denmark (unless Saxo Grammaticus)? And if it is said that Zeus lives on Mount Olympus nobody ever meant by that that Zeus lives in the same way as mortal men, in a house, upon food, or that he died on Mount Olympus at a certain date. Great Pan did not die in the same way as the Emperor Tiberius. Vendler does consistently think of religious language as a kind of fiction, and of both as barely distinguishable from lies: what is true is decided by reference to things. This, again, is an ancient philosophical position which I am not trying to refute philosophically. But in fact many children learn to pray before they learn to make propositions about objects (i.e. before they have any truthfulness to the physical world: it isn't making a proposition in this sense to say 'Gimme jam') and on what *linguistic* grounds are we to say that the 'Our Father' is less English than, or parasitic upon, statements like 'the cat is sitting on the mat'?

Just as sameness of meaning in sentences is taken to be paraphrasability of propositional content, synonymy in nouns is taken to be reference to the same object. 'Even though there is no corresponding concept in one's own language for a concept in another language, one can nevertheless provide a description (if necessary a very detailed description) of its referent', says Leech (*Semantics*, pp. 31–2), implying, one supposes, that the detailed description will be the same as the meaning. Similarly Katz says, 'There are synonymous words like "bunny" and "rabbit", "piggy" and "pig", "stomach" and "tummy", etc., that have different conditions of use because of certain social conventions that have nothing whatever to do with meaning' (*Linguistic Philosophy*, p. 93; cf. below, p. 156). 'Meaning' here is equated with reference as opposed to use. The position, descending as it does from the seventeenth-century quest for an ideal universal language with which Chomsky is so much in sympathy, is found already fully developed as early as Sir Thomas Urquhart—though his tongue was perhaps in his cheek when he proposed 'to appropriate the words of the universal language with the things of the universe' (cited Steiner, *After Babel*, p. 200). But does the morning star (*pace* Frege) mean the same as the evening star because both phrases refer to the same 'object', Venus?

Chomsky himself does not often discuss reference, but when he does mention it he seems to agree with Vendler:

Goodman has argued—to my mind, quite convincingly—that the notion of meaning of words can at least in part be reduced to that of reference of expressions containing these words...Goodman's approach amounts to reformulating a part of the theory of meaning in the much clearer terms of the theory of reference. (*Syntactic Structures*, p. 103)

It is often obviously true, even outside physics, that the sense of what we say will depend on our being able to refer to something. 'Pass me the salt, please', we say at dinner, seeing the condiments. Of course the salt-cellar may be empty, a practical joke which on being touched will explode, etc., but ordinarily our request will refer to salt. One contemporary dilemma of politicians who are usually no more idealists in philosophy than elsewhere is therefore unnecessary. To think that the I.R.A. cannot be banned because it might then change its name is like being afraid to ask for the salt in case everyone else insists on calling it sodium chloride. All that is necessary is a phrase like 'the organization commonly called "the I.R.A."'—leaving identification to the courts.

What I am objecting to is not reference as an important use of language, but the belief that it is somehow more reliable than other uses, and to the frequently concomitant belief that the existence of things somehow guarantees the sense of the language that refers to them. The existence of salt makes possible the ordinary meaning of 'Pass the salt, please' but it is a necessary, not sufficient, condition of that sense.

The effort to make objects somehow inherently meaningful

takes us back to information theory, for it is like demanding bits of information without the questions they answer. Is the dish-cloth in the sink? I can only find out by fumbling under the crockery and soapsuds, and then I answer my question by direct reference either to the dishcloth or its absence. But my question comes first: there is no need for anyone else observing the sink to do the same things with these objects.

Language allows us to make such different senses of objects that I remain unconvinced of the power of objects *qua* objects to do much for our understanding of language. Sometimes the boot is on the other foot. Objects adrift from any of the places given to them in our lives by our language, are prevented from meaning anything.

Presently he rose and approached the case before which she stood. Its glass shelves were crowded with small broken objects—hardly recognizable domestic utensils, ornaments and personal trifles—made of glass, of clay, of discoloured bronze and other time-blurred substances.

'It seems cruel,' she said, 'that after a while nothing matters... any more than these little things, that used to be necessary and important to forgotten people, and now have to be guessed at under a magnifying glass and labelled: "use unknown".' (Edith Wharton, *The Age of Innocence*, chap. 31)

The only approach to meaning in these forlorn things is the tentative identification of them as 'domestic utensils...' This means that even reference is rather vague here. The objects can of course be referred to in any of the ways practised by any of the exact sciences; they can be put on tables and inspected. But to refer to what they really were would be to understand more than the vague 'domestic utensils' allows us to. As Chomsky says, 'artifacts are defined in terms of certain human goals, needs and functions instead of solely in terms of physical qualities' (*Aspects*, p. 29). To make these objects meaningful, that is, we have to put them in a context inexplicable by physical reference. Until we know what a thing is (the same as what it does or means) it won't help much to refer to or name it. 'And when the children of Israel saw it, they said one to another, It is manna: for they wist not what it was' (Exodus xvi. 15). Moses at once gives sense to the word and to the thing: 'This is the bread which the Lord hath given you to eat.'

I believe that Johnson, tempted by an antithesis, got this the wrong way round in the Preface to his Dictionary (which is a pity in a writer who claims for himself with great justness 'a grammarian's regard to the genius of our tongue') when he wrote: 'I am not yet so lost in lexicography, as to forget that *words are the daughters of earth, and that things are the sons of heaven.*' On the contrary words are a revelation of sense, about the things of earth amongst others. Words must transcend mere things and give them a sense they will only possess intrinsically when named.

Presumably all languages have words for *sun* and *moon* (though there seems little need in Welsh, where the demand for *cloud* would be more obvious). But is there any language in which these words are purely referential (I am not sure I know what that would be like) or in which the meaning of the words is given by the existence of the objects? If we say the meaning of *sun* or *moon* is guaranteed by what is known of them by astronomers are we not merely imposing post-Newtonian conceptions upon all languages? The sun and the moon will come into languages as they are known, very variously, in human life: but in fact they are referred to most frequently as gods, not as astronomical objects, and the sun-god and the moon-god have a much better right to be seen as linguistic universals than the sun and moon of the almanacs.

It is a little odd to say, as Hockett does, that 'the invention of counting was at the same time a discovery of something about the world in which we live: that certain natural groupings of things have a property, called their *number.* . .' (*The State of the Art*, p. 106). It isn't, surely, that these groupings somehow reveal this natural property to us. We cannot take them into a laboratory and distil the property out. Counting is indeed an invention: once invented it does describe objects in the world: when we count three sheep there ordinarily are three sheep in very truth. But 'three' is a way of taking the sheep which counting allows us to do. *Qua* objects they will be exactly the same whether we count them or not, and whether we refer to them as 'three', 'sheep', 'woolly', 'Joan, Jill and Jacqueline' or whatever.

We need 'aspect' again. One might say that 'table' can mean *table* because one can point to tables; and I agree that *table* would be a different word if there were no tables to point to. But what if, fresh from the opening discussion of the *Philosophical Investigations*, I point to the table and say to the child not 'table' but 'brown', 'dirty', 'wood' or 'funny'? (Cf. especially para. 28,

p. 13e.) Am I pointing to different things? The table will have whichever of these senses my word manages to give it, though it is true that 'brown', 'wood' and even 'funny' can refer and are not fictitious.

But to say 'table' is not in itself talking. The name is just a 'lexical entry'; it has less meaning, for instance, than STRAWBERRY JAM on a jar, which distinguishes the jar from other jars. With *table* (unless one imagines an object in a furniture shop that might or might not be a table) it is only when we begin talking, when we do something with the label, that the word becomes even a label.

'That isn't a bear, it's a bush.' We certainly want to know whether the object is really a bear (the rules for 'really' here being something like 'Will it attack us?') but the object has that meaning only when we are asking the question.

Reference, far from guaranteeing the intrinsic meanings of words, itself depends on what we are doing in language.

Even pronouns, which might seem so straightforward, are tricky. They merely refer to nouns, we may think, which in turn can refer to things. But what of 'it' in 'it's raining' or 'it's getting worse and worse all the time'?[13] And are the personal pronouns such 'simple referential devices' as Vendler thinks them (*Res Cogitans*, p. 68; cf. below, p. 160)? What am I referring to by calling somebody 'you'? His/her body? Though people do indeed live in the body they cease to be referable to in ordinary conversation by second-person pronouns at the moment of death—when, that is, we say they *are* (not *have*) bodies. Would the person the pronoun is supposed to refer to be here if I could not use the 'simple referential device'? And if not, is 'reference' any explanation of the use of the first- and second-person pronouns?

Perhaps instead we should say that language gets its sense in comparison not with things but with facts. ' "*The* question arises, was what I stated true or false?" And this we feel, speaking in popular terms, is now the question of whether the statement "corresponds with the facts" ' (Austin, *How to do things with Words*, p. 139). 'A statement or belief is true if it agrees with what is the case, if it fits the facts' (Vendler, *Res Cogitans*, p. 83). 'Fact', in writers who hold these views, tends to slide into 'the

---

[13] Cf. Dwight Bolinger, 'Ambient *it* is meaningful too', *Journal of Linguistics*, 9 (1973), 261–79.

verifiable' and verification into physics. But even if 'fact' is only 'what is true' (for if something is untrue we do not call it a fact) the linguist still has to distinguish the meaningful from the true. (Lies may be perfectly good grammar.) It wouldn't be inexcusable parody to represent the position we are discussing as 'you can only say what you can find in a good encyclopaedia'. I object, even before we come back from philosophy into linguistics, both that truth is not restricted to fact and that not all facts are verifiable. (I have in mind in what follows as much as I have yet been able to understand of Wittgenstein's last book *On Certainty*.) It is true, though not a fact, that Michelangelo's David is very beautiful and that Shakespeare's sonnets are a deep and important set of poems. On the other hand it is an undoubted fact that the world existed before any of us were born, but it is not its verifiability which constitutes the undoubtedness of the fact. The natural retort here, in our language, is '*Of course* we can verify that the world existed before we were born.' We can consult records and documents of all kinds and observe old buildings, read antique poems, see mountains that were not made recently. But there *are* people who don't believe the world existed before they were born—quite literally, not only in the way that this might be said of all the present British political party leaders with their tiny perspectives and ignorance of history. To see old documents or poems as evidence of the antiquity of the world is to consent to traditions of historical evidence: but anybody who believed the world did not exist before he was born would be far beyond historical persuasion. And nobody has *taught* us that the world is more than 100 years old. Young children may be laughed at if they say things implying the contrary; but we 'swallow down' the notion with our language, which is not like being taught, e.g., that William conquered England in 1066. This implies that England existed in 1066 but 'implication' is itself a language-game; and so are all the proofs that the world existed before we were born. It is another undoubted fact that nobody has ever been to Mars. But if somebody said he had been?—whether in a spaceship supplied by Martians, or on a shamanic trip? He could not be disproved except by a sort of conversion: he might suddenly be brought to accept our framework of factuality. But here too, though we often do accept as true what accords with the facts, the facts depend on language not vice versa.

Chomskyan Semantics II: Making Propositions

A reference or a fact may demonstrate something *within* language, given our consent to the relevant rules of discourse; but 'fact' and 'reference' cannot be used to explicate language from without.[14]

I have mentioned the problem of reference not to settle its hash with the sort of diagram by which linguists traditionally puzzle readers (Ogden and Richards's famous gapped triangle in *The Meaning of Meaning* has been spreading confusion now these fifty years[15]) but to reiterate that all the linguist can do is to try to understand reference as it occurs in language, and to try to refrain from hunting *things* instead.

(iii)

ABSOLUTE MEANING

One can often do without a particular word: one forgets the word and says *whatd'youmecallit* or *thingummyjig*. Koestler talks of 'the frustrating experience. . .of knowing what we want to say, but not knowing how to express it, searching for the right words that will exactly fit the empty spaces on the conveyor belt' (*The Ghost in the Machine*, p. 47). I think he is confusing two questions here. On the one hand he seems to be discussing unformulated intention (above, p. 78) and to be in danger of the

---

[14] T. S. Eliot's notion of the 'objective correlative', propounded in his *Hamlet* essay, was an attempt to extend to poetry the belief that external reality guarantees meaning. Poets are supposed to supply sets of objects rather than tell readers what to think, and the objects themselves set off the right thoughts and emotions in the reader's mind. The immediate fallacy is, of course, that poets offer words not things. The deeper misunderstanding is the supposition that objects *qua* objects are inherently meaningful. Perhaps from a film set we can infer the film? But what of an epic whose sets are used in the evenings for a send-up version of the same plot?

   Eliot lived to make very effective reparation for the 'objective correlative' in many parts of the *Four Quartets*.

> We had the experience but missed the meaning,
> And approach to the meaning restores the experience
> In a different form. . .

[15] 'In subsequent Anglo-Saxon literature, the revised concepts "reference" and "referent" have become standard' (in Sebeok, *Linguistics in Western Europe*, p. 19) without, as far as I can see, having done anything to answer the objection that the firm and dotted lines between the different corners tell us nothing except that the authors feel a vague relationship between the words represented by different parts of the triangle.

Ulric Brendel fallacy;[16] on the other, I propose a jigsaw as a better figure than a conveyor belt. The sentence, for instance, with *thingummy* doing duty for some noun is not like a mechanism that fails for want of a part, it is like a jigsaw with a missing piece whose shape and relation to other pieces is defined by the other pieces. (If we find the missing piece we know it is the right one because it fits.) Or even better, one might think of the missing word as a missing chessman—for which one can substitute any object, by agreement, without detriment to the game, as long as one remembers what has been agreed.

The *absolute* word, isolated, physically embodied in the brain or reflecting an unmistakable external object—that is a way of losing one's grasp on Chomsky's first insight, that words become language only in their interrelationships. Katz follows the bad old line that morphemes are the smallest 'meaningful units of the language' (*Semantic Theory*, p. 35)—as if it would *mean* something to say, apropos of nothing, '-ed!' or '-'s!' or even 'table!' Words are words (just as NPs, VPs etc. can only be themselves) only in relation to other words. Meaning is not something the individual word possesses and could therefore imaginably be deprived of (here the word, there the meaning): meaning inheres in, or just *is*, proper combinations of words. So for Chomsky in his strong area, syntax, words and sentences mutually define one another: the sentence is the syntactic relationship of the words; without both, neither.

Words, as has often been pointed out, presuppose language. (Cf. Wittgenstein's frequent analogy of a word with a move in chess: a game of chess is a certain series of moves which only make sense within the game.) Given a language, new words can make their way in it.

Hence the question whether we first learn words or language. Chomsky's efforts to prove that both syntax and words antedate speech are necessary if one is to 'explain' language acquisition in his sense of 'explain', and it isn't explanation to say that children

---

[16] *Brendel*: So you see, when golden dreams descended and enwrapped me— when new, dizzy, far-reaching thoughts were born in me, and wafted me aloft on their sustaining pinions—I fashioned them into poems, into visions, into pictures. . .
   Kroll: Hm!
   Rosmer: But you've written nothing down?
   Brendel: Not a word. The soulless toil of the scrivener has always aroused a sickening aversion in me. (Ibsen, *Rosmersholm* Act I, transl. W. Archer)

acquire words and language both at once. This is not an explanation, it is only true; i.e. a kind of rejection of the question. To see
how words can go together is to learn a language, but until we
are already masters of a language we can't use anything properly
called words. The child creates the system and its parts simultaneously: the noises become words at the moment when they
become language.

This in turn makes 'analogy' a potentially more illuminating
word than Chomsky can allow, for to see a likeness is to make at
once parts and a whole—the whole the likeness, the parts the
things which seeing the likeness links, and without which linking
they are not parts—in just the way we are trying to imagine.
And this is generally true of language.[17] When we remember and
use a word what makes it the same word we have used before?
The new use is *like* the earlier uses within the system of likeness
that is the whole language—*not* 'like' because it must refer to
the same concept or thing. So with rules in grammar. What is it
to speak grammatically except to be able to go on forming sentences that are like other sentences in ways described by grammar? There is no need for 'rule' in grammar to mean more than
such a description of likeness. As Hockett points out, Chomsky's
own examples of ill-formed sentences are formed by analogy
with grammatical ones; 'degrees of grammaticalness' can make
sense understood as 'degrees of likeness within grammar' and
Chomsky himself says, of 'deviant sentences', 'interpretations are

---

[17] Wittgenstein devoted much effort to these questions of parts, wholes and
likenesses within language, but there is no need of his help here, for
Chomsky's fallacy about the absolute word is exposed by any good
dictionary—sometimes explicitly.

'Does there exist such a thing in reality as a single word? Words are not
used according to their historical, but according to their immediate and
practical, value. Their meaning is different according to the moment when
they are used, and the use to which they are put. Outside their moment
and their object they fall into nothingness.' (A. and M. Chevalley, *The
Concise Oxford French Dictionary* (Oxford, 1934), p. xi).
They go on to offer, with equal sense, a quotation from a much older
linguist than Chomsky:
'A word is primarily a tissue of associations; it is swathed in associative
relations. To borrow an instance from Saussure, the word *enseignement*
is related by its sense to *éducation*, by its origin to *enseigner*, by its
process of formation to *armement*, by its rhythm and sound to *juste-
ment...*' (*ibid.*)
If we take 'primarily' there to mean 'grammatically' we have the necessary
criticism of the Chomskyan approach. For there is no absolute definition
of a word preceding what we do with the word, and no extra-linguistic
universal system to which we can refer words to get their meaning.

imposed on them by virtue of analogies that they bear to non-deviant sentences' (*Aspects*, p. 76). May we not also understand well-formed sentences by analogy with well-formed sentences?

(iv)

THE SUPER-LANGUAGE

The fallacy running through all the semantic efforts I have mentioned is that of the super-language or metalanguage. It can make sense to talk of the metalanguage of logic or maths: we write down a mathematical formula which can be read in various languages—if we happen to be doing maths. (Above, p. 96.) But we learn to do maths well after mastering our first language (in which counting, number-games etc., the elements of primitive mathematics, may appear very differently). There is no reason so suppose that language itself can be explained by metalanguages.

If one insists on describing this knowledge [the perfect innate knowledge of the acquisition device] as 'direct knowledge of a more basic language', I see no reason to object...but would merely point out that there is no reason at all to doubt that the child has this direct knowledge. (*Language and Mind*, p. 192)

Brain currents and/or the real world and/or the logic of propositions and/or the universal catalogue of concepts will tell us what language must mean. But all these attempts at super-languages or metalanguages, all the efforts to show us what underlies natural language, are themselves language-dependent. (They would be none the worse for that if they knew themselves.) We always understand the conceptual analyses or whatever in English; the universals are understood *via* the particular language; nobody would have thought of the AD were it not for the wonderful and odd fact that children begin talking, and the AD can only refer back to that fact in a circular effort to make sense of it. The only way of understanding the conceptual analyses is by putting them together again into words: ' "Cause become not alive"—oh! perhaps he means "kill".' The word supplies the meaning to the conceptual structure, not vice versa. Coming on a tree diagram and assembling from it the words *I past persuade the doctor of it that the doctor AUX examine John* (*Language and Mind*, p. 151) we extract, and understand,

the English sentence 'I persuaded the doctor to examine John'
or perhaps 'I persuaded the doctor that he should examine John.'
We understand deep structures only by way of the surface. There
is nothing amiss with any of this so long as we remain clear about
what is going on.

At best grammar says things like 'this sentence hangs together
in this way, doesn't it?' or 'you can make a passive out of an
active like this, can't you?'—inviting us to refer to language in
order to agree. (It is a quite serious objection to Chomsky that
his ear for English is not very good and his use of example rather
careless: I append a note about some of his mistakes, at the end
of this chapter.) Even Katz says,

> In general, a semantic component for a given language is under the
> empirical constraint to predict the semantic properties of sentences
> in each case where speakers of the language have strong, clear-cut
> intuitions about the semantic properties and relations of those sen-
> tences. (Steinberg and Jakobovits, *Semantics*, p. 307)

Chomsky's key terms, therefore, 'semantic component',
'semantic interpretation' and 'semantic representation' all seem
to me very misleading.[18] If you talk of 'semantic interpretation'
the natural question is 'interpretation into what?'. The answer
will have to be 'into a super-language' which as usual we shall
understand, if at all, by referring back to the original sentence.
The 'semantic representation' of a sentence similarly just *is* the
sentence, in context, and with all its nuances.

Meaning is not a *component* of language, but a characterization. When language is itself it is meaningful, and the meaning
is whatever makes language language. Hence grammar is indeed
the study of meaning.

This was well said, in a quite different way, by J. R. Firth, a
writer of not much transatlantic repute. Firth's levels of linguistic
inquiry are an ascent towards a full picture of meaning that will
be the same as a full understanding of language:

---

[18] '. . .a semantic interpretation, presumably, in a universal semantics, concerning which little is known in any detail. . .' (*Studies*, p. 12); 'semantic
representation that expresses the intrinsic meaning of the sentence in
question. . .' (*Language and Mind*, p. 136). Why is not the sentence's
intrinsic meaning just the same as the sentence? Cf. Katz: 'The semantic
component will have two subcomponents. . .We will call the result of
applying the dictionary and projection rules to a sentence, i.e. the output
of the semantic component for that sentence, a *semantic interpretation*'
(*Semantics*, p. 298).

To recapitulate, we have resolved meaning into five principal component functions:

First, phonetic function for a sound as a substitution-counter, e.g. **b**, **ɔː**, and **d**, the sounds having their place in the context and in the system of relations we call the phonetic structure of the language.

Secondly, lexical function of the form or word **bɔːd**, as a lexical substitution-counter, distinct from, say, **pɔːt**, or **bɔːt**, or **kɔːd** . . .

Thirdly, when you have **bɔːd** contextualized as the *d*-form of a verb, the complex of articulation and voice correlation which we symbolize as *d* has morphological function, but, be it repeated, not semantic function.

Fourthly, if I pronounced the forms **bɔːd!** and **bɔːd?**, you would be in a position to assess the syntactical function of intonation and place the forms in syntactical categories without knowing any semantic function, i.e. apart from any actual situation.

Fifthly, if I now contextualize the word **bɔːd** and turn to you, on this occasion, with the question **'bɔːd?'**, you may possibly reply 'not really' or just 'no' with a rising intonation, or 'go on', and in the several cases furnish contextual relations which determine the meaning. In such a context of situation you have what I propose to call *semantic function*. (J. R. Firth, *Papers in Linguistics 1934–1951* (Oxford, 1957), pp. 26–7)

This has the great and (in linguistics) unusual merit of seeing that meaning is the high level controlling all the rest; all the aspects of language are thus aspects of meaning and the 'component' and 'interpretation' fallacies are avoided.[19] It also has the equally unusual virtue of taking for granted that linguistics is the study of the meaning of language, in contrast with which semantics is not of the first concern to Chomsky, who has scarcely gone much further than Carroll here. The latter observed accurately that 'A general characteristic of the methodology of descriptive linguistics. . .is the effort to analyse linguistic structure without reference to meaning' (p. 31). And, as we saw Chomsky saying (above, p. 57), 'A central idea in much of structural linguistics was that the formal devices of language should be studied independently of their use. The earliest work in trans-

---

[19] Cf. Polanyi, below, p. 172, and contrast Derwing, following Chomsky as closely as may be: '. . .the important point that no meaning actually resides in an utterance *per se*, but is imposed on the utterance by the hearer. . .' (p. 268). On the contrary meaning resides nowhere else than in the utterance; if it is heard as an utterance its meaning is heard. Derwing here makes language uninterestingly obscure and arbitrary.

formational-generative grammar took over a version of this thesis, as a working hypothesis. I think it has been a fruitful hypothesis' (*Studies*, p. 198). It has, on the contrary, been an ignoring of the way in which 'formal devices' are indeed 'of language', a lack of interest in language itself, a neglect of the object of study.

The only hope for linguists is to fix their attention steadfastly upon language. Chomsky's studies of syntax can become part of a fuller grammar when they are used to observe things that actually happen as we use language; and my 'actually' means 'linguistically' not 'physically'. What actually happens in language is, generally speaking, meaning.

This brings us to our final head of discussion of Chomsky's work, for it is on the verge of raising true philosophical questions.

NOTE

CHOMSKY'S MISTAKES

Some of the following examples may be ascribed to an ordinary insensitivity to language, but it is interesting to see in others how Chomsky's concentration on universals and/or logical operations itself distracts his attention from language. To avoid the *ad nauseam* I select them all from *Studies on Semantics in Generative Grammar*.

p. 18   It is not clear whether Chomsky is using the conventional preceding asterisk and the word *unnatural* to denote the ungrammatical or the unacceptable; anyway 'John's happening to be a good friend of mine' is objected to though 'it's [sic] having surprised me that John was here' is 'tolerable'. I disagree at both places and can see nothing wrong with such a sentence as 'John's happening to be a good friend of mine is no reason for promoting him.'

p. 24   'He was amused at the stories' is not, as Chomsky thinks, synonymous with 'the stories amused him'. In both cases he could have been amused because the stories were amusing or because they were risibly inept; but the latter sense belongs more easily to the first sentence and the former to the second.

p. 25   'Thus we can say *John's clumsiness caused the door to open*...but not *John's clumsiness opened the door*.' Imagine that John is trying to open a jammed door, gently lifting it, sharply tapping it etc. John then trips over his feet against the jammed door and it comes open. John's clumsiness opened the door, not his efforts.

p. 29   'We have *John's uncanny*...*resemblance to Bill* but not **John resembled Bill uncannily*...We might propose to account for this by deriving *John's uncanny resemblance to Bill* from something

141

like *the degree to which John resembles Bill, which is uncanny.'*
Chomsky rejects the proposed accounting, but his instinct is to
explain a feeling about an utterance by logical analysis. In my
English 'John resembled Bill uncannily' is perfectly all right.
Chomsky's reason against the analysis is that 'it provides no way to
exclude such phrases as **their amazing destruction of the city'*
which, again, I could see nothing wrong with (in, e.g., a historian's
account of an army's destroying a city against the army's interests).

p. 32 'If John and I each have a house in the woods, I can refer
to his, with contrastive stress on *John's,* as *JOHN'S house in the
woods*; if we each have a book on the table, I cannot, analogously,
refer to his as *JOHN'S book on the table.'* Why not? I could, were
it not for the difficulty not mentioned by Chomsky that 'John's
book' may be taken as 'the book written by John' not 'the book
owned by John'. The hidden, underlying cause of this mistake may
perhaps be that Chomsky moves in circles where people are more
likely to own houses and write books than to build houses and own
books.

p. 37 'Thus the phrase *John's leg* is ambiguous: it can be used
to refer either to the leg that John happens to have in his possession
(alienable possession), that he is, say, holding under his arm; or to
the leg that is, in fact, part of John's body (inalienable possession).
But the phrase *the leg that John has* has only the sense of alienable
possession.' Not necessarily, in several ways. 'John's leg' can be
used for the leg under John's arm, though taking the phrase out of
context it surely refers primarily to the leg that is part of his body.
But if John has only one leg, or if one of his two legs is numb or in
plaster, there are contexts where 'the leg that John has' will refer to
his one good leg naturally enough. Our legs are not in any sense
possessions (they cannot be sold, pawned, left in wills) but nor are
they inalienable, for we can lose a leg without dying. Chomsky
might have taken the discussion further if he had chosen John's
heart or brain. Even then we might say 'the brain John has', probably implying there isn't much, without meaning the kind bought
in a meat-market. Chomsky is here groping for the distinctions our
language does make between parts of the body and objects we
possess. (The history of *meat* and *flesh* is instructive here.) But this
would be Austinian or Wittgensteinian 'grammar' of a kind
Chomsky has set his face against.

p. 39 '**the picture of John's'. Why not, in phrases like 'the
picture of John's we were talking about'?

p. 43 'Such expressions as *a man to do the job came to see me*
seem highly unnatural.' Not to me. Perhaps Chomsky only means
that he has great difficulty in getting men to come and do his jobs.
This could count as a linguistic reason to the extent that language is

a picture of the real world, but could hardly come into pure TG grammar.

p. 58 'The postulated underlying form, *John was educated by himself*, is ruled out by the principle, whatever it may be, that makes passives incompatible with reflexivization.' Chomsky rules out this perfectly good English sentence by following, in the manner of the old prescriptivists who used to try to stop us saying 'It's me!', an untrue rule.

p. 59 'John grows tomatoes' does not, as Chomsky thinks, mean 'John causes tomatoes to grow'. 'Cause' is difficult for linguists as well as philosophers. Dragging in a 'feature [+cause]' Chomsky is confusing the real conceptual structure of English, in which I may say with perfect clarity that I grow tomatoes without implying anything about causation. What causes tomatoes to grow? Some would answer biochemically, some would say the LORD: 'So then neither is he that planteth any thing, neither he that watereth; but God that giveth the increase' (1 Cor. iii. 7). Perhaps we may one day cause tomatoes to grow in the same way that we may one day be pushing up the daisies, but how else?—unless 'cause' is being used in several senses, which would render pointless the effort to identify semantic universals.

p. 95 'It is a homicidal MANIAC that John is believed to be' and 'It is INCOMPETENT that John is believed to be' are both declared 'very marginal, or even totally unacceptable, from a strictly grammatical point of view' though 'certainly interpretable, presumably by analogy to properly formed sentences'. Neglecting Chomsky's carelessness with his own terms (acceptable, grammatical, analogy) my objection is that one can imagine contexts where both would be good English.

Welfare Officer: I believe John is a charming and sensitive person frustrated by poverty, and that what he did was to fulfil a deep inner need.

Magistrate: But my dear Mrs Brimmer, it is a homicidal MANIAC that John is believed to be, not uncharming or insensitive. . .

Chairman: John is so nice and, I believe, such a help at office parties.

Managing Director: It is INCOMPETENT John is believed to be, not a social failure.

p. 104 'not many arrows didn't hit the target' of which it is said that 'It might perhaps be argued that (77iii) is ungrammatical' is surely good English in a context like:

A: Your shooting was very wild today. Not many arrows hit the bull.

B: Yes, but on the other hand not many arrows didn't hit the target.

pp. 107–8 'Thus it has frequently been noted that (88i) and

(88iii) merely predict, whereas (88ii) is ambiguous, in that it may also mean that John refuses to go downtown:
(88) (i) John will go downtown
      (ii) John won't go downtown
      (iii) it is not the case that John will go downtown'
Not in my English. For me (i) is as likely to say that John insists on going downtown as merely to predict his going, and (ii) is just the negative of that.

p. 110 'the men each hate his brothers' is, apparently, grammatical and acceptable. I would correct it to the form Chomsky says it is derived from, 'each of the men hates his brothers'.

p. 189 'The statement of (102) [two of my five children are in elementary school] presupposes that I have five children; if I have six children, the statement is without truth value.' Even after we neglect the objection that (102) need not be a statement at all, and the other that if one of my six children is dead the true statement is conventional English, there are still other circumstances which render untrue Chomsky's claim (p. 190) that 'there are no circumstances under which the presupposition of (102) that I have exactly five children can be withdrawn'. Here he is as usual confusing logical and linguistic operations. Some people do disown their children and talk of them as if they were not theirs without positively asserting that they do not exist. 'Oh yes', I might add, 'and there is John and Bill, also at elementary school, but I don't count them as mine.' (Cf. Genesis xxii where an Angel speaks of Abraham's only son, viz Isaac, though Abraham is also the father of Ishmael; 'For the son of the bondwoman shall not be heir with the son of the freewoman' (Galatians iv. 30).)

7

Linguistics and Philosophy: Chomsky's Failure with Wittgenstein

Some philosophers recently have been worried lest linguists should be doing better philosophy than philosophers; it is even true that some linguists wonder whether philosophers may not have things to tell them about language. I do not believe that these worries have led to much illumination in either linguistics or philosophy. It might, though, be illuminating to ask why.

Here is one common view of an essential link between linguistics and philosophy:

The philosopher asks what...terms *mean* as used by the practitioners of the special inquiries. This is not to ask, as psychologists, physicists or critics ask, questions about dreams, events or novels. It is to ask about the investigations that are pursued into these things and in particular about the meaning of the terms used in such inquiries. Often the task of clarification here is quite essential.[1]

Philosophy, then, might try to tell linguists the meaning of the words they use. We have indeed met cases where it is necessary for somebody to tell linguists the meaning of their terms. Perhaps philosophy might even take the further step of telling us the meaning of all the terms everybody uses (and so leading us back into a super-language). Philosophy would then be a sort of cure-all for the intellectual problems of mankind, which some have indeed wanted to make it.

Mr Lyas is suggesting (a little unclearly, for 'what terms mean' is crucial but obscure) a conception of philosophy which seems a little more modest, but closely connected, called by Peter Winch the 'underlabourer' conception (*The Idea of a Social Science*, 1958). Philosophy's task, in this view, is to serve the other academic disciplines by sorting out their terminology. It seems a fair retort that if linguists don't know what they mean by their own terms they are in so desperate a state that no philosopher

[1] Colin Lyas, Editor's Introduction to *Philosophy and Linguistics* (1971), pp. 12–13. Mr Lyas is not pinning his whole colours to this position.

can rescue them. Is not the meaning of a word in an academic discipline just the use of it by people mature in the discipline in making the sense the discipline is? What is there for philosophy to add? But if the philosopher *can* come along, for instance, and tell the physicist what electrons are (without knowing much about electrons?) he seems to be setting up in competition with the physicist, but in a position of special privilege, enjoying a dispensation from the judgement by physicists that is the only guarantee of sense in the subject, yet claiming an additional dimension of understanding denied to the ordinary practitioner. If the privilege is challenged the philosopher as physicist or linguist will have to be judged in exactly the same way, within the discipline, as anyone else; and if the philosopher claims to be making an essential clarification of the terms of physics which is not recognized as such by the competent physicist, the physicist is quite justified in telling the philosopher to mind his own business —just as much as the philosopher would be in telling the physicist what to do with the notion that the physicist's discipline of thought gives him a specially privileged place in philosophy.

The set of knotty problems we are skirting is even worse as regards the study of language than elsewhere. For there certainly can be philosophy of science, philosophy of history and so on, and it is tempting to the unwary to say that the parallel thing in the case of the study of language must be the philosophy of language.

Philosophy of physics isn't a super-physics putting things better than the physicists can. Philosophy, says Wittgenstein (below), leaves things just as they are. Philosophy of physics is physics considered from the point-of-interest of the philosopher. And that is indeed more like an interest in meaning—to ask what it is, from the philosopher's viewpoint, for physics to do what it does— than telling the physicists within the terms of their trade how to do what they do. This distinction is not easy, especially for one who isn't either a physicist or a philosopher; and I am not suggesting there could be a philosopher of physics who was un-interested in physics or who knew little physics. But the state of progress within physics won't be affected by the philosophy of physics, and conversely nothing that happens in physics will produce any automatic improvement in the philosophy of physics.

Collingwood distinguishes 'a book of metaphysics' from 'a book about metaphysics'. The latter belongs to philosophy, not the former: 'What I have chiefly tried to do in it is neither to expound my own metaphysical ideas, nor to criticize the metaphysical ideas of other people; but to explain what metaphysics is, why it is necessary to the well-being and advancement of knowledge' (*An Essay on Metaphysics*, p. vii). To explain what something is, from the point of view of one whose concern is with 'the well-being of knowledge', is 'philosophy of. . .'.

My point in saying this is to deny that philosophy of language is parallel to philosophy of physics. Philosophy of language is not the clarification of linguistics and it is not linguistics from the philosopher's point of interest: that would be philosophy of linguistics. And philosophy of language is a necessary part of philosophy in a way that philosophy of physics (or of linguistics) isn't.

Epistemology is central to philosophy; philosophers are necessarily concerned with what it is to know anything or mean anything. (That, after all, is implied by the etymology of *philosophy*, even though the word is often interpreted, not without grounds in what is often done in its name, as if it meant *philosophistry*.) To get far in thinking about knowledge, meaning or thought, anyone has to wonder about language. Philosophy of language is wondering about how language and thought make each other possible.

Where can linguistics come into that? Anything we call 'philosophy' of meaning is obviously different from semantics, the 'science' of meaning, as well as from the philosophy of semantics. This is why the beginning of the large, oft-quoted collection *Semantics* is disastrous: 'The part of philosophy known as the philosophy of language,[2] which includes and is sometimes identi-

---

[2] Another confusion frequent in 'the literature' is the equation of philosophy of language with linguistic philosophy. The former is the philosophic consideration of language, the latter a school that thrived at Oxford during the middle of this century and which developed a method of close observation of ordinary speech. ' "Linguistic philosophy" is primarily the name of a method; "The philosophy of language" is the name of a subject' (Searle, *Speech Acts*, p. 4). I dissent, however, from Searle's definition 'the philosophy of language is the attempt to give philosophically illuminating descriptions of certain general features of language, such as reference, truth, meaning and necessity' merely because I think his 'general' begs some important questions in both philosophy and linguistics. 'Many of the conclusions about e.g. what it is to be true or to be a statement or a promise, if valid, should hold for any possible language capable of producing truths or statements or promises.' Unless this is a circularity ('valid' = 'it is a promise if I call it a promise. . .'?) I just don't see why it should be true, and Searle doesn't argue the case.

Austin is a linguistic philosopher, Wittgenstein a philosopher of language.

fied with the part known as semantics. . .' (p. 3). So what is the connection?

I can only say that the connections, the bearings from either point of view, are what the linguist or the philosopher can make them. But the linguist is likely to get much more out of philosophy, if he can keep his wits about him, than the philosopher from linguistics.

Philosophy does not go in for experimental proof: it is pure speculation,[3] within the limits of what philosophers can recognize as real thought. Philosophy asks what can be said and what can't about the great problems of thinking. And so, in wondering about language, philosophers will often say things of interest to the linguist (or the literary critic), incidentally from the philosopher's point of view.

But though Wittgenstein does often throw up examples which a linguist should find illuminating of sundry problems, that does not turn him into a linguist or the linguist into a philosopher. One problem for the linguist in trying to use the *Investigations* is that, for all the fluent and easy-going look of that book, it is remarkable for its intense devotion to the problems of philosophy purely as such. If linguists can use Wittgenstein they are picking up crumbs from the philosophic feast.

This does, however, leave the linguist master of his own humble house of linguistics. He will have to judge whatever the philosopher says about language by whatever standards of sense his discipline has managed to evolve. It may be that philosophical sense will throw down linguistics utterly,[4] but if not the linguist must remain critical and a linguist. That is no reason for him to follow Chomsky and turn up his nose at both the feast and the crumbs.

---

[3] 'Philosophy may in no way interfere with the actual use of language; it can in the end only describe it.

For it cannot give it any foundation either.

It leaves everything as it is' (*Philosophical Investigations*, p. 49e).

I think this does not contradict Winch's remark that 'the philosopher's concern is not with correct usage as such' (*The Idea of a Social Science*, p. 11).

[4] Wittgenstein had no interest in linguistics and was as contemptuous as Chomsky of what used to pass under that name. 'The only significant linguistic [*sic*] philosopher who neglects (in his argument) to take account of the state of linguistic research in his time', Wittgenstein is called, perhaps with a little injustice to other philosophers of language, in the Sebeok compilation, pp. 20–1.

It may still be a rebuke to a linguist that he has made nothing of philosophy. Chomsky's failure to escape with Wittgenstein's help from any of his fly-bottles is in fact a penalty of a quite basic misunderstanding—of, I would say, both philosophy and language—expressed here as an objection to philosophy as such. This is clear every time Chomsky mentions Wittgenstein (cf. *Current Issues*, p. 24; *Language and Mind*, p. 24; *Aspects*, p. 51), but I shall confine the discussion to Chomsky's formal consideration of Wittgenstein in 'Some Empirical Assumptions in Modern Philosophy of Language'.

In particular Wittgenstein ought to have made Chomsky suspicious about the 'Acquisition Device' and the whole notion of the extra-linguistic physical existence of language. If Chomsky had pondered Wittgenstein's discussions of 'following a rule', competence/performance would have benefited. But things would have been better if Chomsky had seen the force even of the vulgar slogan 'look for the use not the meaning' and had understood its bearings on his formulation of the questions of linguistics. Chomsky is prevented from learning anything from philosophy by the fixity of his notion of science.

In the second part of the essay under consideration Chomsky is trying to extract from Wittgenstein's *Blue Book* and *Brown Book* theories (in Chomsky's sense, i.e. hypotheses that can be tested empirically) about how linguistic competence, in Chomsky's sense, is acquired. There are good reasons why this should be difficult, but they do not include Chomsky's:

Still another difficulty, in the specific case of the *Blue and Brown Books* is, of course, the question whether in detail they do or do not reflect Wittgenstein's views. In the *Philosophical Investigations*, the positions that I want to discuss are less prominent than in the *Blue and Brown Books*, though I find little there that might challenge these positions. In any event, what I will be discussing is the text of the *Blue and Brown Books*, which may or may not express what Wittgenstein really believed about these matters. (p. 283)

It is rather a give-away to suppose that 'what Wittgenstein really believed' is either on the one hand obscure (why doubt that he believed what he said?) or on the other simple and immutable. Chomsky has no suspicion that Wittgenstein might have been struggling to find out what he believed, or that his beliefs might ever have altered. Chomsky's puzzlement here stems from the remarkable fixity of his own positions during a career fore-shadowed in all its essentials to date by the first Skinner review of 1959.

The central misunderstanding, however, is just Chomsky's will to extract hypotheses.[5] Chomsky quotes from the *Investigations*, without understanding, 'there must not be anything hypothetical in our considerations'. The point is the difference between philo-sophy and science—and the question relevant to Chomsky, which he is incapable of asking, is whether linguistics is closer to the one or the other.

Chomsky discusses a passage in which Wittgenstein is consider-ing what it is to say that somebody is reading.

> The criteria that Wittgenstein actually discusses, both here and else-where, are not in fact 'criteria for correct assertion'...but rather 'criteria for justified assertion,' that is, conditions under which a rational person would be justified in stating, possibly erroneously, that so and so is reading, and so on. These are criteria in the sense in which having a certain visual image might serve as a criterion that justifies my asserting that there is an oasis over there while walking through the desert, although my perfectly justified assertion might still be incorrect. It is, however, surely criteria for correct assertion that relate to problems of meaning. (p. 279)

This is an extreme not usually occupied by Chomsky of the position that would make language essentially a reflection of a separately-existing reality. If I look out of the window on the grey Welsh morning and say 'There's an oasis!' Chomsky, to be consistent, would have to say that what I say is false (i.e. incorrect assertion) rather than lies, poetry, a joke, philosophy or madness.

Wittgenstein is indeed giving an account of what justifies the use of words like 'reading' and 'expecting' (and in that way investigating, in pursuit of his own philosophical end, the con-ceptual structure of German); Chomsky's objection is actually

---

[5] Cf. the drive to make 'models'. The need for caution about 'models' is somehow inordinately difficult for even philosophical grammarians to understand. Max Black, the author of a book on Wittgenstein, attributes the pursuit of model-construction to Wittgenstein just at one of the *loci* of Wittgenstein's thought where he is doing his best to show what is wrong with the idea of 'model': 'However interested in the variable details of the topics to be discussed, we shall always try to press on to general ideas that will provide a satisfactory *model* of language. Our task, to adopt Wittgenstein's expression, is that of reaching a "perspicuous view" of language' (*The Labyrinth of Language*, p. 4). 'Perspicuous view' is pre-cisely *not* 'model'.

that Wittgenstein is considering language not the objects of the world, meaning *as against* 'criteria for correct assertion'.

Thus consider the act of reading. The philosopher is concerned to dispel the temptation 'to regard the conscious mental act as the only real criterion distinguishing reading from not reading', and his 'explanation of the use of this word. . .essentially consists in describing a selection of examples exhibiting characteristic features.' This selection of examples will, presumably, provide (or suggest to a human intelligence) the criterion for distinguishing reading from not reading. When Wittgenstein refers to the 'criterion for distinguishing reading from not reading,' he no doubt has in mind criteria that relate to the meaning of the word 'read,' empirical conditions which are conceptually related in some manner to correct (i.e. true) assertion that so and so is reading. (*ibid.*)

The crucial confusion there is at the end. Wittgenstein certainly is discussing the criteria for distinguishing reading from not reading as they relate to the word *read*; what he is deliberately arguing against is that this concerns anything like empirical conditions that must be satisfied. Wittgenstein is deliberately *not* asking what is the real essential act of reading—what actions, shall we say, references or states of mind will guarantee that we are applying the word correctly. Wittgenstein's discussion shows that to talk of states of mind or symptoms is unilluminating because it adds nothing to the word *reading* except what is potentially confusing. That is why he is not offering any hypothesis about reading, anything amenable to experimental test in the way Chomsky demands. 'There must not be anything hypothetical in our considerations.'

The question is not whether there is one demonstrable activity, and only one, of that name, but what *counts as* reading in our language, what the word stretches to. And the interest in the question is neither empirical nor (after the manner of J. L. Austin) an interest in the conceptual structure of our language for its own sake. Wittgenstein is as usual at work on the kind of understanding of the world that language makes possible. I think the whole problem comes clearer in the *Investigations* with the well-known discussion of *game* (cf. above, p. 101); but Chomsky's other example, *expecting*, may help.

Wittgenstein discusses what it is to expect somebody to tea. He shows that no one action or feeling can cover *expecting* and that if there is a set of such actions or feelings they are made so only in the sense of the word. Expecting is, moreover, not something added to what we do or feel. Perhaps I expect somebody to tea by putting the kettle on. The expectation is not then separate from the action; the action expresses expectation and is naturally linked with the word if we say something like 'I expect he'll soon be here—I'll put the kettle on.' (Cf. remarks on indirect speech, above, pp. 110 ff.)

By using the word we see putting the kettle on *as* expecting somebody to tea. So too one might expect somebody by trembling, changing one's shirt and so on. Chomsky misses the point when he says 'alongside of expecting B to come to tea, I may also be expecting innumerable other things (e.g., that B will be less than twelve feet tall, that he will greet me warmly, that if admitted to Harvard he will accept, etc.)' (p. 278). These are, indeed, other things. All that needs to be said about the last is that it is another expectation not relevant to the discussion. The expectation that he will greet me warmly is perhaps part of or closely related to the expectation that he will come to tea, and could be expressed by a similar range of thoughts or activities. It is Chomsky's first example that is interestingly confused, the expectation that B will be less than twelve feet tall.

Here we are right at the heart of J. L. Austin's territory. I think he would have said, and justly, that we neither expect that B will be less than twelve feet tall nor that B will not be less than twelve feet tall. Such fancies simply do not come within the grammar of *expect*. (And that is an observation about our language, not about some separately existing mental state reflecting a universal concept.)

Chomsky will not have this sort of discussion of a word's meaning, whether it makes any sense or not, because for Chomsky, as we have seen, meaning, independent of use, is a word's intrinsic conceptual structure that remains fixed whatever is done with the word.

Above all, Chomsky simply can't understand Wittgenstein's objections to the idea of 'science' which is the only notion of discipline Chomsky can entertain: he can't even see that they *are* objections. Chomsky takes Wittgenstein's basic belief that the philosopher's 'method is *purely descriptive*; the descriptions we give are not hints of explanations' as a kind of admission of defeat, a refusal to pursue the inquiry to the point where it might say something; and so when Wittgenstein, imagining devices much like Chomsky's innate grammar, says of the postulated mechanisms that they 'are only hypotheses, models designed to explain', Chomsky's comment is: 'the word "only" is curious here' (p. 279).

The *Investigations* are themselves an example of the philosophical, i.e. unhypothetical, thought (or *disciplined* speculation) Wittgenstein is considering and Chomsky failing to understand. The most immediately approachable statements of Wittgenstein's on the subject are perhaps the ones he made as he was beginning to confront these problems, in the 'Remarks on Frazer's *Golden Bough*', the first English translation of which I had the honour of publishing:[6]

We can only *describe* and say, human life is like that. [Cf. *Philosophical Investigations* i para. 124.]
Compared with the impression that what is described here makes on us, the explanation is too uncertain.
Every explanation is an hypothesis. (p. 30)

But 'there must not be anything hypothetical in our considerations'. Compare these other paragraphs:

An historical explanation, an explanation as an hypothesis of the development, is only *one* kind of summary of the data—of their synopsis. We can equally well see the data in their relations to one another and make a summary of them in a general picture without putting it in the form of an hypothesis regarding the temporal development. . .

'And so the chorus indicates a hidden law' is what we feel like saying of Frazer's collection of facts. I *can* set out this law in an hypothesis of development, or again, in analogy with the schema of a plant I can give it in the schema of a religious ceremony, but I can also do it just by arranging the factual material so that we can easily pass from one part to another and have a clear view of it— showing it in a '*perspicuous*' way.

For us the conception of a perspicuous presentation [a way of setting out the whole field together by making easy the passage from one part of it to another] is fundamental. It indicates the form in which we write of things, the way in which we see things. . .

This perspicuous presentation makes possible that understanding

[6] 'Remarks on Frazer's *Golden Bough*', translated by A. C. Miles and Rush Rhees, *The Human World* no. 3 (1971).

which consists just in the fact that we 'see the connexions'. Hence the importance of finding *intermediate links*. (pp. 34, 34–5, 35)

Chomsky confuses Wittgenstein's attention to ranges of examples and 'intermediate links' (cf. *Investigations* 1 para. 122) with the old atomistic linguistics. He accuses Wittgenstein of 'restricting himself to data in and for itself' and says:

If we interpret Wittgenstein as intending literally what he formulates as factual assertions (about language-learning, for example), then what he says seems to fall within the framework of a narrow and dogmatic empiricism. If we interpret him as merely circumscribing the task of the philosopher, limiting it to a 'purely descriptive method,' to descriptions which 'are not hints of explanations,' then what he is proposing falls together with other, quite independent tendencies in recent study of language, specifically, with certain tendencies in descriptive linguistics which are also concerned to limit investigation to arrangement of data and 'pure description' that avoids any attempt at explanation (the latter being occasionally stigmatized as a kind of infantile obsession). (Chomsky, 'Some Empirical Assumptions', pp. 280–1)

Chomsky is here suffering from what Wittgenstein elsewhere calls an 'aspect-blindness': he cannot see the philosophical aspect of what Wittgenstein is doing, or the force of words like *perspicuous*. The trouble with the old linguistics wasn't its attention to detail and fact, but its lack of perspicuous presentation, its inability to put the facts together in such a way as to make a coherent whole. (And in this way the fissionists were very unlike the nineteenth-century philologists: the development of the study of Indo-European is a very good example of the 'mere' perspicuous presentation of facts. All Rask, Grimm, Verner and the rest did was to see, with increasing delicacy and clarity, certain links in the spellings of the extant languages which, put together, constituted the idea of a common ancestor-language.) With the disciples of Bloomfield the 'facts' never fell convincingly into their arbitrary taxonomies, hence the strength of Chomsky's attack on their failure to understand language.

The patterns that facts fall into *are* the study, and can't exist before the development of the study. (And before the development of the study we don't know what the facts are.) A scholar mature in a discipline may sometimes think, reasonably enough, that the facts speak for themselves, and if something new turns up it may be immediately meaningful to him. (I think here of G. R. Elton on history.) Yes, but the facts speak because the scholar knows the language in which they speak. It is only the scholar practising his discipline who can give a fact a place in (in this case) a coherent story. It is the capacity to understand facts in a certain way that constitutes a certain academic discipline; but Chomskyan 'explanation' is always the accounting for one discipline in the terms of another.

His 'science' is a framework of would-be perspicuous presentation brought ready-made to the facts and procedures of the study of language. Chomsky is better than his predecessors in seeing the need to put the facts together in a real order; but his failure to see what Wittgenstein is driving at is the final evidence that linguistics for Chomsky cannot be a discipline, i.e. a form of thought with its own self-validating procedures. It does not follow that linguistics, as Chomsky wishes, could be successfully subsumed under psychology.

One must apply to Chomsky the words used of the ignorant by Diotima to Socrates; and the application shows that they are hard words: 'He seeks not, therefore, that possession of whose want he is not aware.'

Chomsky's insistence on extra-linguistic 'explanation' is, moreover, the effective influence of linguistics on other studies; it bedevils not merely linguistics itself but also the attempts to bring linguistics to bear upon psychology, sociology and other subjects to which 'the science of language', if there were one, would have obvious relevance.

8

Linguistics and Everything Else

Psycholinguistics is a word that looks, for all its unfortunate technological ambience, as if it ought to cover interesting ground. The study of the connections between language as common possession and the psyche of the individual must be of obvious importance to psychology as well as to the study of language. Unfortunately the explanatory ambitions have effectively impeded progress. The subject has been treated better by novelists and philosophers than by linguists, as well as by quite ordinary writers, innocent of exact psycholinguistic research, like M. M. Lewis (*How Children Learn to Speak*, 1957).

Roger Brown, who seems to have invented psycholinguistics, began before Chomsky's explanatory onslaught, and his troubles are more old-fashioned. For instance he begins his book *Psycholinguistics* (New York, 1970) with a chapter 'How shall a Thing be Called?' in which he discusses the psychological importance of the fact that we call the same things or people by different names according to circumstances. 'The same man is a *man* to most children, *policeman* to some at some times, *Mr Jones* to the neighborhood kids, and *papa* to his own' (p. 6). The discussion is misleading, for Brown thinks that underlying these different names there is one true name, and that it could be discovered by statistics: 'A still more particular name count must be imagined. The name given a thing by an adult for a child is determined by the frequency with which various names have been applied to such things in the experience of the particular adult.' This is untrue, would be undemonstrable if it were true, and, worse, confuses precisely the questions about why people use different names at different times which Brown is trying to treat. The biggest count may leave Mr Jones still

> in a rapt contemplation
> Of the thought, of the thought, of the thought of his name:
> His ineffable effable
> Effanineffable
> Deep and inscrutable singular NAME

known to nobody but himself, but now imparted to the child. In exasperation we might say that the wretched 'Jones's' real name is what appears on his birth certificate. But what if he becomes a monk, takes a name in religion, renounces it, changes his name by deed poll and then, after suffering a sex change, marries a Mr Smith? *All* our names depend, as Henry James says, on relations and 'directions': the psychological interest is that one may perhaps be a different person as 'Captain Everard' from 'Mudge'—but in a way shown by the use of the names themselves, not by any application of a 'frequency principle'. The name the adult thinks appropriate will certainly give information potentially interesting to a psychologist, but the 'information' will just be the inwardness with the language of the individual in question. 'Some things', says Brown, 'are named in the same way by all adults for all children. This is true of the apple and the orange' (p. 5). No, many parents talk to children about apples and oranges in baby-talk; but again the more interesting objection concerns aspect, context, style; for an adult might point to the orange and say 'orange' meaning the colour not the fruit, or he might say 'round' or even 'not quite spherical' (cf. above, p. 132).

Brown is now, however, out of fashion, and psycholinguistics is increasingly engaged upon the great quest for the Acquisition Device we discussed in Chapter 4. Dr Judith Greene, for instance, is lucid about the quite different claims made by Chomsky for his grammar, but calls the 'second interpretation', that 'the rules of transformational grammar represent the actual operations used by speakers to utter sentences' (which I called conceptual confusion) the 'strong' claim, the task of psycholinguistics being to give experimental evidence for it. All the reported experiments, alas, have been without significant result. This is to state the matter more severely than Dr Greene does. She mentions, for instance, experiments in which the time it takes people to understand (i.e. to respond in ways that show they have understood) different constructions, e.g. the passive, the negative, are measured. From the different times taken attempts have been made to infer the existence of real transformational operations in the brain. But the measuring of time says nothing about processes of understanding; all the experiments show is that some constructions take longer to understand than others, which is hardly surprising. Similarly the experiments to prove the existence of underlying semantic content (p. 171) give no reason to believe in any such thing.

Another line of psycholinguistic approach, certainly not adopted by Chomsky, is to try to catch language at its moment of emergence by observing (or conversing with) chimpanzees. I am not able to raise any great interest in the question whether there are other talking creatures in the universe. The matter may perhaps become interesting if and when they are found—though it may still be problematic to know what we have discovered, for 'if a lion could talk we would not be able to understand him'— and how then to know he was talking? 'No other species has evolved this means of communication and we can therefore compare man with his nearest animal relatives to find out wherein lies the difference' (Roger Gurney, *Language, Brain and Interactive Processes* (1973), p. 11). No, this difference is just what this comparison will not discover, except to him who understands it already. However, if linguists like to beguile their leisure-hours with speculations after the manner of the Doctor Doolittle books, I have no objection to so harmless a pursuit. The chimpanzees do tend, though, to impede serious thought. The best collection of work in psycholinguistics I have come across, for example, *Biological and Social Factors in Psycholinguistics*, ed. John Morton (1970), hardly recovers from the editor's introductory infatuation with the famous chimpanzee Washoe. He credits Washoe with, *inter alia*, the following 'achievements' and 'feats':

She can use signs reliably to indicate:
   (a) objects—'toothbrush', 'hat', 'key', 'napkin-bib'.
   (b) commands or requests—'tickle', 'hurry', 'open', 'out'.
   (c) internal states (or complex situational concepts)—'funny', which is used during games and occasionally 'when being pursued after mischief'; 'sorry', used 'after biting someone or when someone has been hurt in another way (not necessarily by Washoe), and when told to apologise for mischief'.
   (d) people—'you' and 'I–me' as well as at least two signs appropriate to particular individuals. (p. 8)

But how are 'out' and 'open' commands or requests? The animal makes a movement and the psycholinguist talks about an 'internal state' without further ado. But what we have is the animal's movement and whatever sense it seems to make. Washoe may indeed indicate people, but *as* people? What does it mean to say so? If the idea had much sense one could put it to Washoe and ask her what she thought of it, but if that were possible it would be unnecessary. This is surely the extreme, for which Chomsky is certainly not responsible, of Chomsky's position on underlying universals. If universal commands or requests under-lie Washoe's gestures they are universal indeed. Perhaps they extend to the bees, the birds and the flowers.

Washoe is said by other authorities to use words:

> Washoe. . .learned her first word at about the age of fifteen months, an insistent 'come-gimme'. . .Her second word, 'more'. . .came with-in a week or two—and by the time she was about. . .four years old she used more than fifty signs, including those representing 'hear– listen', 'toothbrush'. . .'flower'. . .'dog' and 'please'. (John E. Pfeiffer, *The Emergence of Man* (1971), pp. 397–8)

The fallacy comes clear with the absence of inverted commas for 'word' and with 'representing'. What do these 'words' represent? Here they are parts of our language, but how can they be that for Washoe? But if not why are they words?

This seems to be another variety of Vendler's indirect speech fallacy (above, p. 110). If the cat goes to the empty saucer and miaows, it makes sense to say that the cat is asking for milk. Some cats, I would not deny, are overbearing personalities, and *demand* to be let in or out of rooms. Perhaps they even *order* us to feed them. But it doesn't follow that the animals are talking (or, as Vendler would wish, that meaning is somewhere other than expression: the cat means these things which I have just expressed in English by expressing himself in bodily gestures).

Morton also says that Washoe 'spontaneously generalized from the particular to the general—the sign for "dog" was used for pictures and for the sound of an unseen dog barking' (p. 9). It is interesting that an animal can be trained to recognize a dog in a pict㏑e, but where does the talk of particularity and generality come from? Washoe has been trained to make a certain sign when she perceives a dog, real or pictured (which does mean she can distinguish dogs from other creatures). But Morton's charac-terization is a human and linguistic activity that there is no reason to attribute to the chimpanzee. What she does, it seems to me, well illustrates the *difference* between trained reference (perhaps a kind of conditioned reflex) and naming. Naming belongs in language: it is *not* naming, but idiocy, to say 'dog' every time one sees a dog; and nobody reports that Washoe has anything to say to or about dogs but 'dog'. (If she were to begin 'thinking about' dogs when no dog was present, surely an essential linguistic power, and if she then began making the dog-sign with a thoughtful expression on her face, the experiment would be thought to have failed.) The cat at the empty saucer is not naming milk or using concepts; the pointer does not name the bird it points; the old warhorse neighing at the sound of battle is not naming a battle; and the defeated wolf exposing its jugular is neither apologizing nor crying 'Mercy!' This sort of investigation throws no light, scientific or otherwise, on either language or the psyche.

Washoe's signing is predictable or else the experiment fails. 'It may often look as if an utterance is unpredictable in terms of antecedent and present conditions; but to accept this would indeed mean abandoning the hope of providing a scientific explanation of what determines behaviour', said a psycholinguist in a *TLS* special issue (23 July 1970, p. 835). Yes, and the abandonment might be an excellent thing: it might clear the ground for a genuine psychology of language.

I suspect that if there can be anything called 'psycholinguistics' it will have to work by meditating on the psychology *built into* our language, the ways in which the psyche makes itself in speech. This would of course be the opposite of language-independent explanation, but it might in its way lead us up to a few linguistic universals, that is, allow us to discuss human nature. I cannot imagine a language in which I am not I and you you, and the 'I' is not the 'simple referential device' Vendler wants to make it (above, p. 133), for what is it referring to? 'To me' is the grammatical, and correct, answer, but 'what is me?' is not a grammatical paraphrase of 'who am I?' Neither I nor you are referents like the table, the moon, or even like RED. I prove that I exist when I say something: but what is proved to exist? My body? My life? No, just me. *Pace* D. H. Lawrence in *Apropos of Lady Chatterley's Lover* my body doesn't feel things: *I* do. I do and I experience; so do you and every human being. Speaking is the evidence; any speaking, in any language.

We define ourselves (our selves) with reference to others and to the external world. Jakobson discusses the case of Gleb Ivanovich Uspenskij whose 'first name and patronymic. . .for him split into two distinct names designating two separate beings' (*Fundamentals of Language*, p. 94). Gleb seems to have been a kind of Jekyll to Ivanovich's Hyde. Jakobson comments, 'The linguistic aspect of this split personality is the patient's inability to use two symbols for the same thing.' But *what* 'thing'? Is the psyche a thing? and if the personality was split how was it the same thing? May not this unfortunate man really have called up two persons with his two names?

Sociolinguistics also sounds a promising word; and I don't even regard it as a drawback that one cannot easily imagine any activity in which more than one human being participates as lying outside the purview of the study. But the interest is again often removed by the imposition of would-be scientific method. The question for (and limit of) sociolinguistics, one would have thought, is the effects on language of its use in social groups (rather than, e.g., by individuals on their own, in notices, books, diaries. . .) and vice versa.

Dell Hymes, editor of the massive anthology *Language in Culture and Society* (New York, 1964) and of the new periodical *Language in Society* (Cambridge, 1972– —a magazine which has printed some good things amongst an ominous number of graphs and tables) begins the latter with a good account of the sociolinguistic ambition. After discussing the self-imposed limitations of linguistics he says,

We find, in short, that language is not solely an instrument for naming and describing and conducting rigorous argument. We find it to be an instrument of expression and appeal, of persuasion and command, of deference and insult, of gossip and rebuke; we find it an instrument preferred, eschewed, enjoyed, distrusted, pervasively evaluated, not only in terms of referential adequacy and logical validity, but also in terms of aptness, pleasure, rewards and costs, self-identity and community respect. (Vol. i, p. 4)

In the context of most linguists' discussions one would want to applaud this passage; nevertheless there is an ominous flaw in it. Language is not merely not an instrument of any of the kinds named, it is not an instrument at all—unless of the kind meant by Polanyi's images and analogies, which is plainly not what Hymes has in mind. To speak of language as an instrument, and to discuss 'aptness' like this, is to imply the Saussure–Chomsky view of what language does as external to language; expression, appeal, persuasion, command etc. are then not *in* the language, but something done by the instrument.

Language as our way of understanding society—there surely is the sociolinguist's leading idea. But when Hymes writes 'The significance of features of language cannot be assessed without knowledge of their social matrix' the social matrix is the extra-linguistic sense, the equivalent of the Chomskyan semantic universals, which will tell us what language means.[1] Here we lose both our social and our linguistic way. His statement is demonstrably untrue in that we can have *some* knowledge of Homer's poetry or of the Book of Joshua without any knowledge of the relevant 'social matrices' beyond what we pick up as we read, and what we know because we too live in a human society. Hymes's sentence would point to a better sense for sociolinguistics if it were turned round. Even in the case of objects which seem to carry their own social role with them—motorways, say, or drawing-rooms—can we understand the *social* role unless we know what the objects mean to people, i.e. how they are spoken of? The best practitioners of sociolinguistics have always investigated society through language, though under different banners, for Malinowski did not call himself a sociolinguist.

Hymes also says:

The point to be made here is that speech acts cannot be analyzed or explained within grammar, or indeed within speech, alone. What is linguistically the same utterance, for example, may have the status of a request or of a command, depending not on any feature proper to grammar, but on the social relationship of the parties involved. And rules that govern words as speech acts may be found to govern nonverbal activity as well, as when rules applying to summonses in American society apply to the ringing of a phone or a knock on a door as well. (pp. 6–7)

The remarks at the beginning of the passage are saying in a different way what I observed about the limitations of Chomskyan grammar and of course to that extent I heartily agree with them. (This will be clear if Hymes's 'linguistically' is seen to mean 'Chomskyan-grammatically'.) The element of muddle enters with the word *speech*. Yes indeed we might do 'the same' thing

[1] Sapir got the matter clear when he wrote 'It is an illusion to think that we can understand the significant outlines of a culture through sheer observation and without the guide of the linguistic symbolism which makes these outlines significant and intelligible...It will not be possible for a social student to evaluate such phenomena unless he has very clear notions of linguistic background', *Selected Writings of Edward Sapir* (Berkeley and Cambridge, 1949), pp. 161–2, 163.

by uttering a sentence or ringing a bell; but it does not follow that the ringing of the bell, the 'social relationship', is then somehow more real and observable than speech; it means that the ringing of the bell has become a part of our language. And what the ringing means will depend on whatever it is that makes language meaningful. This is not explained by the phrase 'social relationships' unless they are seen within language. Hymes almost says so when he recognizes that the same rules might govern verbal summonses or a knock at the door: the 'rules' will in both cases be those of the language. 'Once embarked upon analysis of speech acts, linguistics must enter into the analysis of communicative acts, or fail' (p. 7). Yes, but communicative acts seen as social events are not a specially observable, simple or privileged instance of language. What Hymes is on the edge of seeing is that his study, like that of more ordinary linguists, is up against the enduring problems of how language comes to be possible—how mere sound of the vocal cords, or *a fortiori* of telephone bells or knocks at the door, comes to be meaningful. And these problems are not to be solved by the invocation of social science. Hymes's faith in the observation of social structure outside language is therefore an admission of just the same defeat we have seen in Chomsky:

The priority of functional consideration, however, the dependence of recognition of structure upon recognition of function, means that adequate description of a way of speaking must often be from a standpoint heavily dependent on close analysis of social roles, setting, events and institutions, if the rules of co-occurrence that define its features, and the rules of alternation that govern its use, are to be described. Norms of verbal interaction, including silence; beliefs and attitudes about speech and language, or particular ways of speaking; the emergence, expansion and decline of standard varieties of languages, and of ways of speaking generally—analysis and causal explanation of many such phenomena must rely primarily upon methods of observation and analysis developed in the social sciences. (p. 9)

No. Such methods could imaginably be useful, but their usefulness will depend upon their being taken within the study of language, where talk of 'causal explanation...of phenomena' (or, as a *TLS* review put it, 3 August 1973, p. 909, 'the relationship of linguistic symptoms to non-linguistic causes') is utterly inappropriate.

It is even observable that sociologists are sometimes better equipped (by terms like *intersubjective*) to approach these knotty problems than scholars coming at them from the direction of linguistics. For instance the Open University textbook *Language and Social Reality* (Milton Keynes, 1973) would make a useful text for seminar discussion coming, as it does, close enough to the real problems to be worth discussing, and putting some things crudely enough to make improvement essential. This book is still in difficulties with the belief that 'social reality' is separable from language (pp. 7, 18) and uses sociolinguistic phrases like 'the social basis of reality'; it also talks of 'imposing order on experience' (p. 37) and sees language as an institution for doing so, which unfortunately suggests that there could be a social though disordered human existence without language. But the book does take language as an 'index of reality' (p. 7) rather than vice versa, and without suggesting that the index is merely of the kind in which one looks things up. This is more than the socio-linguists can do.

Similar observations are to be made of the linguistics-and-literary-criticism movement which has been increasingly active since 1956, when an issue of *The Kenyon Review* caused a stir by printing some essays using the Trager–Smith system of structural analysis to discuss metre and rhythm.[2] I will restrict my discussion, in the brief space I give to this topic, to the work of Professor Roger Fowler, the best known of the English writers who are trying to make linguistics contribute to literary criticism.

Fowler follows on easily from a mention of Hymes's sociolinguistics because his idea of style 'rests on a theoretical premise which seems indispensable to stylistics (though not to criticism generally): we must assume that a distinctive use of language reflects distinctive extra-linguistic circumstances'.[3] The premise points us back to earlier considerations of reference, the 'objective correlative' and the super-language: Fowler belongs to the 'reflecters' not the 'expressers'. The belief that meaning exists outside language has in Fowler's work the same confusing effect that it has in Hymes's. It makes him take works of literature to

---

[2] The best work I know along these lines has come out in *Language and Style* edited from the English Department of University College, Cardiff.
[3] Roger Fowler, *The Languages of Literature, some linguistic contributions to Criticism* (1971), pp. 19–20.

be objects, i.e. enjoying an objective existence somehow independent of their place in language in reading by individuals.

Fowler several times quotes the opening sentences of Winifred Nowottny's book *The Language Poets Use*: 'In considering the language of poetry it is prudent to begin with what is "there" in the poem—"there" in the sense that it can be described and referred to as unarguably given by the words.' I doubt whether *anything* in poetry is in this sense 'unarguable' but, neglecting that and other difficulties, Fowler takes her to mean that works of literature are objects susceptible to scientific mensuration. He knows that this is rather odd, and raises the question what kind of object a poem is, *almost* concluding that it is the kind of object that reading and discussion permit it to be (p. 84). But he later says, 'the answer to the question "What kind of object?" is "An abstract object"' (p. 87). Occam's razor, always kept so freshly whetted by linguistics, is again called for: I cannot see that 'object' is adding anything to the discussion. Or one might suggest that the world's starvation problem would be rapidly solved if we were all content to live on abstract food. Fowler needs 'object' because he wants something to measure. But are abstract objects measurable?

Elsewhere the 'object'—and language—doesn't seem abstract at all. Fowler offers as a programme for criticism that it 'present literature in terms of categories which are basic and which can be empirically justified' (p. 83; cf. p. 101 first paragraph). But when he tries to show that poems exist as objects he is driven to the argument that they are objects if they imitate objects (which in any case I don't believe they do). 'A literary object', he says, 'has semanticity' (p. 86), and he paraphrases that at the end of the paragraph as imitating reality. (He says that music hasn't semanticity because 'Vivaldi's *Four Seasons* is stylized away from the reality it pretends to imitate': apparently Donne's 'Elegy to his Mistress Going to Bed' isn't.)

I don't think this view of literature or language is tenable because I don't see the point of calling poems or sentences objects. I think the onus is on those who *do* think they're objects to put them on the table.

F. W. Bateson, in two papers reprinted by Fowler, makes the telling objection that there is a lot of talk about what linguistics is going to do for literary criticism, but precious little actual doing. Sometimes the offer is just a *non sequitur*. Fowler makes a list, convincing as far as it goes, of the questions the critic has to ask, and he is aware of the limits to the answers linguistics can give:

Why does a certain text have many long, balanced sentences and a florid vocabulary? Why does a certain speaker constantly use a breathy tone? Why do some texts (e.g. newspaper advertisements) use short, verb-less sentences? Why are certain journals dense with multi-syllabic, uncommon technical terms? Why are some styles of pronunciation intonationally monotonous? The range of such questions (and, indeed, their answers) is apparently endless. And it is quite obvious that simple grammatical description goes only a short way towards answering them. (p. 8)

But then he goes on

Yet it is equally obvious that they are best answered by someone who is well informed about the facts of linguistic structure—who knows fairly accurately what the phenomena are which he is asking questions about.

Why is that obvious if grammar says little about the critic's questions? The essential question how the linguist's knowledge can be brought *into* literary criticism is untouched. So it is unclear why the grammarian is thought to know anything about what phenomena the critic is talking about.

The most useful applications of linguistics to literary criticism, I think, have been studies of metre. The problem given to metrics by the structuralist linguists of the Trager–Smith era is that Trager and Smith say that there are four levels of stress in English speech and hence in verse, but traditional scanning of a line only notices two: why should this be? I have never seen any convincing evidence that there *are* four levels of stress in English speech (I think the number probably depends on the predilections of the enumerator: i.e. the real grammatical question is not one of number at all) but the question did set linguists thinking (for instance E. L. Epstein and T. Hawkes, *Linguistics and English Prosody* (Buffalo, 1959)). Fowler too has work on metre which is very good as far as it goes.

How do we recognize metre in a line, or make it as we read? Why can, say, iambic pentameter be realized in such very different verses? Fowler, following Seymour Chatman, argues convincingly that some stresses are 'metre fixing' and others 'metre fixed'. 'Metre fixing' syllables will be from words whose stress-patterns are fixed by common speech, and about which, granting that metrical patterns are based on common speech stress, there is therefore no problem. They will suggest a metrical pattern which will then tell us how to stress the 'metre fixed' syllables. For instance *compare* must be stressed on the second syllable, and so in the first line of Shakespeare's Sonnet XVIII the reader begins by at least knowing that the second foot is iambic, because it is occupied by the word 'compare'.[4] Such words determine the metrical 'set', and that tells you the accent-pattern of the other words, e.g. monosyllables. (Of course the procedure could not be used to override the stress-patterns of words we know, on which the procedure is based.)

At this point Chomsky gets in the way, for the obvious Chomskyan line of discussion is to see metre as a deep abstract structure, never perceptible in the surface verses, but recognizable in them by means of a series of transformations from an underlying string.

Just when Fowler comes to the verge of saying something interesting about how different lines of verse move—just as he is about to bring linguistics into literary criticism—he desists. He thinks that his work is complete when he has made a formal linguistic description, which can never be enough in literary criticism. It will never do for the critic just to say 'that's a sonnet' or 'that is iambic pentameter according to the following formula':[5] the critic has always to ask what the sonnet form is doing in a particular case. (And I don't even believe that there is any way to understand the sonnet form except by way of sonnets.) In this way literary criticism must follow closely actual uses of language, the only sort there are, and must give its own account of the pieces of language it studies in their real existence as meaning. But so, I think, must linguistics. Fowler's abstraction is

---

[4] Fowler sometimes makes mistakes, of course:
> Her eyes, her haire, her cheeke, her gate, her voice

is not 'a perfect "metre-fixing" line' (p. 137); it is a perfect metre-fixed line, for given the right metre or sense you would read it as trochees:
> *You're* not the girl for me: I only want
> *Her* eyes, *her* hair, *her* cheek, *her* gait, *her* voice.

Even as written by Shakespeare it could *possibly* be trochaic.

[5] See my note on Halle and Keyser's formula for Chaucer's pentameter, *Chaucer and the English Tradition* (Cambridge, 1972), p. ix. I believe their analysis is wrong in its own terms; but the real objection is that it cannot be taken into criticism, i.e. can say nothing about real lines of verse.

inadequate as linguistics because it doesn't say what is happening here within language. If it had done so it would indeed have ascended into literary criticism.

The mistake is the taking into linguistics-and-literary-criticism of the abstractness of Chomsky's study of syntax. Whatever may be the case about pure syntactic analysis, the application of linguistics to literary criticism must surely be a *useful* science and must touch our sense of this poem or that. Linguists who do manage to bring their knowledge into literary criticism *use* it there. I think of Leo Spitzer's fine essay on Claudel (*Linguistics and Literary History*, Princeton, 1948), which calls on his linguistic training, including his detailed understanding of syntax, in order to express his fine response to poetry.

Linguistics can sometimes be the 'underlabourer' of criticism, or of other disciplines.[6] The 'linguistics and. . .' studies all go astray at present and are not as useful as they might be because they follow Chomsky in trying to move the linguistics part away from use, and because they exalt linguistics unduly. In the case in point literary critics are often exhorted to learn from linguists; but I never hear linguists told to learn from critics. Such a lesson is much needed, as I shall conclude by showing.

[6] Linguistics, in a wide sense, can offer help to criticism when linguistics is kept in its properly subordinate place. Every year in tutorials we waste time when bright pupils fumble around for grammatical terms that would have been commonplace thirty years ago. And how many critics nowadays are equipped with such useful terms as *oxymoron, synechdoche, zeugma*? But I don't believe matters will be much improved if Dr George Steiner gets his way ('It should not be possible to leave the university with an English degree and not knowing what a phoneme or a semantic structure is'— *TLS*, 25 February 1972) even if *anyone* succeeds in attaching sense to the last phrase.

9

'The Science of Language' Revisited

Anything calling itself 'the science of language' must satisfy at least two conditions before the title can be recognized. It must be a science; and if it lays claim to the definite article it must surely study the whole of language. This chapter attempts to draw together some of the threads of the preceding ones in order to say how TG grammar fails to satisfy these conditions, since it is not a science and since it can go no further towards accounting for the whole of language than to give one account of the syntax of written sentences.

There cannot be a scientific discipline which will define language from the discipline's own point of view. This ('language-independent explanation', as we have been calling it) is indeed the *sine qua non* for, in Chomsky's sense, a science of language.[1]

[1] Chomsky's view of science is in any case misconceived in attributing to it a sort of general and absolute power of discovering what is a fact. I write very much under correction here, for I am not a physicist and can't even claim any proper understanding of quantum theory. Chomsky, anyway, has plainly an insufficient conception of the real scientists' increasing awareness of the limitations of their respective disciplines to what can be achieved by their respective methods:

'Up to about the turn of this century it was accepted that the models were imperfect representations of restricted aspects of a unique reality, but now it must be doubted whether such a reality can be recognized as existing.' (G. H. A. Cole, 'Physics', in *The Twentieth-Century Mind*, ed. C. B. Cox and A. E. Dyson (Oxford, 1972), vol. 1, p. 251)

Physicists used to think of themselves as disinterested, objective discoverers of a world absolutely 'there' and untouched by them. They are now much more aware of the philosophical problems of perception, and know that what is 'there' is limited by how it is observed, recognizing in this way that the development of physics is an increasingly subtle understanding of the *physical* properties of matter, i.e. the properties amenable to consideration by physicists, and that therefore the development of physical knowledge is the same as, and limited to, the development of the 'language' of their discipline. Physics is thus one true way of seeing things which need have nothing to say to other ways (still-life painting, visions of the beauty of the world...) nor to modes of thought that are not ways of seeing things (history, theology, poetry...). Physics gives a home to the facts of physics and thus brings them and itself into existence, but it has no absolute access to truth and no universally applicable method.

The sciences are disciplines of external observation. There is no common-sense hydrogen atom; it exists only within the observation of the relevant experiments understood within the relevant body of theory, and there it exists as the hydrogen atom. In the cases of things that do exist in the ordinary world a scientist will give a new view that goes beyond the ordinary world, so that the frog to the biologist is not the same creature as to common sense.

'Linguistics', on the contrary, 'is the science of language; hence we had better start by trying to define language' (Carroll, *The Study of Language*, p. 7). If linguistics were the science of language it could not so begin; the definition of language would be the object of the study and would come last.

Though the biologist must not be a frog, the linguist must be a speaker before he becomes a linguist. Only physicists can discover atoms; there is no analogous way in which one needs to be a linguist in order to discover language. Linguistics might, let us hope, refine our sense of language and show us some of its ways we did not know—but only by staying within language and refraining from scientific efforts at external explanation.

If there is to be a natural science, says Collingwood, people 'must take it absolutely for granted that somewhere in the world there is a dividing line between things that happen or can be made to happen or can be prevented by art...and things that happen of themselves, or by nature' (*An Essay on Metaphysics*, p. 192). Natural science can then investigate nature in its own way, testing its hypotheses by experiments on 'things that happen of themselves'. (Natural science is not itself, of course, a part of this world of nature; and the investigation of natural science is not itself science but philosophy of science.) In Christian times, says Collingwood, 'it became a matter of faith that the world of nature should be regarded...as the realm of precision' (p. 253). Hence natural science is nothing if not exact, and its explanations are always hypotheses, but always explanations of 'the world of nature'.

The study of language cannot be a science, in the sense of *science* consistently intended by Chomsky and all his friends and all his enemies within linguistics, because language is inherently metaphysical. 'We can, however, be fairly sure that there will be a physical explanation for the phenomena in question [those of human mentality], if they can be explained at all' (*Language and Mind*, p. 98). Chomsky offers what he thinks an 'uninteresting terminological reason' for this, namely that 'the concept of "physical explanation" will be extended to cover whatever is discovered in this domain'. What it cannot be extended to is the metaphysical. *Discovery* cannot be extended to what cannot be discovered. Language will never be 'explained' in this sense of the word, because attention to its physical manifestations *per se* (whether brainwaves or soundwaves) will never allow us to understand language;[2] and the well-defined rules which might be analytically true will never be a good fit for language.

To say that language is metaphysical, or that it does not belong to the world of nature, is not to deny the real existence of language, to assert that language is 'merely subjective' or to suggest that linguists are licensed to equate their beliefs about language with what is the case about language. Language is the object of the linguist's thought, but not all objects of thought belong to the world of nature.

That language is not physical may be shown by something as commonplace as the mode of existence of a book. In that fine poem *The Owl and the Nightingale* the Owl boasts of her book-learning, to which the Nightingale objects, in effect, that the Owl knows books only physically, not, that is to say, in their real existence as books, which is their meaning.

> An ape can gaze upon a book
> And turn its leaves and have a look
> Without through that knowing the more
> Of any bit of learned lore.

This is not to say that language is found anywhere other than in its physical manifestations. Language is itself in our understanding, which is inward. And if the physiologists tell me that when we talk our brains as well as our vocal and auditory apparatus are active, I will believe them: but I will not look for an understanding of language to what they say (above, Chapter 4). The discussion of language is not the discussion of brain events, but has its own terminology concerning words, sounds,

---

2 ' "But the materialists," said the Astronomer, "urge that matter may have qualities with which we are unacquainted."

"He who will determine," returned Imlac, "against that which he knows because there may be something which he knows not; he that can set hypothetical possibility against acknowledged certainty, is not to be admitted among reasonable beings." '

books etc. when they are taken as language. That we have ways of discussing language separate from ways of discussing either brainwaves or sounds or written marks is the reason for supposing that linguistics is possible. But I am not saying that language is some mysterious other thing added to its physical manifestations—some substance, as it were, peculiarly thin and refined. If language transcends the physicality of the physical it is yet always immanent in the physical.

Ross prepares Macduff for terrible news with these words:

> Let not your ears despise my tongue for ever
> Which shall possess them with the heaviest sound
> That ever yet they heard.
> *Macbeth* IV. iii

'Heaviest sound' is perfectly accurate. The sound will be 'heavy' only when it is taken as language; but then there will be no way of hearing the language without the sound.

It is still language which confers itself upon sound and defines the reality of sound as language. Similarly we can see printed words as typeface or ink, but when we see them as the written language that is what they really are, and the other possible ways of looking at them depend on this, their real metaphysical existence, in our inner possession, as printed language.

Higher systems organize lower. Polanyi says, arguing that the methods of physics need not be universally illuminating:

[the giving of a speech] includes five levels; namely the production (1) of voice, (2) of words, (3) of sentences, (4) of style, and (5) of literary composition. Each of these levels is subject to its own laws, as prescribed (1) by phonetics, (2) by lexicography, (3) by grammar, (4) by stylistics, and (5) by literary criticism. These levels form a hierarchy of comprehensive entities, for the principles of each level operate under the control of the next higher level. The voice you produce is shaped into words by a vocabulary; a given vocabulary is shaped into sentences in accordance with grammar; and the sentences can be made to fit into a style, which in its turn is made to convey the ideas of a literary composition. Thus each level is subject to dual control; first, by the laws that apply to its elements in themselves and, second, by the laws that control the comprehensive entity formed by them. (Michael Polanyi, *The Tacit Dimension* (1967), pp. 35–6)

Language organizes the elements (whether sound, marks on paper, movements of the fingers or whatever) which compose it.

Linguistics will from time to time concentrate on the lower levels, but if it is to be the study of language the lower levels must be seen as those of language, controlled by the high level. (Cf. Firth, quoted above, p. 140.) When the lower levels are recognized as such their study can itself contribute to the disciplined sense of wonder at language which, I suggested, would mark the depth of understanding granted by a real subject. The goal is not utterly beyond even the grammarian. Reading Jespersen, looking up some point or other, I am always surprised and fascinated by the wonderful ordered diversity of English—as I am when going through one of J. L. Austin's discussions or his list of the varieties within 'performatives'. Even such a humble act as consulting a dictionary can be a genuine glimpse of the wonder of language. (And think how difficult it is, if one is not pressed for time, not to wander on from one 'lexical entry' to another.) I recently had occasion to consult the N.E.D. on the word *of*—not a very remarkable word, on the face of it; but I defy anybody of goodwill to read through that dozen or so huge pages without, in the act itself of distinguishing the two dozen or so uses of *of*, paying an awed tribute to the ordered wonder of our common possession. But this is only likely in a context of other looks at language. Furtwängler is said to have spent his leisure hours playing scales on the piano, but he also conducted Beethoven.

Any successful attention to the lower levels of language must recognize their place in the hierarchy *as* lower levels. The highest level of language, controlling the rest, is always meaning, even if all we can know of the meaning is one of the lower levels.

Think of proofreading someone else's text, or of editing a dead author, two of the places where grammar is important. When we think something is wrong—and why do we think well-formed sentences are wrong if not by our sense of the whole language?— we try to correct it. This simultaneously uses our knowledge of the regularities of language and tries to get at what our writer means. A brilliant editorial emendation ('A babbled of green fields' for 'a table of green fields') is recognized by some such feeling in the qualified reader as 'Yes, he must have meant that!'

There is no further appeal in language beyond meaning, and until we get to meaning we are not studying language. So the decision of structural linguistics to postpone the study of meaning was a quite stupendous refusal to pay attention to language.

Linguistics can be no more than ways of meditating upon uses of language from within, from the point of view of the user. There is no other way of paying attention to language as language. (One uses the latter rebarbative phrase only as a retort to the effort of linguistics to see language as everything else—as brain activity, reflection of objects, clothing of logic or whatever. If a spade is called an innate idea it may be necessary to insist that it is a spade.) But how to decide which of all the infinite meanings of all the languages to concentrate on and in what sort of order?

Chomsky is surely right to believe that linguistics must attend to the whole of language, and I do believe that one task of linguistics, bringing it rather close to philosophy, is to beat the bounds of language, to say that something is or is not language. (Perhaps the difference is that philosophy will try to unite two senses of the question what language is and will discuss, in ways beyond the necessary interest of the linguist, how language must connect with thought.)

If linguistics is to study the whole of language it must not, as Chomsky constantly emphasizes, restrict its study of any language to any corpus of evidence; on the other hand linguistics cannot automatically ignore anything that might get into a corpus.

Why linguists disdain the study of the written language I have never been able to understand, especially as even when they are reporting speech the examples in linguists' books always happen to be written down, not spoken. In the case of the study of syntax, the disdain of writing is worse than mere dogma, for syntactic analysis is always of the written language. 'The sentence', the central concept, belongs to writing not speech. To get from sound to a Chomsky surface structure, the raw material for syntactic analysis, one writes the sound down as a sentence. There is no better definition of a sentence than that it begins with a capital letter and ends with a full stop; this used to be taught in schools as part of writing. All languages have letters, says Chomsky at the beginning of *Syntactic Structures* (p. 13: if this were true there would be no force in the contention that speech came before writing); but even letters are inventions of the grammarian, 'A wisdom which Pythagoras held most high. . .to comprise/All sounds of voices, in few marks of letters'. It has been too easily forgotten that a γραμμάτικός is a grammarian because he knows γράμματα, letters.

'The Science of Language' Revisited

The familiarity of linguists with two millennia of the Greek/ Alexandrian tradition of literacy has bred a most misleading contempt. One of its forms is the supposition that the relation between the written and spoken language is not very problematic. Actually, even with the most meticulous phonetic script, the transition from discrete written characters to the flow of language read aloud (not at all the same as speech) is deeply mysterious. No script gives more than hints and guesses about what one can call here its interpretation as sound. To be able to read aloud is in one sense to have begun to be a grammarian.

Whether sounds and words exist in at all the same way for the illiterate as for us is doubtful, but it is indisputable that letters exist on the typewriter keyboard or the hornbook and that the typist knows when to use the space-bar between words.[3]

The literate and the illiterate will follow the same sound-rules but only the former will be able to account for sounds as spelling. A novelist who records 'I'd of done so and so . . .' will in his own person write 'I'd have done . . . ' 'For many American English speakers /t/ and /d/ are ordinarily not distinguished between a stressed and unstressed vowel but can be produced distinctively when there is danger of a confusing homonymity: "Is it Mr. Bitter /bítə/ or Bidder /bídə/?" may be asked with a slightly divergent implementation of the two phonemes' (Jakobson and Halle, *Fundamentals of Language*, p. 16). Alternatively the question might just be 'Do you spell it with double t or double d?'—and if the sound is genuinely the same the difference can *only* be one of spelling. Similarly, in English the insertion of the possessive apostrophe is always in the written not the spoken language. There is no way of saying 'Bloggs' book', and when we say 'Bloggs's book' it might just as well, as far as the sound goes, be 'Bloggses book' or 'Bloggses' book'.

The linguist's refusal to study the written language is bound

---

[3] With 'deletions' we again observe the indispensability of writing to formal grammar. The things deleted are not present in the mind or in sound but in the written paradigm. (Above, p. 39.)

'Do you accept travellers' cheques?
Acceptez-vous les chèques de voyageurs?
Ak-sep-teh voo leh shek duh vwah-ya-zhoer?'
(Charles S. Hughes, *Transworld's French Phrase Book and Dictionary* (1973), p. 30.)

To get to the phonetic form from the ordinary written form we delete the sound apparently represented by some of the plural endings. But it only makes sense to talk in this way because they are there on the page: the case is unlike deleting '+ by + NP$_2$' from some forms of the passive.

to confuse the status of his own implements for inspecting the spoken language, as well as making him neglect language in the only form in which it is available for grammatical inspection. It also cuts him off from *most* of the best language.

What is not language may be a tougher form of the question what is. Is music language? In some important ways it is language-like; and though music cannot perform the function so many philosophers are determined to make the centre of language, viz it cannot make propositions except in a non-musical context, Rush Rhees somewhere truly observes that some meditations upon death can *only* be expressed in music.

What is the borderline (is there *one* borderline?) between language and speechless thought? We often make decisions or even solve problems speechlessly. Shall I get up or lie in bed a little longer? I needn't ask myself in words: I just either pull back the sheet or close my eyes again. Shall I eat a chocolate biscuit or a digestive sweetmeal? I just look at the plate on which they both are, perhaps I have sundry impulses or images (and perhaps not), then I pick up one or another, wordlessly. I see that the type-writer-case is too close to the fire, and I can even see without using any words that if left alone the typewriter will be damaged: what I see is then the sense made to me by the situation of those objects, and seeing the situation in itself means that to me. I simply walk over and move the typewriter-case. These may seem trivial examples, but something similar applies to important ones. Vendler, conducting his argument to show that thought is really always outside speech, asks, 'Suppose I tell you that last night I suddenly realized that Joe must have done it. Does it make sense to ask for the exact sentence I mentally pronounced (heard? read off?) in performing this act?' (*Res Cogitans*, p. 66). Well, it *might* make sense: the realization may have taken the form of some words going through my mind; but it may not. I might just have seen a peculiar image of Joe, or said his name in a peculiar way to myself, or I might even just, with any kind of mental reference to Joe, have felt my heart miss a beat.

It is worth observing that although I can do all these things wordlessly I can also do them with words, even to realizing that Joe did it; and even in the cases of wordlessness I have just reported them in words. But I don't at all want to minimize this question, only to suggest that it ought to be one of the concerns of linguistics.

The polar opposite is to do something which once needed language but now no longer seems to. When I read in one of my pupils' essays about what was going through Donne's mind as he wrote 'The Good Morrow' I just think 'Hm!'; and in the 'hm!' is somehow contained, if I am reasonably alert, the quintessence of all the times I have met and tried to correct this fallacy. Once it involved me in thought and effort, now it doesn't. Isn't the sense then, after all, as Vendler says, outside language?

And what of the trains of thought one comes to necessarily, whatever words or thought-processes one happens to employ, as one masters some particular subject? Are they not language-independent in precisely the way Vendler says, if they don't depend on any particular verbal formulae? In any branch of thought one finds 'you won't get far with this subject until you understand so-and-so', but the 'so-and-so' may be talked of, and approached, in many different ways. In our own subject it might well be said that nobody will get far until his mind has boggled a little at the depths of the problems expressible by the phrase 'words and things': but there is no one way of getting to this place or of expressing these problems. Is it not reasonable to say that the words we use in these cases don't matter much, that what matters is grasping the questions of importance that under-lie whatever language we use to express them? So Blaise Pascal, working out his own mathematics because his father wouldn't let him learn the subject, is said by his sister to have got as far as the thirty-second proposition of Euclid using home-made terms like *rond* for *cercle* and *barre* for *ligne*. Doesn't the geometry then really exist outside language?

I don't think so. Love, too, may take many expressions, but that doesn't mean there is no language of love, much less that love could be expressed without any language. The understanding of mathematics is the criterion for saying that Pascal made progress in mathematics outside its usual formulae. There are different ways of putting these: the range just is the language of mathe-matics, including Pascal's as well as Euclid's. This is close to Russell's 'set of acceptable paraphrases': I am only adding that the sense of what is acceptable, here as elsewhere, is 'competence' in the sense of being able to use a language, not a knowledge underlying language. Mathematical expressions (or declarations of love) may vary, but there is no mathematics without *some* truly mathematical expression, any more than there is love without expression; and what counts as truly mathematical is a question about the 'grammar' of the 'language' of mathematics. If Pascal's maths was all right, if his mathematical propositions were, so to speak, well-formed, he was within the language of mathematics. The language of the discipline is the mathematical aspect of whatever expressions were used; the proper use of whatever language constitutes the discipline, and the observation of this proper use is the relevant 'grammar'. This is very different from saying that the sense of the discipline is found outside language altogether, unexpressed.[4]

We certainly make many kinds of sense outside words: we dream wordlessly; we paint pictures or look at them; we see buildings, or mountains, or the sea, in peculiar ways so that they seem expressive to us; and we have emotions and sensations which we don't put into words but which are far from senseless.[5] Faces make sense and are expressive outside language. How are these senses like language; how, if at all, connected with language?

I believe, and must offer what I say here only as belief, that language is the distinctively human level of making sense. Even Washoe makes some sense—the sense a chimpanzee can make— and it is her own individual sense. Human sense, the sense that gives us the chance to make *our* own individual sense, is language. Our private senses need this shared sense. All uses of language are, of course, by individuals; but in using the language, in that exercise of individuality, we participate in and create the distinctively human world, the sense we share. Language defines the

---

[4] The case may be clearer where there is disagreement about what constitutes a discipline. I am told (let us imagine the case, anyway) that there are two quite different organic chemistries. The one tries to look at all carbon compounds, whose number in practical terms is infinite, in a spirit of either pure or commercial curiosity, rather like the pre-Chomskyan linguist observing the facts of his corpus; the other tries to develop a system of classification so as to cover all possible carbon compounds. There is no inevitability about studying organic chemicals one way rather than the other, though my account makes the second way sound more scientifically respectable. The ways are just two different 'grammars', and the same compound will occupy a different place in the two.

[5] I don't mean we have unexpressed emotions. Even the suppression of emotion is a kind of expression: cf. Collingwood, *Principles of Art*, p. 246, and this characteristic passage from a richly comic novel, *Aaron's Rod*: 'The others no doubt attributed his silence to deep or fierce thoughts. It was nothing of the kind: merely a cold struggle to get his wind back [after a punch in the wind], without letting them know he was struggling: and a sheer, stock-stiff hatred of the pair of them' (chap. 7).

limits of our common sense, and that is the only common standard for any sense.[6] It is therefore possible to see the sense even of dreams as dependent on language. In dreams we are free from the *Weltbild* of our waking lives: we may have been to Mars in our dreams, the world may have been created with our dreams; the old dream of being young and the dying of being in health. But we wake and see what we have dreamed from the point of view of the world defined by our language. (I think it is intriguing and perhaps important that the so-called Tennis-Elbow-Foot Game can have an umpire—that there can be ordinary linguistic rules for 'the association of ideas'.)

Even that demands a kind of individual consent (though one wouldn't call it judgement or evaluation): it is possible to withhold consent from one's language and be what its other users call *mad*.

Our different path has brought us out again at the earlier question how one is to discriminate between the infinitely different meanings of language; I hope it has also shown that another aspect of the question is how to define the central area of sense, on which the academic specialisms depend and of which they *are* specialisms, that I mentioned at the end of the first chapter. For the central ground of judgement can be none other than our language itself.

Any study of the whole of language must develop a notion of the range of the uses of language, of which making propositions is only one.

Leech imagines creatures whose use of language *is* restricted to the propositional/logical/informational, and calls them 'an ideal society of robots' (p. 47). Why 'ideal' I do not know. I *do* know (though Chomskyans will think I am joining them in the realm of conjecture) that such an 'ideal society' is impossible. Creatures who tried only to impart information, only to speak logically, wouldn't even be able to do that. Swift's horses are not really intellectual beings.

Different uses of language must interevaluate one another to give the sense of the whole language. Languages are in fact,

[6] 'It has often been suggested that man is most clearly distinguished from other animal species, not by the faculty of thought or intelligence, as the standard zoological label "homo sapiens" might indicate, but by his capacity for language' (Lyons, *Chomsky*, p. 10). What distinction is being made? Isn't this a failure of linguistics to illuminate language?

looking at them like this, always such a tissue of interevaluating styles; linguistics is its own kind of meditation thereon.[7]

One of my reviewers asked what on earth a change in the style of *The Times* has to do with the English language. Johnson observes in the *Life of Pope* that our language has few letters. Not our literature, our language. That is to say, whatever amount of correspondence exists in attics and museums, little of it enters into the interevaluations by which we know the shape of our language.

Imaginative literature must nevertheless be of supreme importance in any such definition. Judgement in literature is the only guarantee I can think of of judgement in general about language. (Chomsky has never to my knowledge betrayed the slightest public interest in imaginative literature.) As I said somewhere else, 'If English had no great literature it would not be the language we know, even with the same grammar and vocabulary' (*Chaucer and the English Tradition* (1972), p. 284). And so students of French, who are all linguists, must consider Racine and Stendhal and Baudelaire just because in any respectable judgement they are a very important part of the French language.

It is neither an accident nor a mistake that for nineteen-twentieths of its history the study of language has been firmly subordinated to the reading of classical texts. The oddity is the modern divorce, the study of language disconnected from a centre in the consideration of classical literature.

This, I hope, will help us *not* to claim for linguistics the status of a super-science which some of its practitioners want for it. If linguistics studies the whole of language, how is it to avoid this claiming of the whole of human knowledge as only part of its domain? For all the specialisms are language-dependent.

The specialisms, rightly so called, are (in this aspect) developments of language which the linguist can follow only if he becomes the relevant kind of specialist. He might rescue himself from claiming absolute general knowledge by concentrating upon language as language (rather than as physics or whatever), but this is very tricky unless understood as follows.

Judgement of literature is ordinary judgement, not specialist

---

[7] My *Survival of English* was an effort at defining a central area of linguistic judgement by relating some judgements to one another, and was therefore in my view a work of linguistics and not, as one editress thought, of sociology.

judgement, for the sufficient reason that the centre of language is not propositions but poetry. Hence linguistics is an underlabourer of criticism (of literature or language) not a super-language.

Geoffrey Leech, defining different kinds of meaning, ends with 'aesthetic' meaning and characterizes it thus: 'the main semantic point about poetry is that it is language communicating "at full stretch": all possible avenues of communication, all levels and types of meaning, are open to use' (*Semantics*, p. 48). I agree with every word. But why should something fully itself be seen as an extraordinary case? Poetry, by Leech's account, just *is* language; it is his other categories that are special cases.

The critic judges the central area of language, primitive poetry and primitive judgement, and follows it up into imaginative literature, the high form of non-specialist language. Judgement of language must depend on judgement of the best language. Thus the only possible 'explanation' of language is teleological.

Rhythm, harmony, even counterpoint perhaps, are made possible by 'perceptual universals', and it's certainly a very important fact about human beings that many of us have a similar enough sense of time, pitch, loudness, to allow us to form and conduct and listen to orchestras. The resultant music, however, is the sense of the perceptual universals and explains them, not vice versa: they are accounted for by music, and music by the *best* music. Imagine a history of music that allotted space to different composers proportionately to their output! The history of music is the history of what matters in music, the relations between the best music.

Language is a fitting object of study because there are things like *King Lear*. But this means that the important judgements in linguistics, the judgements about the high level of meaning, must always be challengeable. In literary criticism it is *always* possible for there to be serious disagreement. It is even possible to dispute seriously that *King Lear* is deep: Tolstoy did so. Our plight is worse even than Leavis's formula for literary criticism allows. It is always possible for a serious answer to a serious proposition in linguistics or literary criticism of the form 'This is so, isn't it. . .' to be not Leavis's 'yes, but. . .' which continues the discussion and the pursuit of judgement, but NO. That is not to say there can be no true judgement. *King Lear* is a deep play despite Tolstoy.

The same kind of judgement brings all other uses of language, including those of the academic disciplines, within linguistics. The linguist's judgement is from the point of view of the most central and the best of the language he is studying. In one direction this points back to our discussion of linguistics and philosophy; here I merely point out that there is no escape in the study of language from judgements essentially of the kind we make when thinking about poetry, about what matters in language. Linguistics, that is to say, cannot be a science, and if an academic discipline at all it must be a humane one.

Perhaps linguistics could be a discipline; perhaps it could grant us something like that new sight of the object of study which (leaving everything as it is) is the end of philosophy: but it could only do so by imitating literary criticism in holding uses of language steadily in judgement. This might give us a deeper understanding than we had, and what other test can there be of the success of linguistics? But it will never be either scientific or explanation; for that which fully communicates can only be understood through and as itself. To appeal for the last time to the analogy of music:

Hear Don Juan; that is to say, if you cannot get a conception about him by hearing him, then you will never get it. Hear the beginning of his life; as the lightning flashes forth from the murk of the thunderclouds, so he bursts forth from the depths of earnestness, swifter than the lightning's flash, more inconstant and yet as constant; hear how he rushes down into the manifold of life, how he dashes himself against its solid dam, hear those light dancing tones of the violin, hear the signal of gladness, the exultation of lust, hear the festive happiness of enjoyment; hear his wild flight, he hurries by himself, ever swifter, ever more impetuously; hear the unbridled demands of passion, hear the sighing of love, hear the whisper of temptation, hear the whirlpool of seduction, hear the stillness of the moment—hear, hear, hear Mozart's *Don Juan*! (Kierkegaard, *Either/Or*, transl. D. F. and L. M. Swenson (Oxford, 1944), pp. 83–4)

Don't, that is to say, ask informants whether *Don Giovanni* is music, or suppose that they could possibly tell you if you didn't know; don't offer to prove it is music by some corroboration of what we know by listening, or by comparison with some set of rules for what constitutes music; don't try to measure its effect on people or explain it as the workings of innate ideas or the functioning of brain cells: hear it. Then, having heard it, we can hope to meditate on it, to contemplate its moments of creation by running them over in our minds as we think of them from different points of view (Kierkegaard himself is doing this): we may even, if we feel inclined and are knowledgeable enough, begin, after hearing the music, talking the technicalities of musicology. By all means let us ask how our hearing *Don Giovanni* depends on our perception of the elements of music, and on our experience of much other music. But to lose one's grasp of the great fact that it is music that is being discussed, music that exists only in the hearing of sounds as music, music that is all we can refer to— that way madness lies. Is not music enough for the musicologist? and meaning for the linguist? And where is music without the classics? or language without poetry?

No linguistics I have ever stumbled upon makes any sort of shot at accounting for or judging the whole of language. But philosophy must, as Wittgenstein says in my epigraph ('Remarks on Frazer's *Golden Bough*', p. 34), plough over the whole of language. So, in its very different way, must literary criticism. That is why linguistics ought to be the neighbour of both literary criticism and philosophy.

Poets have the deepest working knowledge of language (which is to say that poets are, for better or for worse, the people most humanly alive). This gives the poets no necessary advantage as linguists; they need not write about language—though when they do, as might be expected, they are often better worth attention than most linguists. Poets show us language at full: critics are the people who try to follow poets through the fullness of language. Literary criticism does not define the whole of language philosophically or scientifically, but what are the standards the critic judges by, the standards of value, depth, significance, if not the values of life as understood in our whole language? From what knowledge can a critic speak if not his knowledge of the whole language? The critic's individual judgements are his bringing to bear the standards of the best he knows in the life of his time and place: it is only saying this from another starting-point to assert that when we judge a work of literature we are defining its place in our whole language.

The critic's essential knowledge is not literary in the way the scientist's essential knowledge is scientific. If the critic has no sense of life outside books he will make no sense inside either:

'A man with a paltry, impudent nature', said D. H. Lawrence in words that must haunt anybody who publishes literary criticism, 'will never write anything but paltry, impudent criticism' ('John Galsworthy'). Literary criticism depends on wider judgements of language. If I have sometimes seemed to be reducing linguistics to the status of slave of criticism I have not meant to deny that linguistics might usefully be controlled by a high level of judgements about language which is not restricted to imaginative literature. As I said, I have tried to contribute to linguistics in that sense, and hope to do so again.

And for all the individuality and unprovability of critical judgements, of literature or language, criticism can be, please God, a disciplined and intellectual activity.

This is why it is not strange to me, though it will seem strange to Chomsky and the surviving structuralists, that I have learned far more about language both from the philosophy of Collingwood and of Wittgenstein and Rhees, and from the literary criticism of Leavis, than from the whole corpus of established linguistics.

Leavis's own development into contemplation of language is a remarkable fact of recent intellectual history, and it is a development rightly based on his sense of the mode of existence of a poem.[8] In Leavis's often-used definition of the mode of literary criticism, one imagined speaker says of a poem 'This is so, isn't it?' expecting a reply of the form 'Yes, but. . .' 'Analysis [of a poem] is not a dissection of something that is already and passively there. What we call analysis is, of course, a constructive or creative process. It is a more deliberate following-through of that process of creation in response to the poet's words which reading is.'[9] But if the poem is not there, where is it? If a poem is re-created in reading, and if the inner possession that is the poem's existence is best refined in discussion, that discussion, where the inner possession of a poem can be offered to somebody else, is a special and important area of experience, or language, or thought. Leavis's later work is the realization, with increasing depth, that that area is a central point for humanity, an area to which 'humanity' especially refers. The phrase 'the third realm'

---

[8] With several collaborators I worked out this idea in 'The Third Realm', *The Human World* no. 3 (1971) from which the following sentences are quoted.
[9] *Education and the University*, second edn (1948), p. 70.

is Leavis's means of making his step from the great particular example, the existence of a poem, to a general truth about the nature of language. And this in turn is his way of widening literary criticism into a criticism of life.

The work that decisively initiated Leavis's recent development was the 'notorious' Richmond Lecture, *Two Cultures?* (1962).

> The implicit form of a judgment is: This is so, isn't it? The question is an appeal for confirmation that the thing *is* so; implicitly that, though expecting, characteristically, an answer in the form, 'yes, but—', the 'but' standing for qualifications, reserves, corrections. Here we have a diagram of the collaborative-creative process in which the poem comes to be established as something 'out there', of common access in what is in some sense a public world. It gives us, too, the nature of the existence of English literature, a living whole that can have its life only in the living present, in the creative response of individuals, who collaboratively renew and perpetuate what they participate in—a cultural community or consciousness. More, it gives us the nature in general of what I have called the 'third realm' to which all that makes us human belongs. (p. 28)

I don't think it paradoxical, either, that Leavis's concentration on language should belong with an intense concern to see the links between imaginative literature (in its only manifestations, our experience of individual works) and life as lived by individual human beings, with its moral problems, its joys and terrors, its end in death. One cannot study language without studying human nature;[10] but equally one can't get far about human nature without thinking of its infinite range in individuals and in the very different languages in which they make sense.

Leavis's move from the individual poem to language is just the kind of wondering at human nature, judgement, values which as I began by saying I think the measure of success for any study of language.

Unless the world goes finally mad, unless the human mind in our universities loses utterly its grasp of what makes sense and

---

[10] I do believe in a few linguistic universals, and said so elsewhere, for instance, when I argued that 'It is a universal characteristic of human societies to make something solemn of a funeral' or 'abortion could not in any fully human language lose its aura of the horrible' (*The Survival of English*, pp. 47, 151). The genuine linguistic universals are taboos, rituals, poetry and so on—which vary greatly from language to language—not the accurate description of the objects of the natural world, a largely Western achievement.

our academic styles become those of the Grand Academy of Lagado, people (and linguists) will still be reading the later work of Leavis, and pondering it as thought about language, when the later work of Chomsky is generally recognized as only another episode in the history of the long, desperate effort to reduce thought about language to an exact science.

Index

Index

Index